Microsoft Operations Management Suite Cookbook

Enhance your management experience and capabilities across your cloud and on-premises environments with Microsoft OMS

Chiyo Odika

BIRMINGHAM - MUMBAI

Microsoft Operations Management Suite Cookbook

Commissioning Editor: Kartikey Pandey
Acquisition Editor: Meeta Rajani
Content Development Editor: Devika Battike
Technical Editor: Manish Shanbhag
Copy Editors: Safis Editing, Dipti Mankame, Laxmi Subramanian
Project Coordinator: Judie Jose
Proofreader: Safis Editing
Indexer: Rekha Nair
Graphics: Tom Scaria
Production Coordinator: Shraddha Falebhai

First published: April 2018

Production reference: 1170418

Published by Packt Publishing Ltd.
Livery Place
35 Livery Street
Birmingham
B3 2PB, UK.

ISBN 978-1-78646-909-0

www.packtpub.com

`mapt.io`

Mapt is an online digital library that gives you full access to over 5,000 books and videos, as well as industry leading tools to help you plan your personal development and advance your career. For more information, please visit our website.

Why subscribe?

- Spend less time learning and more time coding with practical eBooks and Videos from over 4,000 industry professionals

- Improve your learning with Skill Plans built especially for you

- Get a free eBook or video every month

- Mapt is fully searchable

- Copy and paste, print, and bookmark content

PacktPub.com

Did you know that Packt offers eBook versions of every book published, with PDF and ePub files available? You can upgrade to the eBook version at `www.PacktPub.com` and as a print book customer, you are entitled to a discount on the eBook copy. Get in touch with us at `service@packtpub.com` for more details.

At `www.PacktPub.com`, you can also read a collection of free technical articles, sign up for a range of free newsletters, and receive exclusive discounts and offers on Packt books and eBooks.

Contributors

About the author

Chiyo Odika is a author, consultant, strategist and thought leader who is passionate about data-driven management and architecture. Chiyo excels at helping clients think strategically about how to use technology to optimize the service delivery to the business, and to create fundamental business change and value. His current technology focus is cloud computing. He enjoys talking about hybrid cloud flexibility, exploring business technology trends, optimizing cloud infrastructures, and leading solution delivery teams.

He has extensive experience in leading full lifecycle technology implementations of cutting-edge business solutions for a wide range of global clients and has championed initiatives from ideation to execution and delivery.

> *I would like to thank my family for their support throughout the course of this project. I'd like to dedicate this book to all persons who dare to dream, and to those who possess the fortitude to realize their dreams. May each day bring them renewed vim and vigor, that they may transcend the clouds and reach for the heavens.*

About the reviewer

Oskar Landman has more than 15 years of IT consulting experience in monitoring and automation. He works as a consultant and owner for OWL IT, a company based in the Netherlands where his focus is monitoring and automation in hybrid and cloud-based solutions. He started with monitoring, Microsoft Operations Manager (MOM) 2005, System Center Operations Manager (SCOM) upto Operations Management Suite (OMS) and beyond. He was awarded the Microsoft Most Valuable Professional Award (MVP) on System Center Operations Manager (SCOM) followed by two MVP awards in Cloud and Data Center Management for his outstanding technical skills and community efforts on the products.

Oskar was a contributing author to System Center 2012 Operations Manager Unleashed (2013), System Center Service Manager 2010 Unleashed (2011), and System Center 2012 Service Manager Unleashed (2015).

Packt is searching for authors like you

If you're interested in becoming an author for Packt, please visit `authors.packtpub.com` and apply today. We have worked with thousands of developers and tech professionals, just like you, to help them share their insight with the global tech community. You can make a general application, apply for a specific hot topic that we are recruiting an author for, or submit your own idea.

Table of Contents

Preface

Microsoft **Operations Management Suite** (**OMS**) is a cloud-based collection of management services that is designed with hybrid management in mind. OMS simplifies IT management within your environment by providing you with solutions in order to manage and protect your on -premises and cloud environments. OMS is designed to provide you with a single-pane-of-glass view into the operation of your IT environment, and it is built to work across heterogeneous environments. It provides you with capabilities to manage your Windows and cross-platform devices across such clouds as **Amazon Web Services** (**AWS**) and Microsoft Azure, and because it is implemented as a cloud-based service, you can onboard to the service quickly and with minimal investment in infrastructure services and start to realize many benefits of OMS. In addition, the cloud-based nature of the service means that new features and capabilities are automatically delivered, saving you upgrade and maintenance-related costs. This cookbook aims to deliver recipes across various OMS solution offerings and provide guidance for working with core OMS components for Insights and Analytics, Protection and Recovery, Security and Compliance, and Automation and Control.

Who this book is for

This book is written for the IT professional and general reader who is interested in technology themes such as DevOps, Big Data Analytics, and digital transformation concepts. Azure and other cloud platform administrators, cloud professionals, and technology analysts who would like to solve everyday problems quickly and efficiently with hybrid management tools available in the Microsoft product ecosystem will derive much value from this book.

What this book covers

Chapter 1, *Getting Started with Microsoft Operations Management Suite*, provides an overview of OMS and its underlying services and shows you how to onboard to OMS services.

Chapter 2, *Searching and Analyzing OMS Data*, shows you how to review, search, and analyze collected data using the powerful new Azure Log Analytics query language.

Chapter 3, *Managing Alerts in OMS*, shows you how to use OMS for alert and event management and view and correlate alerts from various connected sources, such as SCOM, Nagios, and Zabbix. You will also learn how to use and configure alert actions in Log Analytics.

Chapter 4, *Protecting and Recovering Data with OMS*, provides an overview of the data protection and recovery capabilities of OMS and shows you how to leverage the various features of Azure Backup and **Azure Site Recovery (ASR)** as part of your disaster recovery and business continuity strategy.

Chapter 5, *Configuration Management and Automation with OMS*, shows you how to leverage the Azure Automation capabilities for inventory and change tracking, update management, process automation, and desired state configuration.

Chapter 6, *Working with Security and Compliance in OMS*, provides an overview of the Security and Compliance service in OMS and shows you how to assess your security state across various security domains, audit security-related events across your environment, identify and remediate security gaps within your environment, and remain compliant with various security standards.

Chapter 7, *Using Wire Data 2.0 and Service Map*, shows you how to unlock insights into your network traffic and understand how application components relate to one another and any network dependencies.

Chapter 8, *Exploring Other Management Solutions*, provides an overview of other management solutions and their various capabilities, shows you how to install and configure a variety of solutions, and perform assessments of various workloads within your environment.

Chapter 9, *Cross-Platform Management with OMS*, shows you how to manage Linux and other non-Windows workloads with OMS and also shows you how to work with collected data, and correlate data from other monitoring solutions to unlock insights and manage your cross-platform workloads wherever they might reside.

To get the most out of this book

To get started with OMS and to make the most of the content in this book, you will need an Azure subscription, and an Azure Log Analytics workspace. You will also need some test Windows and/or Linux machines, depending on your interest area. You will also benefit from deploying some cloud-based workloads in Azure or other cloud to understand how OMS works across management boundaries.

To work with the Hybrid worker group feature in Azure Automation, you will need at least one VM or Physical computer on-premises that can serve as a hybrid worker.

You will also need to ensure that your test machines are running supported versions of Windows or Linux operating systems for the various capabilities that you intend to explore. Furthermore, each chapter in the book spells out any requirements you will need to get started, in the Getting Started section of the various chapter recipes.

Download the example code files

You can download the example code files for this book from your account at www.packtpub.com. If you purchased this book elsewhere, you can visit www.packtpub.com/support and register to have the files emailed directly to you.

You can download the code files by following these steps:

1. Log in or register at www.packtpub.com.
2. Select the **SUPPORT** tab.
3. Click on **Code Downloads & Errata**.
4. Enter the name of the book in the **Search** box and follow the onscreen instructions.

Once the file is downloaded, please make sure that you unzip or extract the folder using the latest version of:

- WinRAR/7-Zip for Windows
- Zipeg/iZip/UnRarX for Mac
- 7-Zip/PeaZip for Linux

The code bundle for the book is also hosted on GitHub at https://github.com/PacktPublishing/Microsoft-Operations-Management-Suite-Cookbook. In case there's an update to the code, it will be updated on the existing GitHub repository.

We also have other code bundles from our rich catalog of books and videos available at https://github.com/PacktPublishing/. Check them out!

Download the color images

We also provide a PDF file that has color images of the screenshots/diagrams used in this book. You can download it from `https://www.packtpub.com/sites/default/files/downloads/MicrosoftOperationsManagementSuiteCookbook_ColorImages.pdf`.

Conventions used

There are a number of text conventions used throughout this book.

`CodeInText`: Indicates code words in text, database table names, folder names, filenames, file extensions, pathnames, dummy URLs, user input, and Twitter handles. Here is an example: "The OMS Gateway supports HTTP tunneling using the `HTTP CONNECT` command."

A block of code is set as follows:

```
Perf
| where CounterName == "% Processor Time" and ObjectName == "Processor" and
InstanceName == "_Total"
| summarize AggregatedValue = avg (CounterValue) by Computer, bin
(TimeGenerated, 5m)
```

Any command-line input or output is written as follows:

```
Get-Service OMSGatewayService
```

Bold: Indicates a new term, an important word, or words that you see onscreen. For example, words in menus or dialog boxes appear in the text like this. Here is an example: " This introductory chapter will provide an overview of how to get started with the management capabilities in **Operations Management Suite (OMS)**. "

 Warnings or important notes appear like this.

 Tips and tricks appear like this.

Get in touch

Feedback from our readers is always welcome.

General feedback: Email `feedback@packtpub.com` and mention the book title in the subject of your message. If you have questions about any aspect of this book, please email us at `questions@packtpub.com`.

Errata: Although we have taken every care to ensure the accuracy of our content, mistakes do happen. If you have found a mistake in this book, we would be grateful if you would report this to us. Please visit `www.packtpub.com/submit-errata`, selecting your book, clicking on the Errata Submission Form link, and entering the details.

Piracy: If you come across any illegal copies of our works in any form on the Internet, we would be grateful if you would provide us with the location address or website name. Please contact us at `copyright@packtpub.com` with a link to the material.

If you are interested in becoming an author: If there is a topic that you have expertise in and you are interested in either writing or contributing to a book, please visit `authors.packtpub.com`.

Reviews

Please leave a review. Once you have read and used this book, why not leave a review on the site that you purchased it from? Potential readers can then see and use your unbiased opinion to make purchase decisions, we at Packt can understand what you think about our products, and our authors can see your feedback on their book. Thank you!

For more information about Packt, please visit `packtpub.com`.

1
Getting Started with Microsoft Operations Management Suite

This introductory chapter will provide an overview of how to get started with the management capabilities in **Operations Management Suite (OMS)**. It will cover the various methods for signing up to Log Analytics, creating and administering a workspace, provisioning and managing access to workspaces, on-boarding agents to OMS, and viewing the initial data. This chapter will also review architectural considerations for OMS, including proxy and firewall configurations, OMS gateway considerations, and placement. This chapter will include the following topics::

- Understanding OMS architecture and data flow
- Connecting sources without internet access to OMS
- Getting started with OMS
- Reviewing the collected data

Introduction

Microsoft OMS is a cloud-based collection of management services that is designed with hybrid management in mind. OMS simplifies IT management within your environment by providing you with solutions for managing and protecting your on-premises and cloud environments. OMS is designed to provide you with a single pane-of-glass view into the operation of your IT environment, and is built to work across heterogeneous environments.

It provides you with the ability to manage your Windows and cross-platform devices across such clouds as **Amazon Web Services** (**AWS**) and Microsoft Azure, and because it is implemented as a cloud-based service, you can onboard to the service quickly, and with minimal investment in infrastructure services. Additionally, the cloud-based nature of the service means that new features and capabilities are automatically delivered, saving you upgrade and maintenance-related costs.

At the heart of OMS lies a set of Azure-based services that provide the core functionality of OMS. These services enable the key solutions that provide you with flexible access to the management capabilities that you need:

- **Automation** provides you with consistent control and compliance capabilities across your environments, both on-premises and in the cloud, including third-party clouds
- **Log Analytics** enables you to gain rich insight into your environment, from collected data and provides you with analytics capabilities across your workloads
- **Backup** provides you with reliable backup and restore capabilities to protect critical data both on-premises and in the cloud
- **Site Recovery** helps with availability and disaster recovery through seamless replication, failover, and failback capabilities for your workloads

These services are the foundation of the manifold benefits of OMS, which include the ability to do the following:

- Enable a unified view of all of your IT assets, both on-premises and across the various clouds
- Gain instant insights across a variety of Windows, Linux, and other workloads
- Improve your security posture with the ability to identify and respond quickly to security threats
- Deliver continuous IT services through consistent control and compliance
- Ensure the availability of your data through automated cloud data protection and disaster recovery

OMS provides you with true hybrid management capabilities, so that while OMS services run in the cloud and effectively provide you with comprehensive management of your cloud workloads, you can also seamlessly and effectively manage on-premises workloads. If you already have investments in System Center, you can seamlessly integrate System Center components with OMS in a hybrid scenario.

Understanding OMS architecture and data flow

This section will explore important architectural concepts and considerations for the various OMS services, and provide you with an understanding of how OMS receives and processes data. A good grasp of how data flows to OMS for the various management functions will enable you to better follow the subsequent recipes.

Getting ready

OMS is a collection of cloud-based services that provide you with hybrid cloud management capabilities, and through four key solutions offerings, OMS provides you with flexible access to the management capabilities that you need. Each of the four solution offerings require specific cloud services to be enabled in Azure in order to access the underlying management capabilities that they provide.

How to do it...

To get started, you should determine which of the key solutions and underlying capabilities you need, and understand how the various OMS cloud services facilitate their respective capabilities. For instance, if you are primarily concerned with insight and analytics capabilities for log collection and searches, and for network health monitoring, you would make use of the Log Analytics service in Azure. If, however, you are interested in protection and recovery capabilities and would like to ensure the availability of your applications and data, you would make use of the Backup and Site Recovery services in Azure. When evaluating the key solutions, note the following capabilities included with each offering:

Insight and Analytics	Automation and Control	Protection and Recovery	Security and Compliance
Log collection and search	Azure Automation **Desired state configuration** (DSC)	Back up to Azure and restore from Azure	Security and audit capabilities with threat intelligence

Network health monitoring and application insights	Update management and automated remediation	Site recovery to Azure and the customer's secondary datacenters	Malware threat analysis
Application and server dependency mapping (Service Map)	Change tracking	Replicate and failover to Azure, and failback from Azure	Integration with Azure Security Center for in-depth Azure services security management

Table 1.1 Solutions

How it works...

To understand how OMS works, you need to know about the various services that enable the various management functions in OMS.

Log Analytics

As mentioned earlier, Log Analytics is an OMS service that enables you to monitor your environments' availability and performance. Log Analytics does this by collecting data from sources that you connect to the service. The following are some examples of such sources:

- Windows and Linux agents
- Azure VMs and resources
- System Center

For Windows and Linux operating systems, Log Analytics collects data through agents that must be installed on the host computers. These agents then collect data from the server and relay the data directly to OMS endpoints. If, however, the computer(s) are part of a **System Center Operations Manager** (**SCOM**) management group, then no additional agent is required because through SCOM-to-OMS integration, and depending on the management solution enabled in OMS, the SCOM agents will collect data from the servers they are deployed to and send it either to OMS via the SCOM management group, or they will simply send the data directly to OMS.

In addition to collecting data from Windows and Linux computers and System Center, Log Analytics can also collect data from Azure resources such as Azure Diagnostics and Azure Monitor. Azure Diagnostics data can be written directly into Log Analytics, or sent to Azure storage, where Log Analytics is then able to read the storage logs. Log Analytics can also collect data from other Azure resources using connectors, which enable data to be sent from services such as Application Insights to Log Analytics. In addition, Log Analytics provides a REST API that enables data collection from other Azure services, third-party applications, and custom management solutions that can't send data through any of the aforementioned means.

Once sources are connected to Log Analytics, data sources are then collected from the various connected sources, based on data source configurations that are delivered to agents either directly, for directly connected computers, or through SCOM management packs, for agents that report to a SCOM management group that is integrated with OMS. Some examples of data sources include Windows Event logs, custom logs, Windows and Linux performance counters, and Syslog, among others.

Once the agent receives the data source configurations, it collects the specified data, and, depending on the collected data source - directly or via SCOM - it sends the data to Log Analytics. Once the collected data gets to OMS, it is then stored as records in the OMS repository. You will then be able to make use of the log search feature in Log Analytics to query and analyze the indexed data to glean insights about your cloud and on-premises environment and consume the data in various ways (visualize, alert, automate, integrate into workflows, and so on), which we will take a look at later in this book.

The following diagram depicts the flow of data from various connected sources to OMS and to the OMS repository for storage:

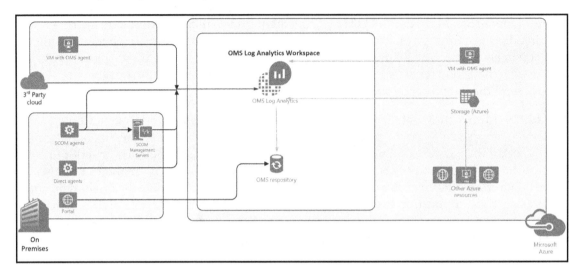

Figure 1.1 Log Analytics data collection

Automation

As mentioned earlier, the Azure Automation service lies at the heart of configuration management, process automation, and other automation-related capabilities in OMS. The Automation service uses Azure technologies and Windows PowerShell to provide you with process-automation capabilities using runbooks, and configuration-management capabilities using **desired state configuration** (**DSC**) for your Windows and Linux resources that may reside on-premises, in Azure, or other cloud service.

To automate processes such as long-running and repetitive tasks, you will make use of a set of tasks called runbooks. These enable you to perform automated processes in Azure Automation. You can perform automation tasks with runbooks just like you can with PowerShell, because runbooks in Azure Automation are based on Windows PowerShell or PowerShell workflows. Azure Automation runbooks execute in Azure and can be run against any cloud resources and any other resources that you can access. To execute runbooks against your on-premises resources, you can make use of the Hybrid Runbook Worker feature, which enables you to designate one or more computers on premises as resources, on which Azure Automation can execute runbooks to manage resources on premises.

Each worker will require the **Microsoft Management Agent** (**MMA**) and will connect to both the Automation account in Azure Automation and OMS Log Analytics. Azure Automation delivers the runbooks to the workers, and all other automation processes are executed in Azure Automation. You can then monitor the behavior of the management agent using Log Analytics. There are other considerations for making the Hybrid Runbook Worker feature highly available using groups, and we'll explore these later in this book.

Azure Automation also provides you with configuration management capabilities, using Azure Automation DSC. Azure Automation DSC is based on PowerShell DSC fundamentals, and is, in fact, a cloud-based solution for PowerShell DSC, and uses a declarative PowerShell syntax to enable you to manage, deploy, enforce, and monitor configuration for your computers. Because it is cloud based, you will manage your DSC resources in Azure Automation and apply your desired configurations to any computers on premises or in the cloud. Your computers then retrieve the configurations from a DSC pull server in Azure. You can then use the reporting capabilities in Azure Automation DSC to monitor the application according to your criteria, and identify and manage drift.

The following diagram depicts the Azure Automation data flow, process automation using runbooks in Azure and Hybrid Runbook Workers on premises, and configuration management using Azure Automation DSC:

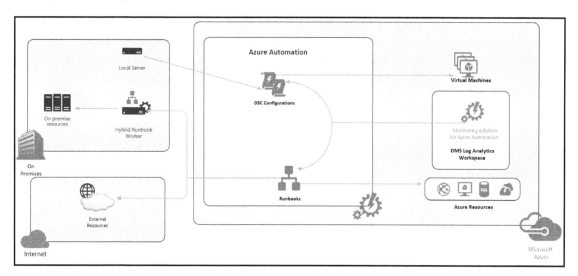

Figure 1.2 Azure Automation workflow

Azure Backup

Azure Backup is one of the services that enables the protection and recovery management functionality in OMS. It is a service based in Azure that enables you to protect and restore your data from the Microsoft cloud, and includes support for the protection and recovery of files, folders, application workloads, and Azure virtual machines. Azure Backup provides various components to meet your protection and recovery needs, and depending on your protection goals, you can use one of the following components to protect your data in a Recovery Services vault in Azure:

- Azure Backup (MARS) agent
- System Center **Data Protection Manager (DPM)**
- Azure Backup Server
- Azure IaaS VM Backup

Note that while all Azure Backup components enable you to protect your data using a Recovery Services vault in Azure, the Azure Backup Server also enables the storage of backup data to a locally attached disk, and the System Center DPM component enables the protection of backed-up data to a locally attached disk and on-premises tape libraries. Azure Backup also provides some support for protecting Linux computers.

When storing backups in Azure, depending on the backup component you utilize, once the data is backed up at the protection point, it is compressed and stored in an Azure-based online storage entity called a **Recovery Services vault**, and, based on your storage needs, you can enable high availability through locally-redundant or geographically redundant storage replication. You can monitor backup metrics and connect to the OMS Monitoring solution for Azure backup..

The following figure depicts an Azure Backup data flow, a backed-up data relay to an Azure Recovery Services vault, storage replication of protected data, the monitoring of backup statistics, and the viewing of backup reports with Power BI, as well as the monitoring of backup parameters with the OMS monitoring solution:

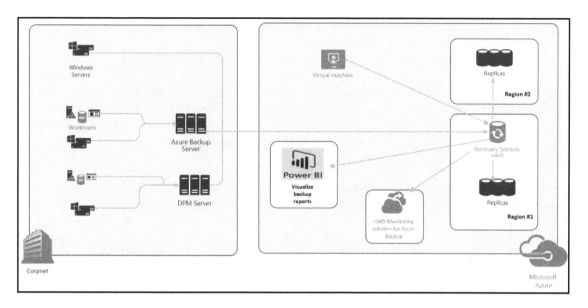

Figure 1.3 Azure Backup workflow

Azure Site Recovery

Azure Site Recovery (**ASR**) enables the recovery management capabilities for OMS. ASR is a service in Microsoft Azure that facilitates your disaster recovery and business continuity strategy by enabling you to replicate, failover, and recover your workloads in the event of a failure. With ASR, you can replicate on-premises VMWare, Hyper-V VMs and Windows and Linux physical servers to either Azure storage or to a secondary datacenter. You can also use ASR to replicate Azure VMs to another Azure region.

ASR supports the replication of VMs in the following scenarios:

- Replication and recovery to and from Azure of on-premises Hyper-V VMs on Hyper-V standalone hosts and clusters that are managed with or without System Center **Virtual Machine Manager** (**VMM**)
- Replication and recovery to and from Azure of on-premises VMWare VMs
- Replication and recovery to and from Azure of on-premises physical servers
- Replication and recovery to and from secondary datacenters of on-premises Hyper-V VMs on Hyper-V standalone hosts and clusters that are managed in VMM clouds
- Replication and recovery to and from secondary datacenters of on-premises VMWare VMs

- Replication and recovery to and from secondary datacenters of on-premises Windows and Linux physical servers
- Replication and recovery of Azure VMs from one Azure region to another

The ASR replication process varies according to the scenario you implement, and will be explored in greater detail in Chapter 4, *Protecting and Recovering Data with OMS*, of this book. In general, if replicating workloads to Azure from an on premises location, you will need to set up requirements for the Azure components, including an Azure account, a storage account, and an Azure network.

For **VMWare VMs and Physical server** replication to Azure, you will also need ASR component servers (configuration and process servers) and a master target server for failback. You will need to set up a Recovery Services vault in Azure, which is the storage entity that houses the data in Azure. In the vault, you can specify the replication target and source, set up the configuration server, add sources, define your replication policy, and perform other recovery tasks, such as test failovers and failbacks.

Similarly, for replicating Hyper-V VMs to Azure, if the hosts are configured in VMM clouds, you can register the VMM server(s) in the Recovery Services vault and install the Site Recovery Provider to orchestrate replication with Azure. If hosts are not located in VMM clouds, then you will install the Site Recovery Provider directly on the hosts.

Once the infrastructure is set up and the replication configured, protected on-premises machines will replicate an initial copy of the data, after which delta changes will be replicated. Traffic is then replicated over the secure internet connection or Azure ExpressRoute to Azure storage endpoints. For Azure VMWare VMs and Windows/Linux physical servers, this traffic can also be replicated over a site-to-site VPN connection.

For Azure VM replication, you will need to enable Azure VM replication in the Azure portal, after which resources are created automatically in the target region that you designate. Once replication is enabled, the Site Recovery Extension Mobility Service will be installed automatically on the Azure VM and will then be registered with Site Recovery, and then the VM will be configured for continuous replication. At this point, any data written to the Azure VM disks will continuously get transferred to the cache storage account in the source environment. Site Recovery will then process the data and send it to the target storage account in the target environment.

ASR also provides you with failover testing and the failover of protected resources to a target protection environment (Azure or a secondary site), as well as the ability to fail back to the source site. The following figure depicts the ASR data flow for the replicated data of protected resources from the source location to the target location in Azure or a secondary site:

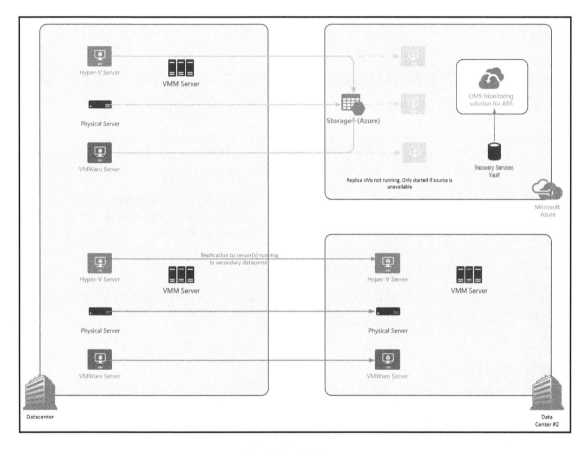

Figure 1.4 Azure Site Recovery

There's more...

While some configuration is needed to enable some of the key OMS service offerings, such as the protection and recovery capabilities, as shown previously, the deployment requirements for onboarding to OMS are minimal because the underlying functionality is provided by services in Azure.

See also

The following is a useful link to information relating to OMS architecture and data flow:

- **Microsoft TechNet - OMS architecture**:
  `https://docs.microsoft.com/en-us/azure/operations-management-suite/ope`
  `rations-management-suite-architecture`

Connecting sources without internet access to OMS

If you implement security policies that restrict computers in your **corporate network** (**corpnet**) from connecting to the internet, OMS has an HTTP forward proxy feature called the OMS Gateway that will enable you to still connect computers in your corpnet to OMS.

While the computers in your corpnet will have no connectivity to the internet, the OMS Gateway must have access to the internet, or be connected to a proxy server that does, so as to be able to forward data to the OMS service endpoints. The OMS Gateway supports HTTP tunneling using the `HTTP CONNECT` command. It collects data on behalf of the OMS agents deployed to the computers in your corpnet, and sends the data to OMS.

The following information will help you understand how to connect sources to OMS that have no connectivity to the internet.

Getting ready

At this time, the OMS Gateway supports the following connected sources scenarios:

- Windows computers directly connected to an OMS workspace with the MMA
- Linux computers directly connected to an OMS workspace with the OMS agent for Linux
- SCOM agent-managed computers reporting to a management group that is integrated with OMS. The following SCOM versions are supported:
  - SCOM 2016
  - SCOM 2012 R2 with update rollup 3
  - SCOM 2012 SP1 with update rollup 7
- Azure Automation Hybrid Runbook Workers

The OMS Gateway feature can also be made highly available using your existing enterprise hardware-based load balancers. To begin, you will need to download and install the OMS Gateway.

How to do it...

You will need to download the OMS Gateway setup file and use the file to install and configure the OMS Gateway. You can also configure high availability for the OMS Gateway using load balancing, if you wish.

Downloading the OMS Gateway setup file

You can download the latest version of the OMS Gateway setup file in one of three ways:

1. Navigate to the following URI (`https://www.microsoft.com/en-us/download/details.aspx?id=54443`) to obtain the setup file from the Microsoft Download Center

2. Obtain the setup file from the OMS Portal:
    1. Sign into your OMS workspace
    2. Navigate to **Settings | Connected Sources | Windows Servers**
    3. In the resulting blade, click **Download OMS Gateway:**

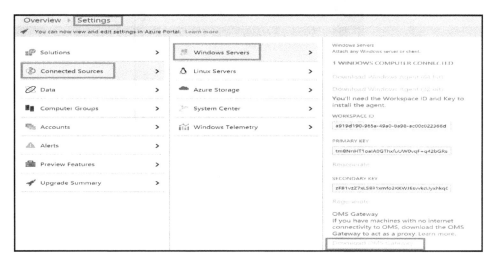

Figure 1.5 Downloading OMS Gateway from the OMS portal

3. You can download the OMS Gateway setup file from the Azure portal
    1. Sign in to the Azure portal
    2. Select **Log Analytics** from the list of services
    3. Select a workspace
    4. Under the General section in your workspace blade, click **Quick Start.**
    5. Under the **Choose a data source to Connect to the Workspace**, click **Computers**
    6. In the **Direct Agent** blade, click **Download OMS Gateway**
    7. Save the **OMS Gateway.msi** file:

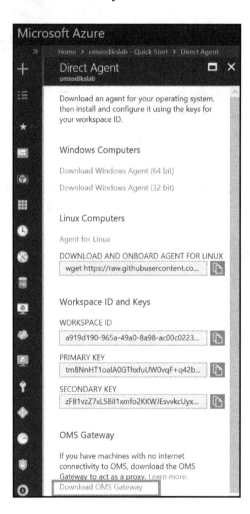

Figure 1.6 Downloading OMS Gateway from the Azure portal

Installing the OMS Gateway

Use the following steps to install the OMS Gateway:

1. Locate the **OMS Gateway.msi** file downloaded in the previous section
2. Right-click the file and select **Install**
3. Click **Run** on the security warning prompt, if any appear

4. Click **Next** on the **Welcome** page:

Figure 1.7 OMS Gateway setup

5. Select **I accept the terms in the License Agreement in the End-user License Agreement** page and click **Next**
6. On the **OMS Gateway Configurations** page, do the following:
    1. Enter the port to be used for the server. The default port is 8080. You can enter any values that range from 1 through to 65535.
    2. Optionally, if the OMS Gateway server needs to communicate through a proxy to get to the internet, check the radio box to **Use a proxy server** and enter the proxy server information. If the proxy requires authentication, check the **My proxy requires authentication** radio box and enter the **username** and **password** information as well.

3. Click **Next** to proceed:

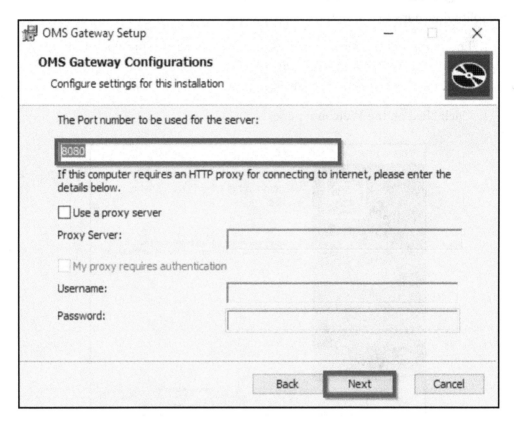

Figure 1.8 OMS Gateway setup

7. On the **Destination Folder** page, leave the default folder settings as `C:/Program Files/OMS Gateway`, or choose another folder to install the OMS Gateway on, and click **Next.**
8. Click **Install** on the **Ready to Install OMS Gateway** page and select **Yes** if you receive a **User Account Control (UAC)** prompt.
9. Click **Finish** after the setup has completed.

Check the list of services or use PowerShell to verify that the OMS Gateway service is installed and running:

```
Get-Service OMSGatewayService
```

```
PS C:\Users\codika> Get-Service OMSGatewayService

Status    Name               DisplayName
------    ----               -----------
Running   OMSGatewayService  OMS Gateway
```

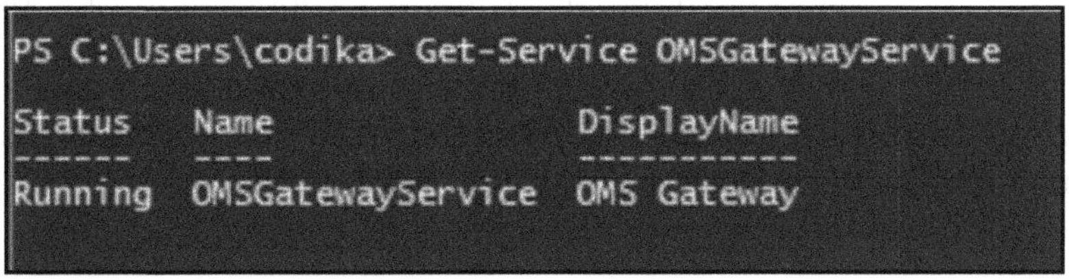

Figure 1.9 Verifying that the OMS Gateway service is running

How it works...

The OMS Gateway is simply an HTTP forward proxy that makes connections on behalf of clients through HTTP CONNECT tunneling. In this case, the OMS agent computer forwards its TCP connection to the OMS Gateway, which tunnels the TCP connection to the OMS service endpoints. This tunneling mechanism means that the data is sent directly from the OMS Gateway to the OMS endpoints without being analyzed.

The OMS Gateway can be used with both OMS agents that are configured to directly connect to an OMS workspace, and an Operations Manager (SCOM) management group that is integrated with OMS. With directly connected OMS agents, the data is sent to the OMS Gateway, which then transfers the data directly to OMS in the manner previously described. When configured for use with an SCOM management group, the proxy information defined for the management group is distributed automatically to every agent-managed computer that is configured as an OMS-managed computer, even if that setting isn't defined.

Depending on the solution(s) configured in OMS, the agent will then collect the relevant data and either send it to the management server or, in the case of high-volume data, such as performance metrics and security events, directly to the OMS endpoints via the OMS Gateway.

There's more...

You can configure the OMS Gateway for high availability through **network load balancing (NLB)**. This will enable you to use the TCP/IP networking protocol to distribute traffic across two or more OMS Gateway servers. Using an NLB configuration will provide you with some measure of high availability and scalability for your OMS Gateway configuration. You can make use of any existing hardware-based load balancers that you use within your infrastructure, and the OMS Gateways configured as NLB hosts should support common NLB configurations, such as your preferred load-balancing algorithms (least sessions, round robin, fastest, and so on), persistence methods, and so on.

 Ensure that your target server listening port adheres to the port configuration used during the installation of the OMS Gateway server(s).

You can also install the OMS agent on the computer configured as the OMS Gateway. This configuration will enable the following:

- The OMS Gateway can identify the service endpoints that it needs to communicate with
- The OMS agent can monitor and collect event and performance data from the OMS Gateway

Additionally, Operations Manager Gateway servers deployed in untrusted networks cannot communicate with the OMS Gateway. They can only report to an Operations Manager management server, and would therefore be subject to the proxy server settings (if any) configured for the management group to which the SCOM management server belongs.

For directly connected computers to send data to the OMS Gateway, they must have network connectivity to the OMS Gateway, and the agents' proxy configuration should be set to the same port used by the OMS Gateway to communicate with OMS service endpoints.

Using a proxy server to access OMS from SCOM

Perform the following steps:

1. Open the SCOM console and navigate to the **Administration** workspace

2. Navigate to **Operations Management Suite**, click **Connection,** and then click **Configure Proxy Server**:

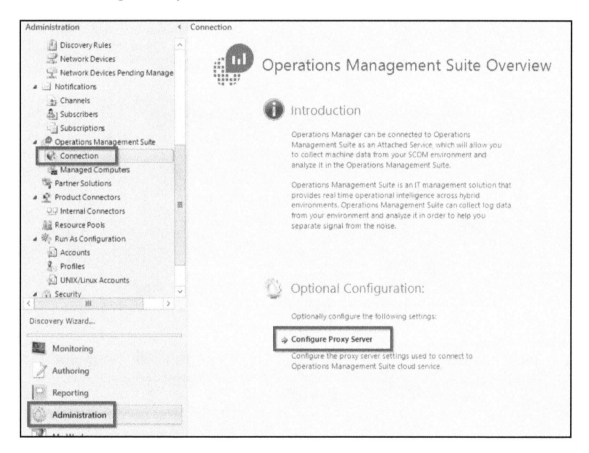

Figure 1.10 - Configuring proxy server options in SCOM

3. Select the option to **Use a proxy server to access the Operations Management Suite** and type either the IP address of the standalone OMS Gateway server or the virtual IP address of the array of load-balanced OMS Gateway servers

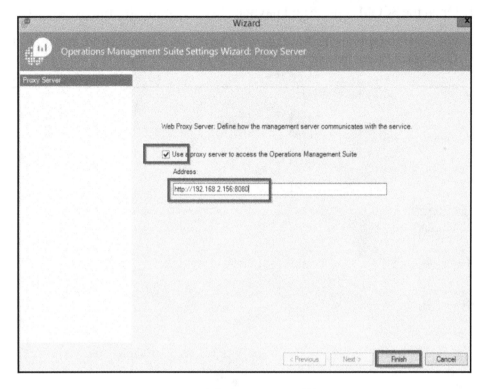

Figure 1.11- Configuring the proxy server in SCOM

Ensure that you start with the `http://` prefix. Additionally, ensure that you bypass the HTTPS inspection if you need to permit access to OMS service endpoints through your firewalls.

Use PowerShell cmdlets with OMS Gateway

You can make use of PowerShell to review and modify the OMS Gateway configuration settings. The OMS Gateway PowerShell module should get imported in the OMS Gateway server(s) upon installation of the OMS Gateway feature. You can always verify this by importing the module to confirm:

```
Import-Module OMSGateway
```

Once you confirm that the OMS Gateway has been imported, you can also verify your OMS Gateway configuration for the listening port, log level, and other settings:

```
Get-OMSGatewayConfig
```

```
PS C:\Users\codika> Get-OMSGatewayConfig
ListenPort=8080
LogLevel=INFO
IncorporateOMSSolution=true
IncorporateScomSupport=true
```

Figure 1.12 - Reviewing the OMS Gateway configuration

To make changes to the OMS Gateway configuration using PowerShell, you can make use of the `Set-OMSGatewayConfig` cmdlet. For instance, to change the port on which the OMS Gateway is listening, you can execute the following command:

```
Set-OMSGatewayConfig -Name ListenPort -Value [port]
```

In the preceding command, `[port]` is the integer value of your desired port on which the OMS Gateway listens.

At this time, the `Set-OMSGatewayConfig` cmdlet supports the following configuration names:

- `ListenPort`
- `LogLevel`
- `IncirporatedOMSSolution`
- `UseIpv6`
- `IncorporatedScomSupport`

See also

The following links also provide some useful guidance on troubleshooting tips relating to the OMS Gateway:

- **Microsoft TechNet: Troubleshooting OMS Gateway event IDs**: `https://docs.microsoft.com/en-us/azure/log-analytics/log-analytics-oms-gateway`
- **Microsoft TechNet: OMS connectivity resources**: `https://docs.microsoft.com/en-us/azure/log-analytics/log-analytics-windows-agents`

Getting started with OMS

The following information will show you how to get started with OMS by setting up a Log Analytics workspace. There are several ways to create a Log Analytics workspace:

- Create a workspace through the Microsoft OMS **Overview** page
- Create a Log Analytics workspace in the Azure portal
- Create and configure a Log Analytics workspace using Azure Resource Manager templates
- Create and configure a Log Analytics workspace using Log Analytics PowerShell cmdlets

This section will focus on creating a Log Analytics workspace and onboarding through the Azure portal.

Getting ready

To get started with OMS Log Analytics, you will need to make use of an Azure account. If you don't have an Azure account, you can create a free account, which will give you access to the Azure service. This free account will be available for 30 days.

How to do it...

We can start the on-boarding process using the following steps:

Creating an Azure account

To create a free account, go through the following steps:

1. Navigate to `https://azure.microsoft.com/en-us/free/?v=17.23h` and follow the instructions to create your account. You will be able to make use of a work, school, or personal email account. You can also create a new Microsoft account that you can authenticate with Azure.
2. Sign in and follow the instructions to create an account.

Creating an OMS Log Analytics workspace

Once you have access to the Azure service, you are ready to create your OMS Log Analytics workspace:

1. Navigate to the **Azure Portal** (`http://portal.azure.com`) and sign in.
2. In the Azure Portal, click the **New** button and type Log Analytics in the marketplace search field. Select **Log Analytics**:

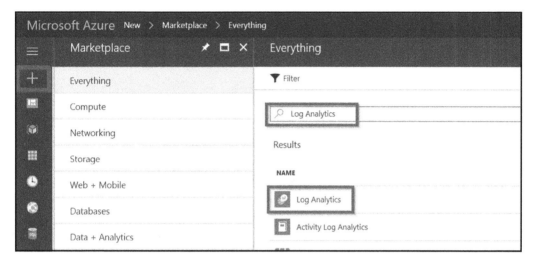

Figure 1.13 Log Analytics workspace

3. Click the **Create** button and enter or select information for the following fields:

   - **OMS Workspace:** Enter a name for your workspace
   - **Azure subscription**: Select the Azure subscription that you would like to assign to your OMS Log Analytics workspace. You can change your OMS workspace Azure subscription at any time.
   - **Resource group**: You can choose to create a new resource group or use an existing one using the radio button. Select the existing resource group from the dropdown.
   - **Location**: Select the Azure region.

- **Pricing tier**: Select a pricing tier that will govern the cost of your OMS Log Analytics workspace, and the solutions you use. You can choose from the following options:
  - **Free**
  - **Per Node (OMS)**
  - **Per GB (Standalone)**
  - **Standard**
  - **Premium**

A resource group is a container that holds related resources for an Azure solution.

Figure 1.14 - Creating Log Analytics workspace

4. Click **OK** to finish creating your workspace.

5. You can now filter for Log Analytics in the Azure portal to see your new OMS Log Analytics workspace.

6. Click on your Log Analytics workspace. You can now review the settings and features for your workspace:

Figure 1.15 - Log Analytics workspace

Adding solution offerings and solutions

After creating the Log Analytics workspace, you can add solution offerings and management solutions to your workspace. Management solutions are collections of logic, data collection, and visualization rules that provide you with information that is pertinent to a particular problem area. Solution offerings are bundles of management solutions.

To add solution offerings and solutions through the Azure portal, go through the following steps:

1. Navigate to the Azure portal and click the **New** button. Type the name of the solution you would like to add, such as **Activity Log Analytics**, into the marketplace search field and press *Enter*.

2. Select **Activity Log Analytics** in the **Everything** blade, and click **Create**:

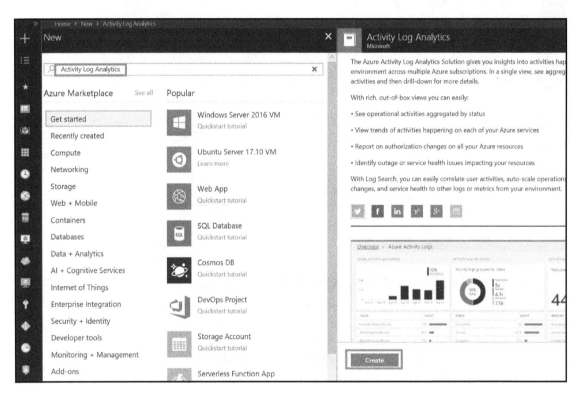

Figure 1.16 - Log Analytics solution offerings

3. In the **Activity Log Analytics** blade, select the workspace you would like to associate with the management solution and click **Create**:

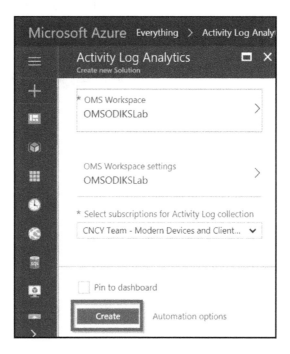

Figure 1.17 - Adding solution offerings to Log Analytics

4. Repeat the preceding steps to add additional service offerings and solutions to your workspace.

From the marketplace, follow steps 1-3 to add the **Security & Compliance** service offering to your workspace to get the Antimalware Assessment and Security and Audit solutions. Additionally, you can add the **Automation & Control** service to get the System Update Assessment, Change Tracking, and Automation Hybrid Worker solutions:

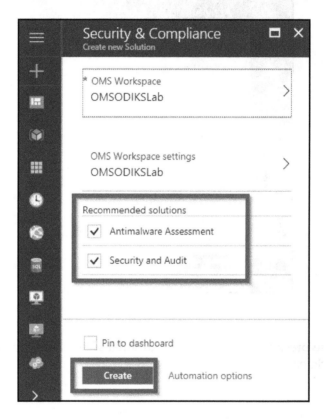

Figure 1.18 - Adding Security and Compliance solutions

5. After adding solutions to your workspace, you can view the management solutions by navigating to **Log Analytics**, clicking on your workspace name, and, in the Workspace blade, selecting **Overview** under **Management**:

Figure 1.19 - Viewing Log Analytics solutions

Once in the **Overview** page, you can see the solutions tiles for the solutions that you have added to workspace:

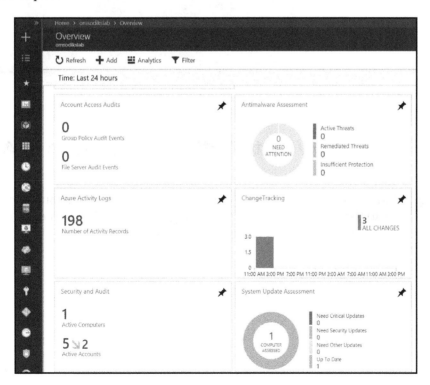

Figure 1.20 - Log Analytics solution tiles in Azure Portal

Alternatively, while in the workspace blade, you can click on **OMS Portal** to take you to the portal on the OMS website. We'll look at some operations that can be performed in the OMS portal in the following sections of this chapter and in subsequent chapters of this book.

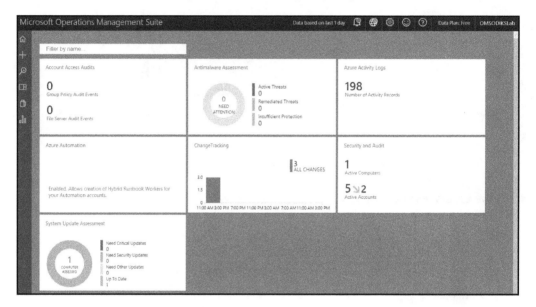

Figure 1.21 - Log Analytics workspace in the OMS portal

Connecting Azure VMs to OMS Log Analytics in Azure portal

After adding solution offerings and solutions to your OMS workspace, you are now ready to connect sources to the workspace to start collecting some data. You can enable the VM extension to connect your Azure VMs to OMS Log Analytics:

1. Navigate to and sign in to the Azure portal.

2. Search for and navigate to **Log Analytics** and select your **Log Analytics** workspace

3. In the **Log Analytics** blade, select **Virtual machines** under **Workspace Data Sources**

4. Review the list of virtual machines and the OMS connection status for each virtual machine on which you would like to install the agent:

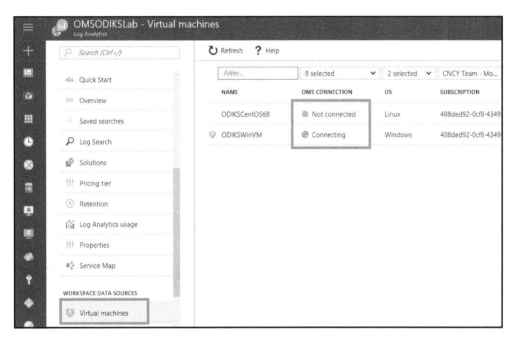

Figure 1.22 - Azure VMs connection to OMS

5. Select the virtual machine that you would like to install the agent on, and in the details blade for the VM, select **Connect**. This will automatically install and configure the agent for your Log Analytics workspace:

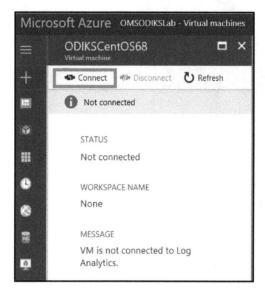

Figure 1.23 - Connecting Azure VMs to OMS Log Analytics

After the agent is installed and connected, the OMS connection status for your workspace will reflect this:

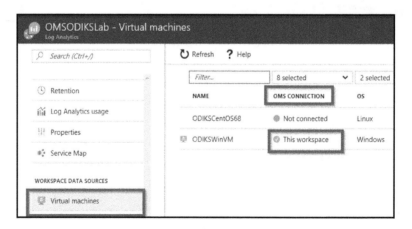

Figure 1.24 - Azure VMs connected to OMS

Connecting Windows computers to OMS Log Analytics

As mentioned earlier, you can directly connect Windows computers to your OMS Log Analytics workspace. To do this, you will need to download the agent setup file from the OMS portal or the Azure portal, install the agent, and configure it for your workspace:

1. Navigate to the Azure portal, select **Log Analytics**, and select your **Log Analytics** workspace
2. In the **Log Analytics** workspace blade, select **Quick Start**, and under **Choose a data source to connect to the workspace**, select **Computers:**

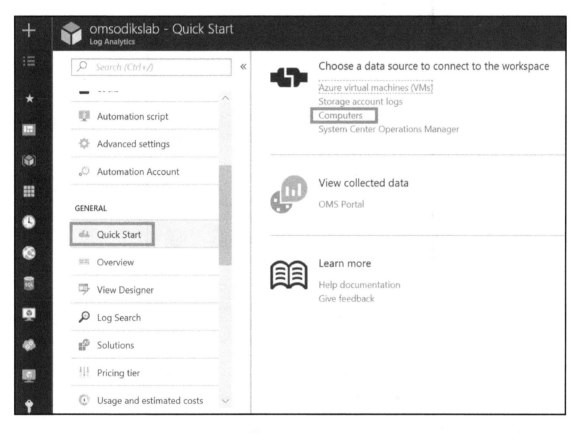

Figure 1.25 - Onboarding Windows computers to Log Analytics

3. In the **Direct Agent** blade, click the **Download Windows Agent** that applies to your computer processor type to download the setup file
4. Save the setup file to your preferred directory

5. In the **Workspace ID and Keys** fields, copy the **Workspace ID** and **Primary Key** values to a Notepad for use during direct agent installation:

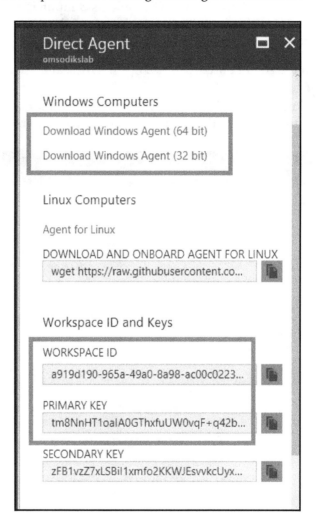

Figure 1.26- Log Analytics Windows agents

6. On the computer that you want to manage with OMS Log Analytics, run the setup file, and click **Next** on the Welcome page
7. On the **License Terms** page, read the terms and click **I Agree**

8. On the **Destination Folder** page, change or keep the default folder and click **Next**
9. In the **Agent Setup** options page, select the **Connect the agent to Azure Log Analytics (OMS)** and click **Next**

10. Paste the Workspace ID and Primary Key into the respective **Workspace ID** and **Workspace Key** fields, select your preferred **Azure Cloud** option (**Azure Commercial** is default) and click **Next**:

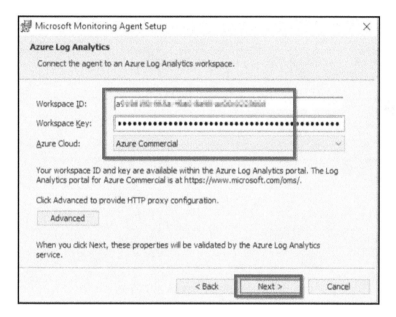

Figure 1.27 - Connecting the Windows Agent to the Log Analytics workspace

11. On the **Ready to Install** page, review your choices and click **Install**
12. Click **Finish** once the configuration completes successfully

13. You will now see the Microsoft Monitoring Agent in the **Control Panel** of the agent computer. Open the properties of the agent, and under the **Azure Log Analytics (OMS)** tab you will now see a confirming status - **The Microsoft Monitoring Agent has successfully connected to the Microsoft Operations Management Suite Service**:

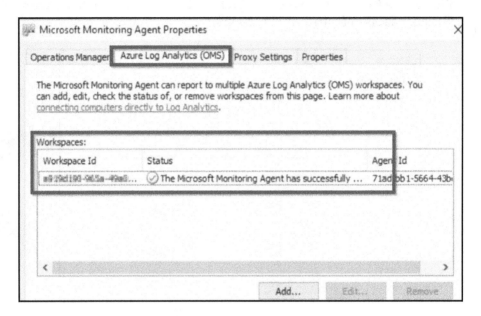

Figure 1.28 - OMS Log Analytics Windows Agent properties

Adding data sources in OMS

As mentioned previously, Log Analytics collects data from the connected sources that you define in your workspace and stores that data in the OMS data stores. The data sources you configure will define the data that is then collected from each connected source. Two data sources that you can start with are Windows events and performance data.

To add a Windows event log data source to OMS, go through the following steps:

1. In the OMS console, click the **Settings** tile.
2. In the **Settings** page, click on **Data** and select **Windows Event Logs.**
3. In the **Log Name** field, type the name of an event log you would like to collect. Log Analytics will suggest common event log names based on your entry.

4. Type your log name, or select from the suggestions, and click the + button to add the event log for collection:

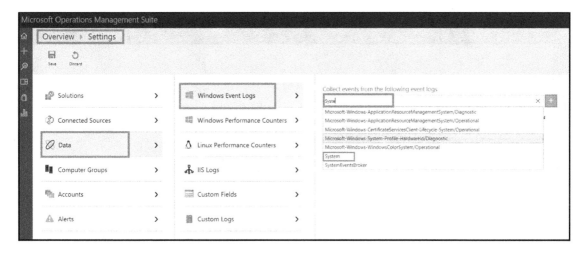

Figure 1.29 - Log Analytics event log collection

Configuring performance data sources in OMS

OMS supports the collection of Windows and Linux performance counters.

Collecting Windows performance counters:

Perform the following steps:

1. In the OMS console, click the **Settings** tile.
2. On the **Settings** page, click on **Data** and click **Windows Performance Counters.**

3. Click the **Add the selected performance counters** button to start collecting a list of suggested performance counters. You can uncheck any of the counters before adding the other selections:

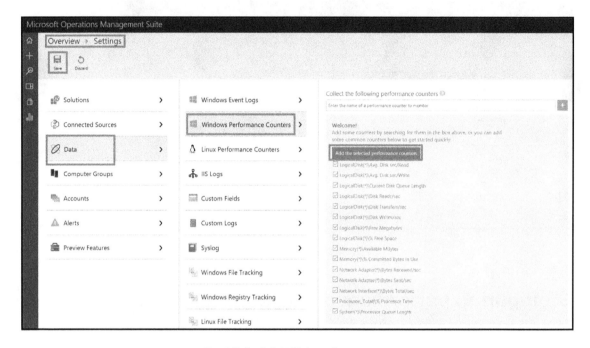

Figure 1.30 - Log Analytics Windows performance counters

4. Once the counters are added, review the counters and the sample collection intervals:

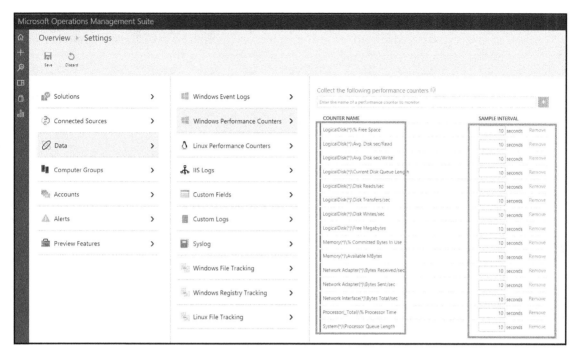

Figure 1.31 Log Analytics Windows performance counters and collection intervals

5. Search for additional counters in the entry field, or use the **Remove** button next to the counter sample interval to remove any counters.

Collecting Linux performance counters:

Perform the following steps:

1. In the OMS console, click the **Settings** tile.
2. On the **Settings** page, click on **Data** and click **Linux Performance Counters**.

3. Click the **Add the selected performance counters** button to start collecting a list of suggested performance counters. You can uncheck any of the counters before adding the other selections:

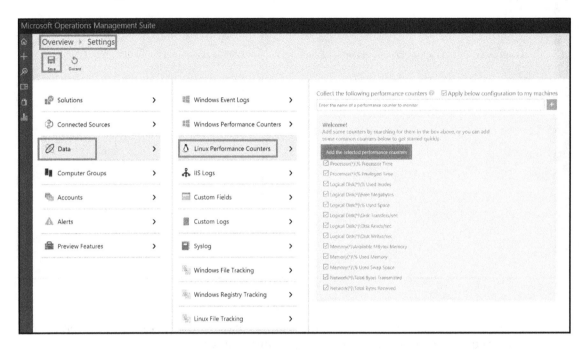

Figure 1.32 - OMS Log Analytics Linux performance counters

How it works...

To get started with OMS, set up a Log Analytics workspace. A workspace is a container and Azure resource in which data is collected, analyzed, and presented in a portal. It includes account information and simple configuration information for a given account. You can have multiple workspaces to manage different datasets. In order to create a workspace, you will need the following:

- An Azure subscription
- A name for your workspace
- An Azure geographical region

You will also need to associate your workspace with an Azure subscription. A workspace can be used as a granular unit of management for specific workloads, functional teams, or other bases. A Log Analytics workspace provides you with the following:

- Granularity for billing
- Data isolation
- Custom workload configuration
- Geographic location flexibility for data storage

You can get started with OMS by creating a workspace using any of the following methods:

- Create a workspace through the Microsoft OMS overview page
- Create a Log Analytics workspace in the Azure portal
- Create and configure a Log Analytics workspace using Azure Resource Manager templates
- Create and configure a Log Analytics workspace using Log Analytics PowerShell cmdlets

You can subsequently view, administer, and configure your workspace through the user interface portals in either Azure or the OMS website.

Once you add solutions to your workspace and connect sources to the workspace, you can then define the data that gets collected from your connected sources by defining and configuring data sources for your workspace. The configured data sources determine the nature of the collected data. The following are some examples of data sources:

- Windows event logs
- Windows and Linux performance counters
- Syslog
- IIS and custom logs

For Windows event logs, Log Analytics will only collect events from the Windows event logs that you specify in your workspace. You will not, however, be able to manually add security events to your workspace. To collect security events, you will need to install the **Security and Audit** solution or the **Security & Compliance** solution, which includes the security solution.

The collected data is then stored in the OMS repository as a set of records, with each record type having a set of properties.

This collected data can then be queried using the log search feature to combine and correlate the data, and with the emphasis on particular workloads or problem areas using solutions, you can glean insights and take action on the information derived from the data. You can then further analyze the data using the various visualization capabilities in OMS.

Furthermore, you can manage accounts, users, and groups to have some measure of role-based access to your Log Analytics workspace. This can be done using Azure permissions, and in the OMS portal.

 The Microsoft or organizational account that creates a workspace becomes an administrator of the workspace by default.

There's more...

In addition to the **Insights & Analytics** and **Security & Compliance** solutions described in the previous section, you can also add solutions for **Automation & Control** (Update Management, Change Tracking, Azure Automation Hybrid Worker), and Protection & Recovery (Azure Backup and Azure Site Recovery) to your OMS Log Analytics workspace.

Managing users in the OMS portal

Perform the following steps:

1. Navigate to the OMS portal (http://oms.microsoft.com) and sign in.
2. On the **Overview** page, click the **Settings** tile.
3. Click the **Accounts** tab and click **Manage Users.**

While in the **Manage Users** section, you can perform tasks such as adding and removing users and groups.

Adding a user or group to a workspace

Perform the following steps:

1. In the **Manage Users** section, choose the account type to add. You can choose between an **Organizational Account**, **Microsoft Account**, or **Microsoft Support**.
2. Choose the user type: **Administrator, Contributor,** or **ReadOnly User**.
3. Choose whether the account is a **User** or **Group**.

4. Enter the name of the account and click **Add:**

Figure 1.33 - Managing users in the OMS Log Analytics workspace

If you choose the **Organizational Account** type, when you enter part of the name of a user or group in the account field, a list of matching users and groups will appear in a drop-down box.

Editing or removing a user or group from a workspace

Perform the following steps:

1. While still in the **Manage Users** section of the **Overview | Settings** page, locate the user or group you would like to edit or remove from the list of users/groups.

2. Toggle to the relevant user or group type radio button to edit the user type, or click **REMOVE** next to the username you would like to remove:

USER NAME	ADMINISTRATOR	CONTRIBUTOR	READONLY USER	STATUS	REMOVE
chiyo.odika@gmail.com	◉	○	○	Active	✕
codika@concurrency.com	○	◉	○	Active	✕

Figure 1.34 - Editing users in the Log Analytics workspace

Considerations for other solution offerings

There are additional configurations required for adding the Automation & Control and the Protection & Recovery solutions respectively to your workspace, and for use with OMS.

Add Automation & Control Solution Offering to OMS

To add the **Automation & Control** solution, you must create an Automation account or select an existing Automation account. An Automation account is an Azure resource through which you can manage all of your Azure, cloud, and on-premises resources:

1. Navigate to the Azure portal and click the **New** button. Type **Automation & Control** into the marketplace search field and press *Enter*
2. Select **Automation & Control** in the **Everything** blade and click **Create**
3. In the **Create New Solution** blade, click the **OMS Workspace** button and select your **OMS workspace**, and check the **recommended solutions** you would like to install and click the **OMS Workspace Settings** tab

4. In the resulting blade, confirm your workspace, Azure **Subscription**, **Location**, **Resource group**, and **Pricing tier** information, and click Automation account

5. In the **Automation account** blade, select an existing Automation account or click **Create an Automation account**:

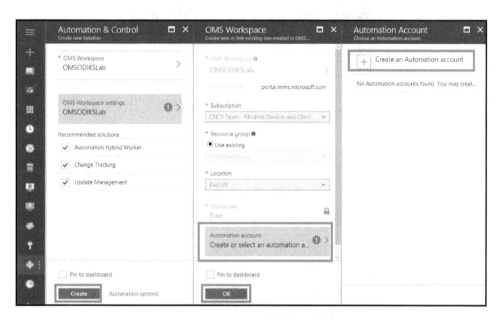

Figure 1.35 - The Automation & Control solution

 Creating the Automation account when you add the Automation & Control solution to your workspace establishes the integration with your OMS workspace, and enables you to install related management solutions into your workspace.

6. In the **Add Automation Account** blade, enter the name of your Azure Automation account in the **Name** field, review the **Subscription**, **Resource group**, **Location**, and **Azure Run As account** creation options, and click **OK:**

Figure 1.36 - Adding Azure Automation Account

7. After the deployments are complete, click **OK** in the **OMS Workspace** blade, and upon completion of the deployment, click **Create** in the **Automation & Control** blade to finish adding the **Automation & Control** solution to your workspace.

OMS data retention

When performing analytics against datasets, the duration of that data is an important consideration, as is its retention. OMS offers a variety of pricing tiers to suit your budget and needs, and the retention periods for the various OMS pricing tiers are very well defined. Remember that there are five pricing tiers that you can choose from for your workspace:

- **Free**: On the free tier, data is retained for seven days
- **Per Node (OMS)**: Log Analytics makes the last 31 days of data available on this tier
- **Per GB (Standalone)**: Log Analytics makes the last 31 days of data on this tier available
- **Standard**: On the standard tier, data is retained for 30 days
- **Premium**: Data on the premium tier is retained for 365 days

When you use the OMS and Standalone pricing tiers, you can keep up to 2 years' worth of data (730 days). This is configurable from the Log Analytics Workspace settings in the Azure Portal. There is, however, a retention charge for data stored for more than the default 30 days.

Pricing

The cost of your workspace depends on the pricing tier and the solutions you use. To use OMS entitlements and access all solutions, you can choose between the Per Node (OMS) and Free tiers. Various solutions are also offered in some of the other pricing tiers.

For instance, to use the Network Performance monitoring or Service Map solutions, which are part of the Insights and Analytics solutions, you can choose the Per Node (OMS) or Free tiers. Additionally, to use such solutions as Security and Antimalware (from the Security & Compliance solution) and Update Management and Change Tracking (from the Automation & Control solution) you can choose the Per Node (OMS) or Free pricing tier. Microsoft offers detailed Log Analytics pricing information and a calculator at `https://azure.microsoft.com/en-us/pricing/details/log-analytics/?v=17.23h`.

See also

Visit the following links for more information:

- **Troubleshooting OMS on-boarding issues**: `https://support.microsoft.com/en-us/help/3126513/how-to-troubleshoot-operations-management-suite-onboarding-issues`
- **Troubleshooting guide for OMS agents for Linux**: `https://github.com/Microsoft/OMS-Agent-for-Linux/blob/master/docs/Troubleshooting.md`

Reviewing the collected data

After you connect sources to your workspace and define the type of data that will be collected from your connected sources through the data sources, Log Analytics will start to collect data based on these criteria and the solutions that you have installed in your workspace, and you will start to see the relevant data in your workspace.

How to do it...

You can start by reviewing the solution-specific data in your workspace:

1. In the OMS console, review the solution tiles in your workspace that correspond to the solutions you have installed in your workspace.
2. Click the **Security And Audit** solution tile to enter the **Solution View** page.
3. Once on the page, Log Analytics will present you with a list of recommended alerts that relate to the solution. Click **Enable alerts** to enable the recommended alerts for the solution, and click **Ok** to close the **Recommended alerts** panel:

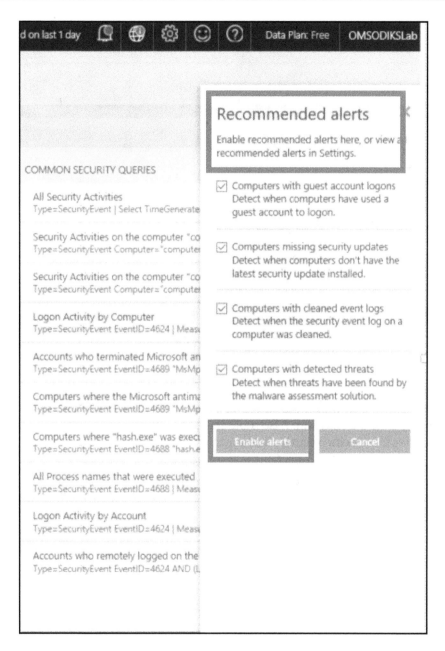

Figure 1.37 - Security & Audit solution dashboard

You can view and manage all of your alerting rules by navigating to **Settings | Alerts**.

Figure 1.38 - Log Analytics workspace overview page

4. On the **Security and Audit** page, review the visualization elements that comprise the view of the solution. Also, note the common security queries tile that suggests queries for specific security and audit scenarios.

5. Repeat steps 1-4 for any additional solutions in your workspace.

6. From the OMS overview page, click **Log Search.**

7. In the Log Search page, enter the **search *** character query into the search field and click Search:

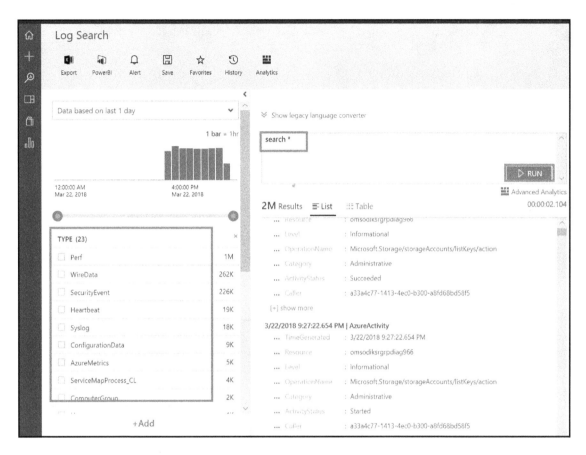

Figure 1.39 - OMS Log Analytics log search

The query returns results that are displayed in the **Query Results** field. You will also see various data types and field values on the left side of the Log Search page:

8. Click on the **Perf** data type on the left side of your screen to return performance data. Note that when you make this selection, the log search modifies the query search to reflect your selection.

9. Click on the **Table** perspective to see a different view of the resulting dataset:

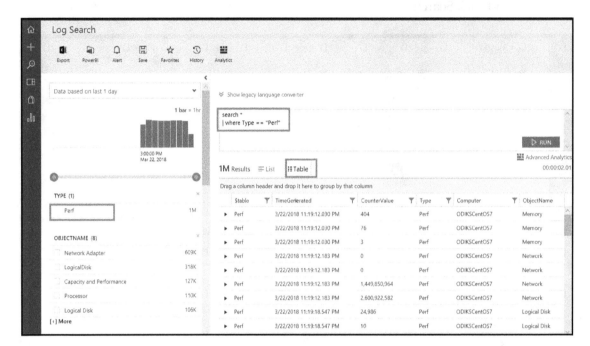

Figure 1.40 - Log Analytics performance data records

How it works...

Once data is collected in OMS, it is stored in the OMS data store as records. Records that are collected by the various data sources configured for a workspace will have unique properties, and will get tagged with a unique Type property that identifies that data record as being from a particular data source. For instance, Windows event log data, once collected in the OMS repository, will be assigned a tag of type Event. This means that in Log Analytics, you can search for non-security Windows event logs by specifying a query, such as Event, as the where condition for your filter. Similarly, performance counter data will get tagged as data of type Perf, and you can use the query Perf to filter for this sort of data.

All of the data collected in the OMS repository is tagged as such, and you can filter for any type of data once you know what the tag value, or type, of data it is. The OMS log search can enable you to further shape, filter, aggregate, and glean insights from your data. In the next chapter, you will learn how to use the OMS log search to glean insights from your data. You will also learn how to analyze and visualize your data using OMS and complementary tools.

See also

Visit the following links for more information:

- **Log Analytics frequently asked questions (FAQs)**:
  https://docs.microsoft.com/en-us/azure/log-analytics/log-analytics-faq
- **OMS pricing**:
  https://www.microsoft.com/en-us/cloud-platform/operations-management-suite-pricing

Searching and Analyzing OMS Data

2

In this chapter, we will take a look at the types of data that are collected from the sources that were mentioned in the previous chapter, and learn how to search and analyze the data using the new Azure Log Analytics query language. This new and powerful query language is a feature included in the enhanced Azure Log Analytics service, and it differs significantly from the legacy query language. Readers will learn how to search and analyze data, perform smart analytics, and glean deep, useful, and actionable insights from their collected data. Topics in this chapter include the following:

- Understanding the Azure Log Analytics query language
- Working with queries in the Analytics portal
- Working with visualizations

Introduction

The log search feature enables you to combine, correlate, query, and retrieve data from Log Analytics. Recall that Log Analytics enables you to collect and aggregate large amounts of data from heterogeneous sources; we reviewed some of those capabilities in Chapter 1, *Getting Started with Microsoft Operations Management Suite*. As mentioned in the previous chapter, the collected data, is only as useful as the insights that can be derived from them, and the subsequent actions that those insights inform. This is where the Log Analytics query language comes to the fore.

The new and improved Log Analytics query language is based on Analytics (codenamed Kusto)—the powerful search feature in Application Insights, which Microsoft has recently made available as an upgrade for Log Analytics workspaces. The Log Analytics query language is optimized to perform and handle data at cloud scale, and it offers several very significant and noteworthy improvements over the legacy language.

In addition to such tasks as working with and manipulating large datasets, which you can perform with the legacy language, the interactive Log Analytics query language introduces a simpler and more intuitive syntax structure with full piping capabilities, and enables you to perform such incredibly powerful tasks as advanced joins, data and time functions, search-time field extractions, and smart analytics for evaluating patterns in large datasets and comparing datasets. The Log Analytics query language also improves upon the visualization capabilities in the legacy language, and features better integration with Power BI, enabling you to export queries for use in Power BI Desktop, for instance. With the Log Analytics query language, you can perform tasks such as the following:

- Filtering indexed data by any field, including your custom properties and application and workspace metrics
- Joining multiple tables
- Performing powerful statistical aggregations
- Working with intuitive and powerful visualizations
- Running queries programmatically from PowerShell using the REST API

Understanding the Azure Log Analytics query language

The Log Analytics query language is an interactive query language that enables you to unlock valuable insights from your data by querying, combining, filtering, joining, and performing numerous other operations on your data in Log Analytics.

Getting ready

To work with the Log Analytics query language, you can write search queries from the log search page in Azure Log Analytics. Alternatively, you can use the Analytics portal to write search queries. The Analytics portal is a web tool created expressly for writing and executing Log Analytics queries. It offers a unique environment for working with both simple and advanced analytics, advanced diagnostics, and feature-rich visualizations.

How to do it...

Perform the following steps:

1. Navigate to the **Azure portal** (`http://portal.azure.com`) and sign in.

2. In the Azure portal, type `Log Analytics` in the **Search resources** search field and select your workspace.

3. In the **Log Analytics** blade for your workspace, click the **Log Search** button to take you to the search field:

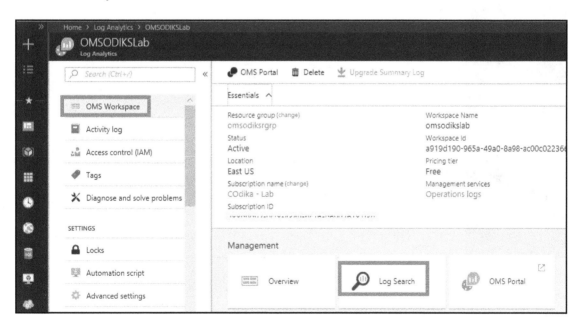

Figure 2.1

4. In the search field, conduct a simple search by typing `Perf`, a simple, table-based query to return all performance data, and click **Search**.

`Perf` is a table-based query that filters the data in the Azure Log Analytics repository and returns all records from the `Perf` table. As can be seen in the following screenshot, the query returns hundreds of thousands of results from the data. Because the result data in the tables is categorized by fields that are organized into columns in the table, you can further search for specific data by using the data fields and filters in your query:

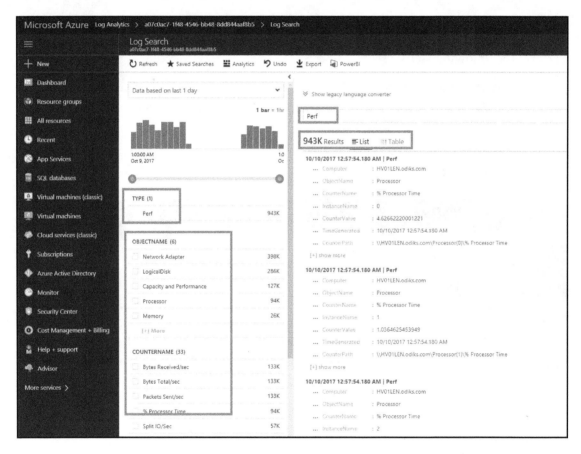

Figure 2.2

To better visualize how the Log Analytics data is structured, you can run the same query in the Analytics Portal. To do this, follow steps 1-4 again. Meanwhile, in the **Log Search** field:

1. Conduct a simple search by typing a simple, table-based query—Perf—to return all performance data and click **Search**.

2. Click on the **Advanced Analytics** link uder the log search box:

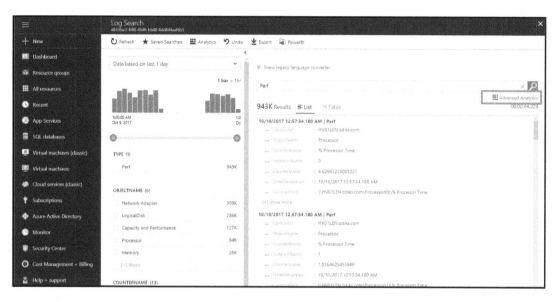

Figure 2.3

This will open the Analytics portal, in which the first 10,000 records of your query result will be displayed. Importantly, you will be able to review the results and determine, at a glance, the structure, table schema, and content of the queried table, as seen in the following screenshot:

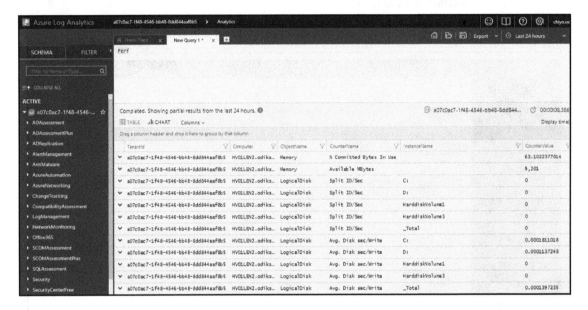

Figure 2.4

For illustration purposes, many of the queries created in this chapter will be both constructed and visualized in the Analytics portal.

How it works...

A Log Analytics query enables you to perform read operations against data ingested into an Azure Log Analytics data repository. Log Analytics queries can start with either a search command or a table name. This is important to note because OMS data sources and solutions store their data in tables in the Log Analytics workspace. When you build a table-based query or a search query, you reference these tables. Fundamentally, the language syntax of a Log Analytics query references a Log Analytics table, which defines what the initial data is, and from where the initial data gets returned. For further processing of the initial result set, various query operators separated by a pipe character (|) can be used to refine and further filter the data.

After the initial result set is returned, the result is passed on to a filter for further processing. This action is indicated with the use of the pipeline character in a new line, which indicates the start of a filter. The pipeline will usually be followed by a `query` operator, which references parameters such as scalar expressions. A new line denoted by a pipeline character indicates the start of another filter or command that will be performed against the initial result set that is being processed by the query.

The syntax structure for the Log Analytics query language is as follows:

```
Table or search query
| operator1 scalar expression
| operator2 [function]
| operator3....
```

A scalar expression refers to numerical or string values in a single Log Analytics table cell. Scalar expressions will evaluate to scalar values. Examples of scalar expressions include the following:

```
Log (10)/1 = = value - 99
Where TimeGenerated > ago(24h)
```

Furthermore, you can use the intuitive filters and facets in the portal to further filter the result sets until you arrive at the specific information of interest. As you interact with and select field values of interest, you can add the selected values to your filter in the query bar. This intuitive feature enables you to easily build queries and learn how to filter indexed data.

You can further make use of query filters to return more specific data from the initial result set. For instance, using the table-based `Perf` query mentioned previously, you could further filter the previously mentioned result set to return records of a specific value, such as `LogicalDisk` from the `ObjectName` column in the `Perf` table. You could use a query such as the following:

```
Perf
| where ObjectName == "LogicalDisk"
| where Computer == "HV01LEN.odiks.com"
```

The preceding query starts with a basic, table-based query that filters for a `Perf` data type and uses instances of the tabular `where` operator and scalar expressions to further filter the initial result set. It also uses the reference `LogicalDisk` and a `Computer` name facet from the `ObjectName` and `Computer` columns respectively in the `Perf` table. The search then identifies all data that conforms to the query and returns the data as the result set that is then displayed in the search or Analytics portal. The pipe character is used to separate the operators, and can be used to identify a new input into the subsequent operator, as well as indicate the start of a new filter. For instance, in the preceding query, the input to the first tabular `where` operator is the `Perf` table, which is the result of the pipeline that precedes the `where` operator:

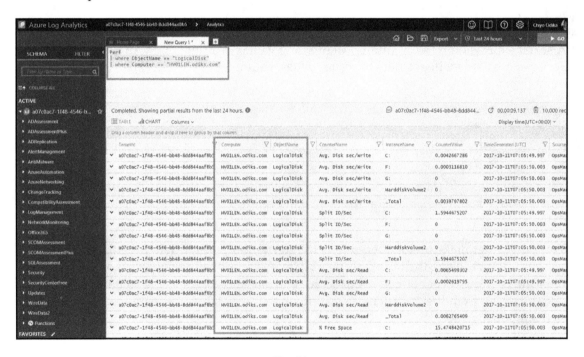

Figure 2.5

There's more...

As shown in the preceding query syntax, a Log Analytics query is comprised of a filter, which can be a table or a search command, and a set of operators or commands that can further filter the initial result set and return very specific information from the data in tables in your Log Analytics workspace, or across workspaces. The structure of the query language is such that you can start with simple basic queries and progress to use more advanced functions and capabilities as your search requirements increase in complexity. As shown previously, after you return the initial result set by referencing data in a table, you can perform incredibly advanced functions by chaining multiple operators together in order to further filter and glean insights into your data. In order to work with more advanced functions and perform more complex query operations, you will need to understand the various Log Analytics service concepts, supported query operators, functions, expressions, and other query components that are available in the Log Analytics query language.

See the links in the following *See also* section for detailed Log Analytics query language reference guides.

As stated in earlier sections of this chapter, the Log Analytics language is a highly-interactive language from which you can derive answers and insights from disparate machines and other data sources. It works at scale, is optimized for searches over large datasets, and includes smart machine-learning constructs for analyzing and correlating ingested data.

The query language supports the use of a wide range and variety of tabular and scalar operators, as well as various functions that enable you to scope, filter, and aggregate data to glean and visualize insights from even the most complex big data sets. To illustrate this, let's look at how we can quickly glean and visualize insights about data usage in a Log Analytics workspace using a relatively simple query. Consider the following query, which shows a distribution of your workspace data by type over the last 24 hours:

```
union withsource=type *
| where TimeGenerated > ago(24h)
| summarize AggregatedValue = count() by type
| render piechart
```

This query effectively says, *Take all tables in a workspace and return records with a timestamp from the past 24 hours from all table rows. From that set, aggregate the data and return the count for each data type. Display the aggregated data in a pie chart visualization.*

When executed in the Analytics portal, this query will return a pie chart rendering of the distribution of data in your workspace. Let's peel back the covers and analyze what the query is doing beneath the surface. The query begins with a `union` tabular operator, which scopes the initial result set that will be filtered further in the query:

```
union withsource=type *
```

The `union` operator references all tables in the current workspace—using the wildcard (*) operator—and returns the rows in all the workspace tables. It then passes this on for filtration. The initial result set is then filtered in the next query line introduced by the pipe character:

```
| where TimeGenerated > ago(24h)
```

The `where` tabular operator is then used with a simple scalar expression to filter all the rows returned in the initial result set that satisfy the predicate defined in the scalar expression (`TimeGenerated > ago(24h)`). This filters all the rows and returns only data from the last 24 hours. The returned data is then passed on for further filtering in the next query line, which is also introduced by another pipeline character:

```
| summarize AggregatedValue = count() by type
```

The `summarize` tabular operator then takes the data returned by the preceding filter, makes a call to the `count ( )` aggregation function, and returns the aggregated count value for each data type in all rows input into the filter.

At this point, the data has a shape that looks like the following screenshot:

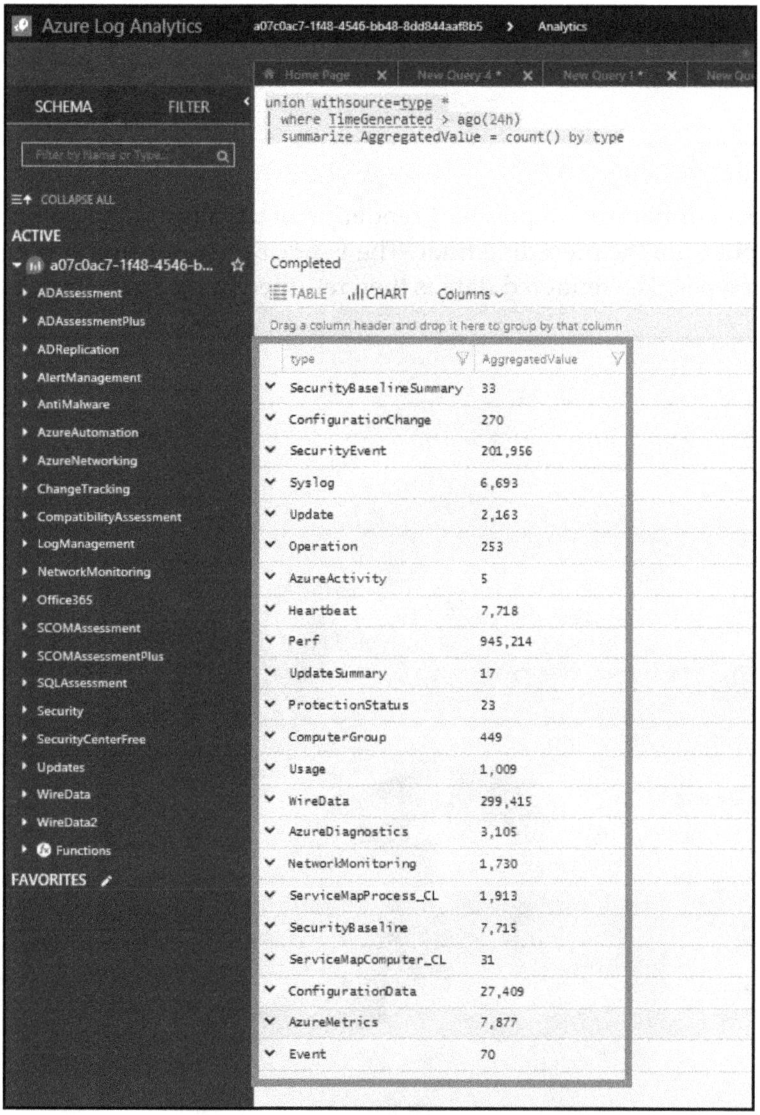

Figure 2.6

The aggregated data is then passed on for further filtering in the next and last query line, which is also introduced by another pipeline operator:

```
| render piechart
```

The `render` tabular operator renders a graphical output of the aggregated data input from the preceding filter.

The `render` operator should be the last operator in the query expression.

The `render` operator performs a pie chart rendering of the aggregated data type count information input from the preceding filter. The `render` operator supports a wide variety of visualization types. The rendered data is then returned in the following form:

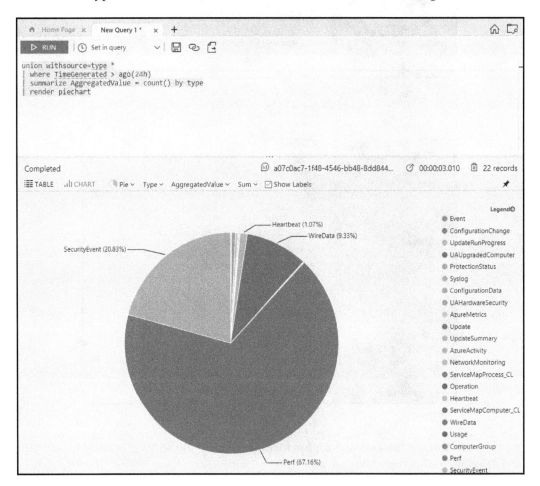

Figure 2.6

In addition to the tabular operators reviewed in the preceding example, the Log Analytics query language supports the use of scalar operators and a wide variety of functions.

See also

Microsoft has a very comprehensive language reference guide that provides a wealth of resources and guidance about the query language:

- **Azure Log Analytics language reference**:
  `https://docs.loganalytics.io/docs/Language-Reference`
- **Azure Log Analytics portal overview**:
  `https://docs.loganalytics.io/docs/Learn/Getting-Started/Getting-started-with-the-Analytics-portal`

Working with queries in the Analytics portal

In this recipe, we will review query writing in more detail, and show how to write basic queries.

Azure Log Analytics queries can start with either a table name or a search command. In either case, a table will always be the reference point because Log Analytics data sources store their data in dedicated tables in a workspace (or in several workspaces). The start of a query must, therefore, define a clear scope for the query.

 While search commands are effective, a table-based query is preferable for efficiency, returning the relevant data and providing optimal query performance.

We will review both query types in this recipe.

How to do it...

Let's begin with table-based queries.

1. Navigate to the **Azure portal** (`http://portal.azure.com`) and sign in.
2. In the Azure portal, type `Log Analytics` in the **Search resources** search field and select your workspace.

3. In the **Log Analytics** blade for your workspace, click the **Log Search** button to take you to the search field.

4. In the **Log Search** page, click on the **Advanced Analytics** link under the search box to take you to the **Analytics portal**:

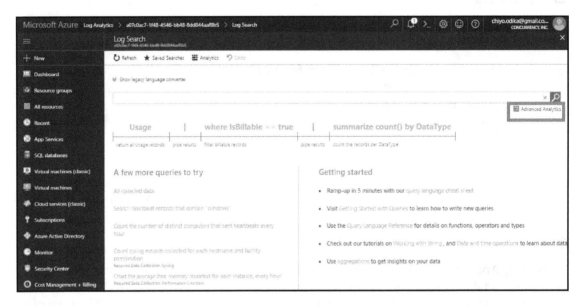

Figure 2.7:

5. In the Analytics portal, click on the + button to open a new query tab:

Figure 2.8

6. In the new query field, type `search *` into the search field and click the **Go** button in the upper right hand corner of your screen to return all records from all tables in the workspace.

7. Review the query result set. Note that by default, only the first 10,000 records are returned, and only data from the last 24 hours is returned. Also, note that the **SCHEMA** and **FILTER** panes on the left hand side of your screen display which tables and data types exist within the workspace:

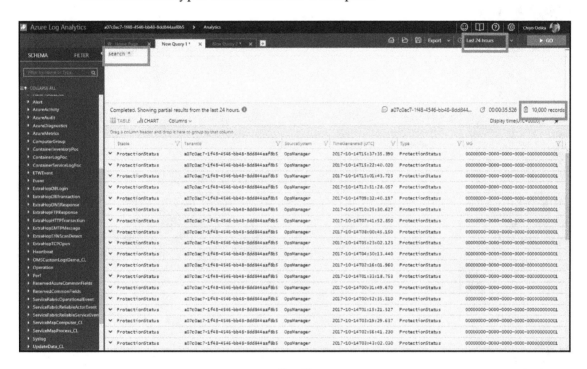

Figure 2.9

8. Next, type the following query to return counts of all data types in the Log Analytics workspace, in no particular order, and click the **Go** button:

```
search *
| summarize AggregatedValue = count() by Type
```

9. Take note of the various data types returned and the aggregated count values for each data type:

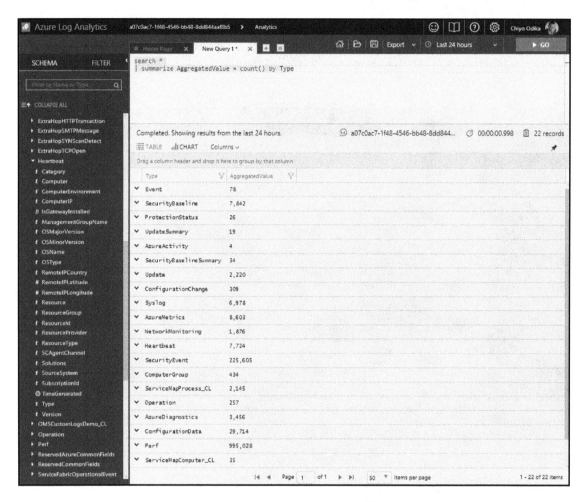

Figure 2.10

10. Open a new search tab and type the following query into the search field. Click the **Go** button to scope your query to the data from the `Heartbeat` table in your Log Analytics workspace and return the aggregated count of the `Heartbeat` data:

```
Heartbeat
| summarize AggregatedValue = count() by Type
```

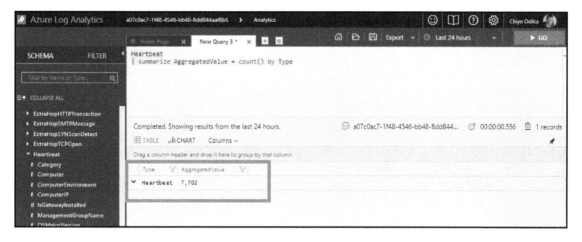

Figure 2.11

11. Revise the query by typing `Heartbeat` into the search field, so as to remove the filter in the second query line, and click the **Go** button to return all records in the `Heartbeat` table.

12. Run the query shown in the following screenshot to determine the breakdown of data based on the `OSType` column in the `Heartbeat` table:

```
Heartbeat
| summarize AggregatedValue = count() by OSType
```

Figure 2.12

The query aggregates the initial result set of records from the `Heartbeat` table, and returns a distribution of records based on the `OSType` column values in the `Heartbeat` table.

How it works...

A table-based query starts with, or references, a table in the first part of the query. This defines the scope of the query and determines what initial result set gets returned or passed on to subsequent parts of the query for further filtering or processing. In the previous example query that we walked through, a table of the name `Heartbeat` is used to define the scope of the query.

Queries can be written in various ways to arrive at the same result, provided that the query is syntactically correct. For instance, the following query is used to return an aggregated count of all records in the table with the name of `Heartbeat`:

```
Heartbeat
| summarize AggregatedValue = count() by Type
```

This query can also be written in the following form to return the exact same result:

```
union withsource = $table Heartbeat
| extend Type = $table
| summarize AggregatedValue = count() by Type
```

While these two queries will return the same data, the query behavior is rather different. While both are table-based queries (they both reference a table with the name `Heartbeat`), the first query simply scopes the initial result set to the data records in the Heartbeat table and passes it on to the filter with the `summarize` tabular operator, which uses the `aggregation` argument and `count ( )` aggregation function to return the count of all records in the `Heartbeat` table. These records are, as seen in the output, of the `Heartbeat` type.

The second query produces the same result, but does it slightly differently:

```
union withsource = $table Heartbeat
```

The query starts by using a `union` tabular operator and uses the `source` argument to return all rows of the table with the name `Heartbeat`:

```
| extend Type = $table
```

It then passes the initial result set on to a filter that features the `extend` tabular operator. This takes the input tabular result set from the preceding query line, creates calculated columns for the `Heartbeat` data, and appends it to the result set before passing it to on the next part of the query for processing:

```
| summarize AggregatedValue = count() by Type
```

The filtered data is then passed into the next filter with the `summarize` tabular operator—which uses the aggregation argument—and the `count ( )` aggregation function to return the count of all records in the Heartbeat table.

When you can arrive at a desired result from using various queries, use the simplest and most efficient queries, as this will result in noticeable query performance gains, especially when working with very large data sets.

As we will see later on with search-based queries, although the search term is case insensitive, when using search-based queries, the Log Analytics query language is, in fact, case-sensitive.

Query operators, functions, expressions, and other language keywords are typically written in lowercase. For table names and table column names, refer to the correct case in the Analytics portal schema pane.

There's more...

As mentioned earlier, Log Analytics queries can start with either a table name or a search command. We looked at table-based queries at length in the previous section, and will now look at search-based queries.

When dealing with large data sets, search-based queries will have a higher query performance cost, and could take longer to complete than a table-based query. The performance and processing time could be even longer if the search queries are not scoped.

Scope search-based queries where possible by specifying the name of the table(s) in the query.

Because search queries are less structured than table-based queries, they are actually preferable, and are better employed when searching for specific values across columns or tables. For instance, given tables named `SecurityEvent` and `WireData`, you can easily search for a specific value by scoping the tables. Consider the following query that makes no use of table scoping:

```
Search "Failed"
```

The preceding query searches all columns in all tables in a workspace for the term `"Failed"`. This query will not execute as efficiently as a query that makes use of a table scope:

```
Search in (SecurityEvent, WireData) "Failed"
```

The preceding query results in a more efficient query operation because the search is scoped to specific tables.

In addition to table scoping, search-based queries support the use of boolean operators (`AND`, `OR`), and operations such as filtering, sorting, and aggregation. For instance, you can use a table scope to define and shape the initial result set and perform further operations on the data:

```
search in (WireData) "*Russia*"
| distinct Computer, ApplicationProtocol
```

In the preceding search-based query, the query scopes the initial result set to records in the `WireData` table columns that contain `"*Russia*"`. It then passes the returned result set on for further processing using the distinct tabular operator, which produces a table with the distinct combination of the `Computer` and `ApplicationProtocol` columns of the `WireData` table:

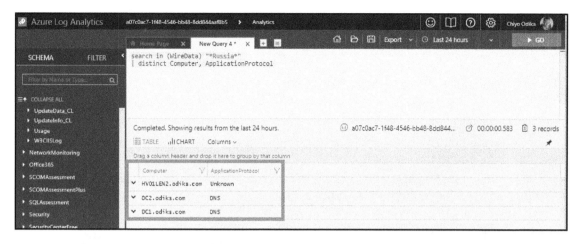

Figure 2.13

TIP

When writing queries, you can use the schema pane in the Analytics portal to review information about tables and table columns in a Log Analytics workspace.

See also

Visit the following link for further reference:

- **Azure Log Analytics language reference**:
  https://docs.loganalytics.io/docs/Language-Reference

Working with visualizations

OMS makes visualizing your indexed and queried data incredibly easy. In the OMS and Log Analytics portals, there's a dedicated view designer feature with which you can create custom views and visualizations of your data. The new Analytics portal for Azure Log Analytics makes available immediate and powerful visualization capabilities for seamless visualization of your queried data.

How to do it...

Perform the following steps:

1. Navigate to the **Azure portal** (http://portal.azure.com) and sign in.
2. In the Azure portal, type Log Analytics in the **Search resources** search field and select your workspace.
3. In the Log Analytics blade for your workspace, click the **Log Search** button to take you to the search field.
4. In the **Log Search** page, click on the **Advanced Analytics** link under the search box to take you to the Analytics portal:

Figure 2.14

5. In the Analytics portal, click on the + button to open a new query tab:

Figure 2.15

6. In the new query field, type the following query into the search field:

```
union withsource=type *
| where TimeGenerated > ago(48h)
| summarize AggregatedValue = count() by type
```

7. Click the **Go** button in the upper right hand corner of your screen to return a distribution of your data over the last 48 hours. By default, the results are displayed in a table:

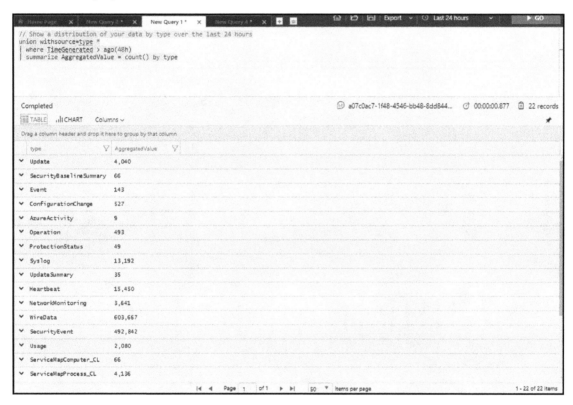

Figure 2.16

8. Click **CHART** to chart the result, and to see the results in a stacked bar chart view:

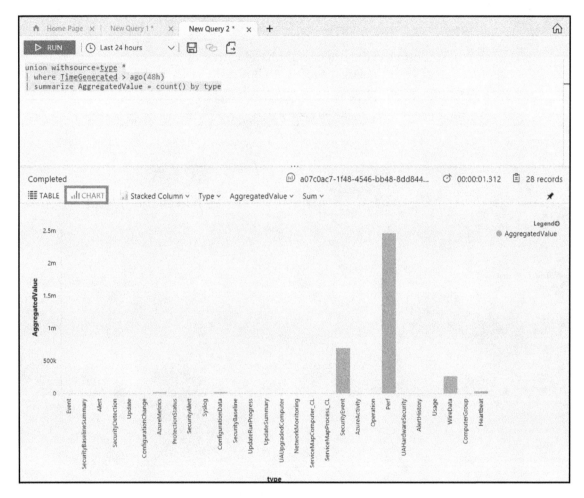

Figure 2.17

9. Click **Stacked Column** and select **Doughnut** to show another view of the results:

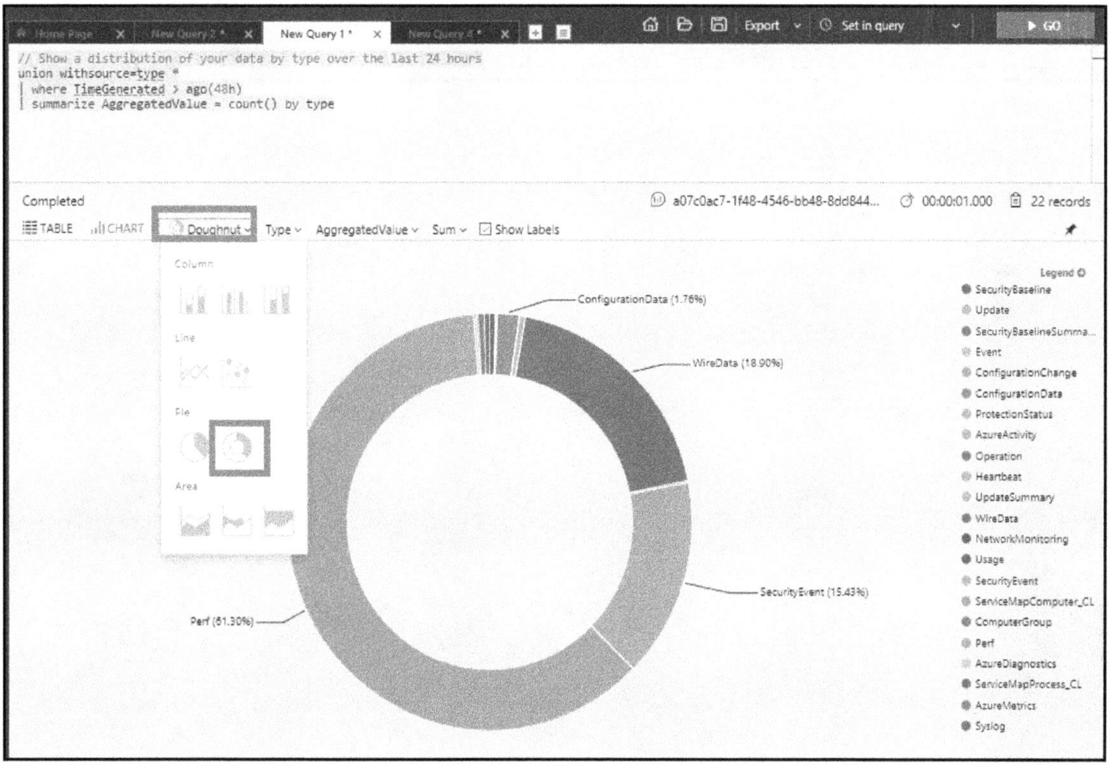

Figure 2.18

10. Return to the search field in the same page and add a new line with the `render` tabular operator to render the data as a pie chart:

```
union withsource=type *
| where TimeGenerated > ago(48h)
| summarize AggregatedValue = count() by type
| render piechart
```

11. Click the **Go** button 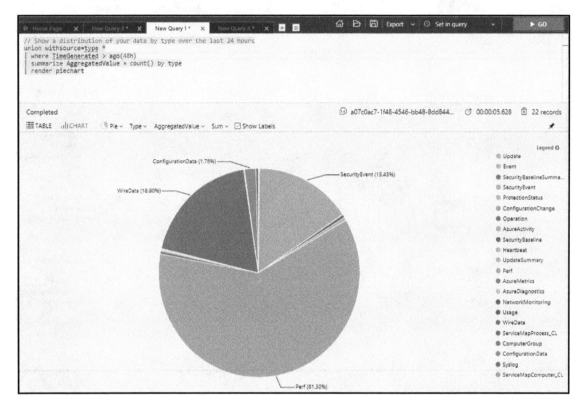 in the upper right hand corner of your screen to return a distribution of your data over the last 48 hours, rendered as a pie chart:

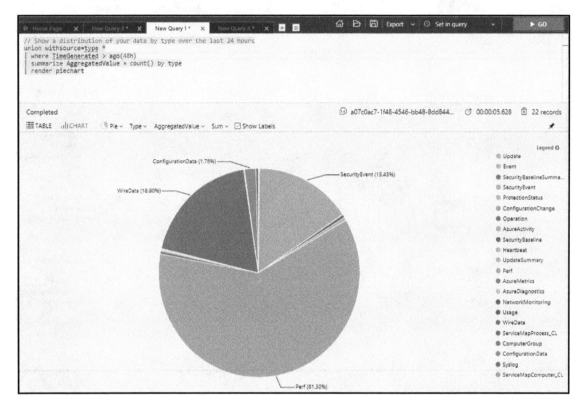

Figure 2.19

How it works...

The analytics charts enable you to create intuitive and interactive visualizations of your data. The visualizations are based on data that exists in the Log Analytics repository and queries that filter and shape the data. The chart views then make use of the query results to intuitively present the data. By default, query results are displayed in a table. You can embed the visualization within your query expression itself, and guide the visualization behavior of a query by using the `render` tabular operator.

This operator takes the filtered query table data as inputs and renders the result in a graphical output. It takes a specified visualization type as an argument. For instance, to render query results in a ladder chart, use the following query:

```
| render ladderchart
```

This operator will always begin with the pipeline character, indicating that it is taking query results as input.

 The `render` operator should be the last operator in the query expression.

If your query result set volume is significant, you can limit the volume that you display by using such tabular operators as `top`, `summarize`, and `where`. Also, note that the `render` operator will only display positive values.

There's more...

Azure Log Analytics also features visualization capabilities for performance data, which you can find in the `Perf` table in your workspace.

Working with multiple dimensions

Using **multiple dimensions**, you can use expressions in the `by` clause to create multiple visualization rows, one for each combination of values:

1. In the new query field in the Analytics portal, type the following query into the search field:

```
SecurityEvent
| where TimeGenerated > ago(1d)
| summarize count() by tostring(EventID), AccountType,
bin(TimeGenerated, 1h)
```

2. Click the **Go** button ▶ GO in the upper right-hand corner of your screen to return a distribution of your data over the last day. By default, the results are displayed in a table.

3. In the results pane, click **Chart** to view a multidimensional depiction of the data with various value combinations.

The query casts the Event ID to a string because dimensions must be of the string type.

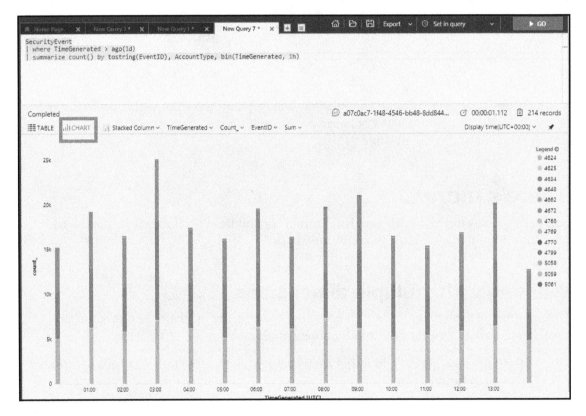

Figure 2.20

The query returns data that is segmented by two dimensions, and you can use the controls in the results pane to switch between the dimensions and visualize the data based on another dimension.

4. In the results pane, click **TimeGenerated** and select **AccountType** to see the data according to the Account type:

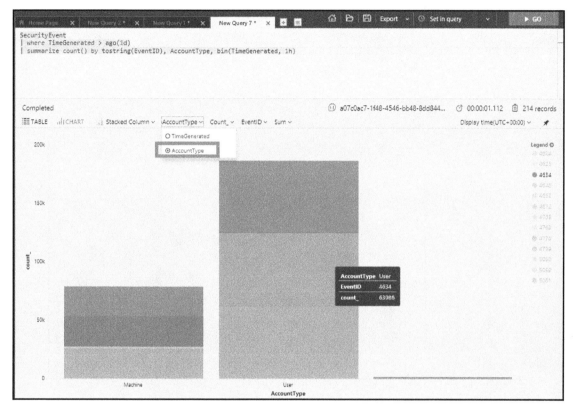

Figure 2.21

5. Click **AccountType** and select **TimeGenerated** to revert to the previous view. Click **EventID** and select **AccountType** to switch to the other dimension of the data segmentation:

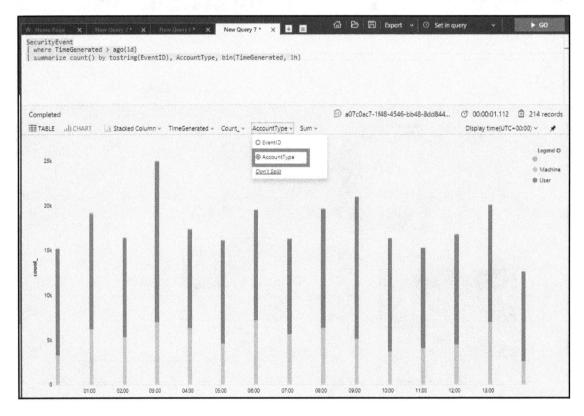

Figure 2.22

Working with time charts

Azure Log Analytics also provides time-charting capabilities. With **time charts** you can show the average fiftieth and ninety-fifth percentiles of a performance counter over a period of time. Consider the need to show the average fiftieth and ninety-fifth percentiles of the bytes total/sec performance counter in bins of 1 hour. To do this, go through the following method:

1. In the new query field in the Analytics portal, type the following query into the search field:

```
Perf
| where TimeGenerated > ago(1d)
| where CounterName == "Bytes Total/sec"
| summarize avg(CounterValue), percentiles(CounterValue, 50,
95)  by bin(TimeGenerated, 1h)
```

2. Click the **Go** button ▶ GO in the upper right-hand corner of your screen to return a distribution of your data over the last day. By default, the results are displayed in a table.

3. In the result pane, click **Chart** to render a multidimensional depiction of the data with various value combinations. Click **Stacked Column** and select **Line** to display a line chart:

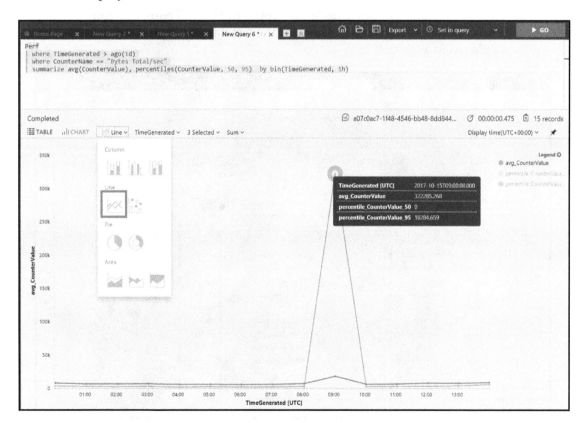

Figure 2.23

With time charts in Azure Log Analytics, you can incorporate thresholds into charts using **reference lines** to easily identify and visualize when a metric exceeds a specific threshold of interest. To do this, use the extend tabular operator to create and initialize a calculated column and append it as a threshold value to the result set. To do this, go through the following steps:

1. Modify the query expression in the search field to extend the result set with a constant column that serves as a threshold:

```
Perf
| where TimeGenerated > ago(1d)
| where CounterName == "Bytes Total/sec"
| summarize avg(CounterValue), percentiles(CounterValue, 50,
95) by bin(TimeGenerated, 1h)
| extend Threshold = 100000
```

2. Click the **Go** button ▶ GO in the upper right-hand corner of your screen to return a distribution of your data over the last day. By default, the results are displayed in a table:

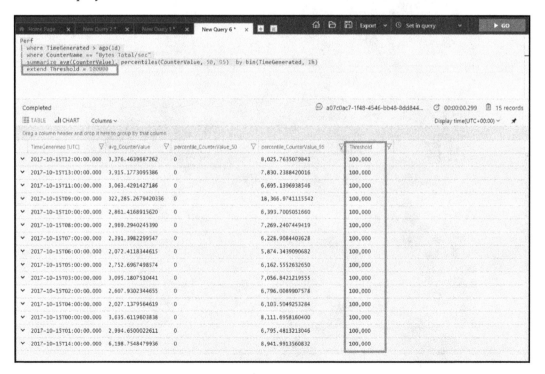

Figure 2.24

3. In the results pane, click **Chart** to render a multidimensional depiction of the data with various value combinations. Click **Stacked Column** and select **Line** to display a line chart with a visible threshold line:

Figure 2.25

Feed Power BI from Azure Log Analytics

Power BI is a suite of business analytics tools that helps you analyze data and share insights. Through Power BI integration with OMS, you can export data from the OMS data store into Power BI in order to leverage its analysis and visualization tools. You can export Azure Log Analytics data to Power BI in various ways, including the following:

- **Power BI integration with OMS**: This integration will enable you to export datasets to Power BI in order to create visualizations in Power BI.

- **Export Analytics query**: You can write queries in the Analytics portal and export them to the Power BI dashboard.
- **Stream Analytics and continuous export**: You can use Stream Analytics to process exported data from Azure Log Analytics. This will require you to create an Azure storage account and a Stream Analytics instance. It will also require you to configure a continuous export of data to Azure storage and perform some additional configurations.

When you create a query in the Analytics portal, you can use the **Export** feature to export the query for use with other Analytics tools, such as Power BI:

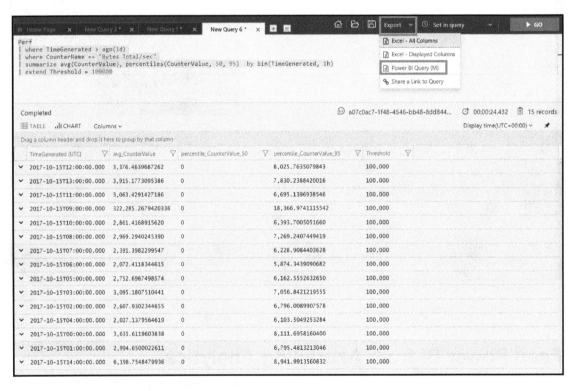

Figure 2.26

See also

Visit the following links for more information:

- **Azure Log Analytics language reference**: `https://docs.loganalytics.io/docs/Language-Reference`
- **Smart Analytics**: `https://docs.loganalytics.io/docs/Learn/Tutorials/Smart-Analytics/Understanding-Autocluster`

Managing Alerts in OMS

3

OMS facilitates alert and event management by providing you with tools for generating and detecting meaningful notifications about the status of your IT infrastructure and services, as well as viewing and correlating alerts from various connected sources such as **System Center Operations Manager** (**SCOM**), Nagios, and Zabbix. The alerting and event management capabilities in OMS are based on automation, and Log Analytics capabilities that enable you to create alert rules and actions, and the Alert Management solution that helps you analyze the alert generated in Log Analytics as well as from a variety of other sources. In this chapter, we will review alerting in OMS, alert actions, and available options for the entire alerting lifecycle. Topics include:

- Working with Search Queries and Alert Rules
- Configuring Alert Actions and Notifications
- Using Automation with Alert Rules
- Using ITSM Actions
- Working with the Alert Management Solution.

Working with search queries and alert rules

Alerts in OMS are created using search queries that are run at regular intervals. These alerts are stored in the OMS repository and can be retrieved and queried with a log search query. Alert data records in OMS can be analyzed using the Alert Management solution which we will review later on this chapter. Furthermore OMS allows for the integration of monitoring into your existing event management workflows, and also enables you to centrally monitor and manage work items across your ITSM products/ services.

In Log Analytics, you can create an alert from a log query. To generate an alert from a log query, you will need to define an alert rule in which you specify a search criteria with a log query, and run the query at regular intervals. An alert is then created when the query returns alert record results that match the defined criteria. With this concept in mind, you can generate alerts based on any data indexed in the Log Analytics repository.

How to do it...

In this exercise, you will create, edit, and review an alert rule to generate an alert when the available memory is at or below a certain threshold.

Creating an alert rule

Perform the following steps:

1. Navigate to the Azure portal at `http://portal.azure.com` and sign in.
2. In the Azure portal, type **Log Analytics** in the search field and select your workspace.

3. In the **Log Analytics** blade for your workspace, click the **Log Search** button to take you to the search field:

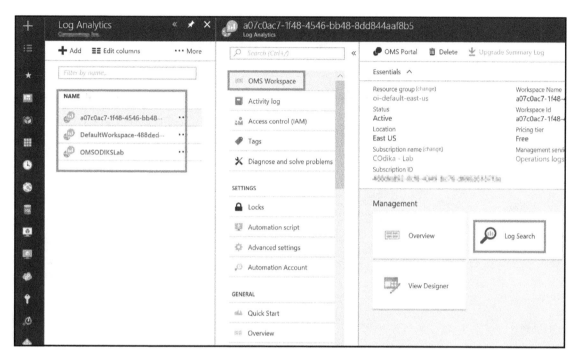

Figure 3.1

4. In the **Log Search** editor, conduct a search by typing in this table-based query and clicking the search icon:

```
Perf
| where ( ObjectName == "Memory")
| where (CounterName == "Available MBytes") and
CounterValue<=1024
|summarize avg (CounterValue) by Computer
```

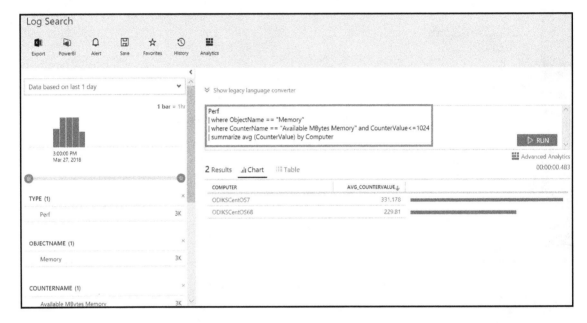

Figure 3.2

5. After the results have been displayed in the results field, click the alert button at the top of the **Log Search** page to open the alert rule page:

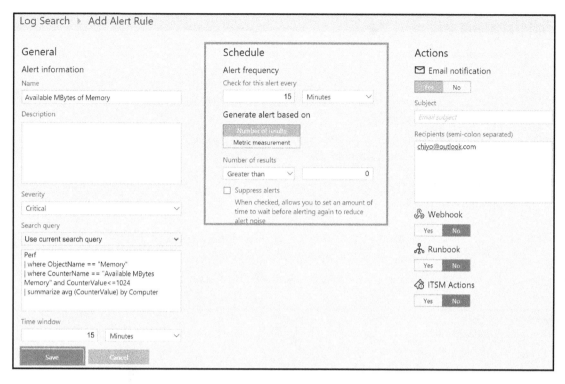

Figure 3.3

6. In the **Add Alert Rule** page, enter a rule name in the **Name** field, such as `Available Mbytes of Memory` <= 1024, and optionally, fill in the **Description** field.

7. Click the drop-down under the **Severity** to select an alert severity, review the query in the **Search query** field, and enter a time range in the **Time window** field.

8. In the **Schedule** section of the alert rule page, enter a time frequency in the **Alert frequency** field to indicate how often the query should be run.

> You can specify a time range and alert frequency of between 5 minutes and 24 hours in both the **Time window** and **Alert frequency** fields.

9. Next, select the **Number of results** field and **Greater than 0** in the **Number of results** field. Then click on **Save**.

Editing an alert rule

Perform the following steps:

1. Navigate to the Azure portal at `http://portal.azure.com` and sign in.
2. In the Azure portal, type **Log Analytics** in the **Search resources** search field and select your workspace.
3. In the **Log Analytics** blade for your workspace, click on the **OMS Portal** button to take you to the OMS portal.
4. In the OMS portal, click the settings icon to navigate to the **Settings** page, and select **Alerts**.
5. We can now:
   - Edit an alert rule by clicking the pencil icon beside it
   - Disable an alert rule by selecting **Off**
   - Delete an alert rule by clicking the **X** icon beside it:

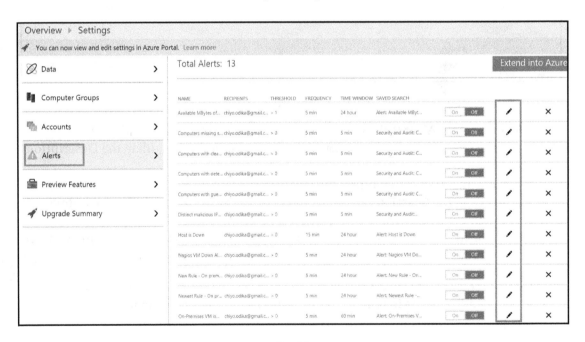

Figure 3.4

How it works...

Alert rules automatically run log searches at regular intervals that you define in the rule. If the log search returns results that match the defined criteria, then an alert record is created and an action can be performed, based on what you define in the alert rule.

The following properties are required in an alert rule:

- **Search query**: The query upon which an alert rule is based will run every time the alert rule executes.
- **Time window**: The time range of current time for which records are returned by the search query. This time window can range between 5 minutes and 24 hours. For instance, if you set the range to the default 15 minutes and the query is run at 12:00 PM, the search query will return only records created between 11:45 PM and 12:00 PM.
- **Alert frequency**: This determines how often the search query is run. The alert rule frequency can be between 5 minutes and 24 hours. Importantly, the alert rule frequency should be less than or equal to the time window, in order for the query to accurately return relevant records.
- **Threshold**: This depends on the type of alert rule created, and when defined, determines when search query results will generate alerts. See the following Alert rule types section.
- **Suppress alerts**: This feature helps to reduce noise. When enabled, and after the alert rule creates a new alert, it disables actions for the rule for a length of time that you define in minutes or hours.

Alert rule types

Log Analytics alert rules are of two types which are as follows:

- **Number of results**: When selected, this will create a single alert for all records that conform to the search query and alert rule arguments. An alert will be generated if the number of records returned by the search query is either **Greater than** or **Less than** the value you specify.

- **Metric measurements**: When selected, this will create a distinct alert for each record in the search query results, with values that conform to the defined metric measurement threshold. The metric measurement alert rule type is composed of the following properties:
  - **Aggregate Value**: This is the threshold that must be exceeded by each aggregate value in the records returned by the search query in order for it to be a threshold breach. You can look for results that are **Greater than** or **Less than** the specified value in order to be considered a breach.
  - **Trigger alert based on**: This is the number of breaches required in order for an alert to be created. You can look for a number of **Total breaches** or **Consecutive breaches** in order for an alert to be generated.

When using the **Metric Measurement** alert rule type, the search query should contain `AggregatedValue` and `bin (TimeGenerated, <roundTo>)`.

For instance, the following query can be used with a **Metric Measurement** alert rule type to create an alert for each computer object in a query with a value that exceeds an 80% threshold:

```
Perf
| where CounterName == "% Processor Time" and ObjectName == "Processor" and
InstanceName == "_Total"
| summarize AggregatedValue = avg (CounterValue) by Computer, bin
(TimeGenerated, 5m)
```

To specify that the values of interest are those above the 80% threshold, we specify **Greater than 80** in the **Aggregate Value** field for the **Metric measurement** alert rule:

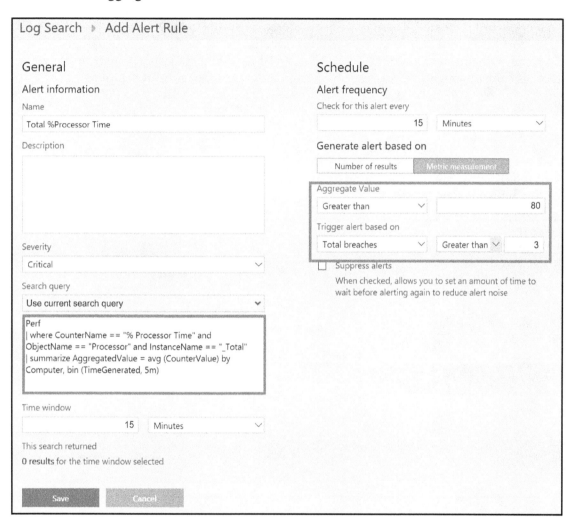

Figure 3.5

There's more...

When the criteria defined in an alert rule is matched by the results of the search query, then an alert record is created. These records are stored as events in the `Alert` table in the OMS repository and are of type alert. Alert records created by alert rules in Log Analytics have a **SourceSystem** property value of OMS. This can be used to distinguish them from alert records from other sources, such as SCOM and the Alert Management solution.

You can use this query to find alert records in your workspace:

```
Alert
| summarize count () by SourceSystem
```

This query aggregates the content of the `Alert` table and returns the count of alert records by the **SourceSystem** property:

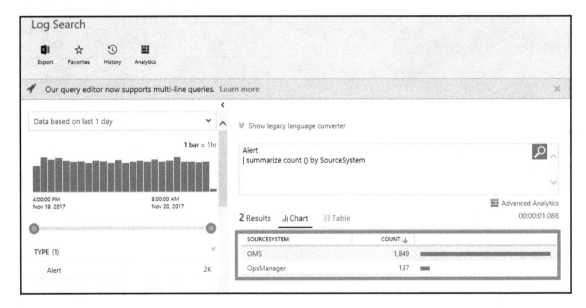

Figure 3.6

You can view the properties of an alert record generated by a **Log Analytics** alert rule by specifying the OMS SourceSystem value in your search query:

```
Alert
| where SourceSystem == "OMS"
```

In the resulting field, click the **[+] show more** button to expand the result view for one of the alert records. This will display all of the alert record properties and corresponding property values:

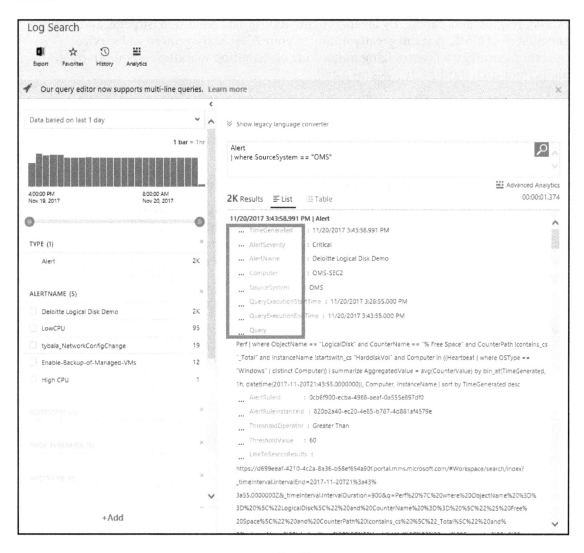

Figure 3.7

Third-party Alert Management

As mentioned in Chapter 1, *Getting Started with Microsoft Operations Management Suite*, OMS enables you to connect various sources, including third-party monitoring systems such as SCOM, Nagios, and Zabbix. By leveraging the robust data collection, storage, and analysis capabilities of OMS, you can greatly optimize your Alert Management and service operations strategy by centralizing monitoring and alerting workflows. You can collect alerts from such third-party systems as:

- Microsoft SCOM
- Zabbix
- Nagios

Operations Manager Alerts in Log Analytics

Integrating OMS with SCOM enables you to benefit from the extensive data collection, storage, and analysis capabilities of Log Analytics, and maintains your investments in System Center. Through SCOM integration with OMS, alert data created in SCOM is forwarded from the SCOM management group to the OMS repository. Once indexed, this data can then be analyzed with the Alert Management solution, which provides an intuitive breakdown of the alert data in SCOM.

To Connect SCOM to OMS:

1. Open the SCOM console and select the **Administration** workspace.

2. Expand the **Operations Management Suite** option and click **Connection** as shown in the following screenshot:

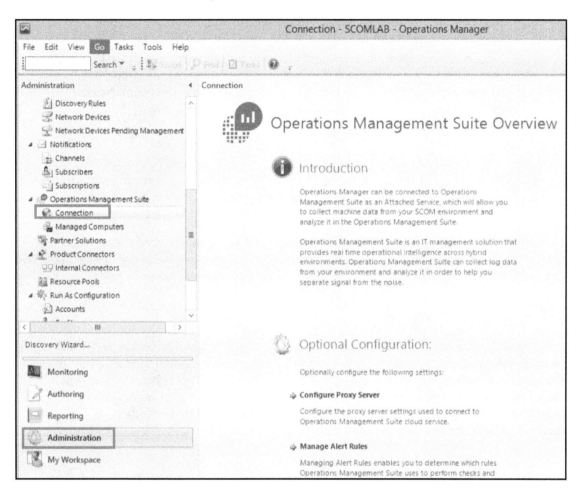

Figure 3.8

3. Click the link to **Register to Operations Management Suite**.

4. On the **Operations Management Suite Onboarding Wizard: Authentication** page, enter the email address or phone number and the password of the administrator account associated with your OMS subscription. Click **Sign in**.

5. Once authenticated, on the **Select Operations Management Suite Workspace** page, select your workspace. Click on the drop-down to select your OMS workspace if you have more than one workspace, and then click **Next**.

6. On the **Summary** page, confirm your settings and click **Create.**

7. On the **Finish** page, click **Close.**

SCOM only supports one OMS workspace at a time. To change the OMS workspace integrated with SCOM, follow the same preceding steps to **Re-configure Operations Management Suite**.

Once you connect SCOM to OMS, SCOM is then used as a data source for Log Analytics, and SCOM alerts are written into the OMS repository as they are created and modified. You can use the following query to find alert records for alerts generated in SCOM:

```
Alert
| where SourceSystem == "OpsManager"
```

Alert records generated by the SCOM alerts in Log Analytics will have a type of alert, and a **SourceSystem** of **OpsManager**. The properties for these records will differ slightly from those of alert records created by alert rules in Log Analytics. This is because alerts in SCOM are generated by monitors or SCOM rules, and with integrated alert management in SCOM, monitors in SCOM. For instance the state of alerts, can be updated manually, or automatically if the alert is generated by a monitor.

To view the properties of an alert record created from an SCOM alert, from the results of the previous query, click the **[+] show more** button to expand the result view for one of the alert records. This will display all of the alert record properties and corresponding property values:

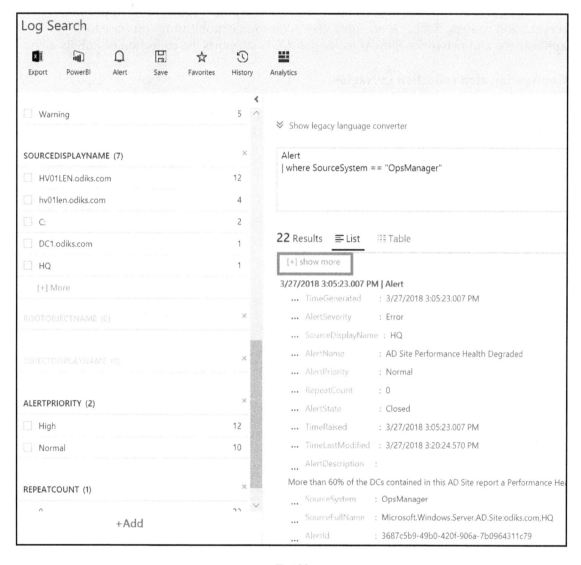

Figure 3.9

After alerts are created by the alert rule, you can then perform various actions on the alerts.

Collecting Nagios and Zabbix alerts in Log Analytics

In addition to SCOM, you can also collect alerts from open source monitoring tools such as Nagios and Zabbix. Nagios which is also known as Nagios Core, is an open source computer software application that monitors systems, networks, and infrastructure. It offers monitoring and alerting for various infrastructure components, including applications, servers, and routers. Zabbix is an enterprise open source monitoring software for applications and networks. Similar to Nagios, OMS supports the collection of Zabbix alerts.

Configuring alert collection in Nagios:

1. Navigate to the **Nagios** web interface and verify the location of the Nagios log file. This location could vary based on installation and configuration.
2. On the home page, click on **Alerts** under the **Reports** tab, and take note of the log file path:

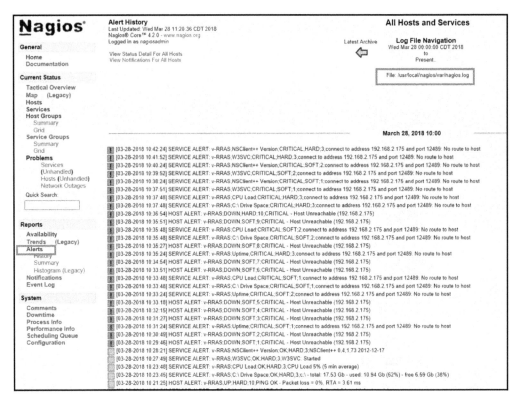

Figure 3.10

The log file path could vary based on Nagios configuration. As seen in the preceding screenshot, the log is located at `/usr/local/nagios/var/nagios.log`. It could also be located in a path such as `/var/log/nagios/nagios.log`.

3. Grant the `omsagent` read access to the Nagios log file identified previously. If the `nagios.log` file is owned by the `nagios` group, you can add the `omsagent` user to the `nagios` group using the following command:

Sudo usermod -a -G nagios omsagent

4. Navigate to the configuration file located at `/etc/opt/microsoft/omsagent/conf/omsagent.conf` and ensure that the following entries are present and are not commented out:

```
<source>
  type tail
  #Update path to point to your nagios.log
  path /usr/local/nagios/var/nagios.log
  format none
  tag oms.nagios
</source>

<filter oms.nagios>
  type filter_nagios_log
</filter>
```

5. Restart the `omsagent` and `syslog` daemons using the following commands:

```
sudo sh /opt/microsoft/omsagent/bin/service_control restart
sudo service rsyslog restart
```

Once you start collecting Nagios alerts in OMS, you can use the following query to find alert records for alerts generated in Nagios:

```
Alert
| where SourceSystem == "Nagios"
```

Alert records collected by Nagios will have a type of `Alert`, and a `SourceSystem` of `Nagios`.

Configuring Zabbix alert collection:

1. Navigate to the configuration file located at `/etc/opt/microsoft/omsagent/conf/omsagent.conf` and ensure that the following entries are present and are not commented out:

```
<source>
  type zabbix_alerts
  run_interval 1m
  tag oms.zabbix
  zabbix_url http://localhost/zabbix/api_jsonrpc.php
  zabbix_username Admin
  zabbix_password zabbix
</source>
```

2. Restart the `omsagent` and `syslog` daemons using the following command:

```
sudo sh /opt/microsoft/omsagent/bin/service_control restart
sudo service rsyslog restart
```

As seen previously, you need to specify a user and password in clear text. This is not an ideal configuration for obvious security reasons, so create a user account and assign only the permissions required for monitoring. Consult the Zabbix documentation on permissions in the following *See Also* section.

Once you start collecting Zabbix alerts in OMS, you can use the following query to find alert records for alerts generated in Zabbix:

```
Alert
| where SourceSystem == "Zabbix"
```

Alert records collected by Nagios will have a type of `Alert`, and a `SourceSystem` of `Zabbix`.

See also

For more information, refer to the following URL:

- **Zabbix permissions documentation**: `https://www.zabbix.com/documentation/` `2.0/manual/config/users_and_usergroups/permissions`.

Configuring alert actions and notifications

After alerts are generated by the alert rule(s), you can perform such actions as creating and sending email notifications, initiating web hook actions, or starting a runbook.

Getting ready

In order to use the runbook actions with alert rules, you must have the **Automation solution** installed in your OMS workspace. Other actions can be performed without this requirement. Additionally, we will go through a complete walk-through of creating an alert rule with a webhook to call a service such as Mockbin at `http://mockbin.org/` or Slack at `https://slack.com`. Mockbin is a hosted service for creating custom endpoints for testing HTTP requests. Mockbin generates an endpoint based on criteria you specify and then allows any online service to hit that endpoint and receive a predefined response. Setup is easy, and we don't need an account to set up a new bin. To follow along, you will need to create a bin.

Enabling webhooks in Slack

Perform the following steps:

1. Navigate to Slack from `https://slack.com` and either select an existing channel or click the + beside channel to create a new channel.

2. Select the channel and click on **+Add an app** as shown in the following screenshot:

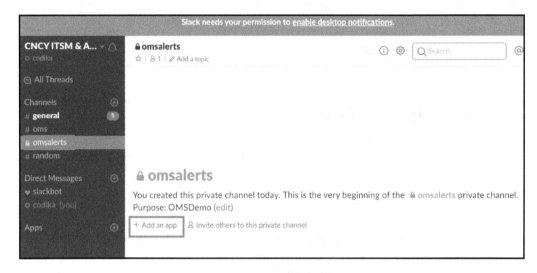

Figure 3.11

3. In the search field, type **webhook** and select the **Incoming WebHooks** option from the list:

Figure 3.12

4. Click on **Add Configuration** and in the resulting window, click on **Add Incoming WebHooks integration**.

5. Navigate to the **Webhook URL** and copy the URL for use in the OMS alert rule:

Webhook URL

Send your JSON payloads to this URL.
Show setup instructions

https://hooks.slack.com/services/T0F13G91T/B84B1P4Q4/kfeYSMQvsdG7AO0

Copy URL • Regenerate

Figure 3.13

How to do it...

You can perform various actions with alerts generated by OMS alert rules.

Using email actions

1. Navigate to the Azure portal at `http://portal.azure.com` and sign in.
2. In the Azure portal, type **Log Analytics** in the **Search resources** search field and select your workspace.
3. In the **Log Analytics** blade for your workspace, click the **OMS Portal** button to take you to the OMS portal.
4. In the OMS portal, click the settings icon to navigate to the **Settings** page and select **Alerts**.
5. From the list of alert rules, click the pencil icon next to the **Available Mbytes of memory <=1024** alert rule created earlier.
6. In the **Actions** section, select **Yes** to enable email notifications.
7. Enter **Available Mbytes of Memory <=1024** in the **Subject** field.
8. Add addresses of one or more email recipients in the **Recipients (semi-colon seperated)** field. Use a semicolon (;) to separate addresses, if you specify more than one address.

9. Click **Save** to complete the alert rule as shown in the following screenshot:

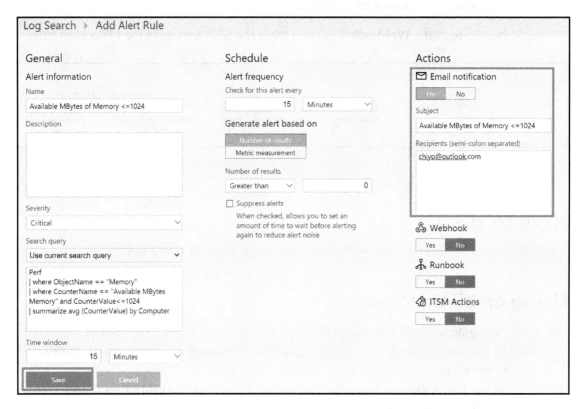

Figure 3.14

Once saved, the alert rule will continue to run as configured and create alert records when the defined threshold is met, but it will now send an email to the recipients defined in the rule, as seen in the following screenshot:

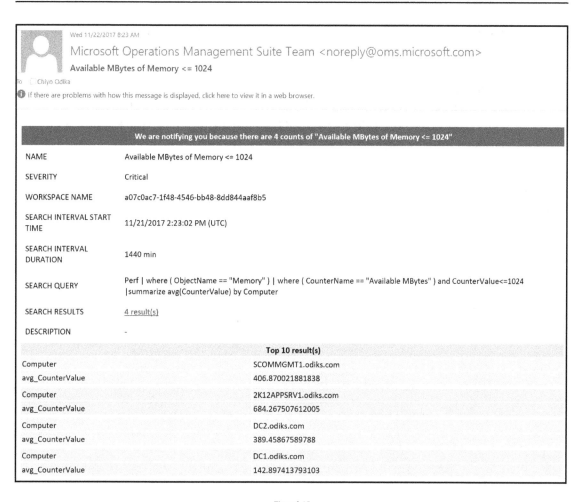

Figure 3.15

Using Webhook actions

1. Navigate to the Azure portal at `http://portal.azure.com` and sign in.
2. In the Azure portal, type **Log Analytics** in the **Search resources** search field and select your workspace.
3. In the **Log Analytics** blade for your workspace, click the **OMS Portal** button to take you to the OMS portal.
4. In the OMS portal, click the settings icon to navigate to the **Settings** page, and select **Alerts**.

5. From the list of alert rules, click the pencil icon next to the **Available Mbytes of Memory <=1024** alert rule created earlier.

6. In the **Actions** section, select **Yes** for Webhook.

7. Paste the Slack URL copied in the *Getting Ready* section previously into the **Webhook URL** field.

8. Check the box to **Include custom JSON payload**, and paste the following JSON payload into the payload field:

```
{
"text":"Alert rule '#alertrulename' running every
#searchinterval seconds fired with #searchresultcount records."
}
```

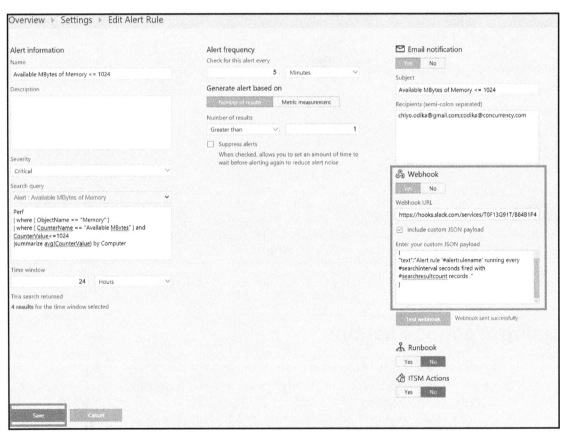

Figure 3.16

9. Click **Save** to complete and save the alert rule.
10. After the alert frequency interval elapses, check the Slack messages for the alert:

 incoming-webhook APP 10:40 AM
Alert rule 'Available MBytes of Memory <= 1024' running every 300 seconds fired with 4 results records .

Figure 3.17

How it works...

You can configure a Log Analytics alert rule to perform certain actions when an alert is created. The following actions are supported for alert rules:

- **Email action:** When you configure an email action,The alert rule will send an email with details of the alert to one or more recipients
- **Webhook**: Use this action to post alerts from Log Analytics to an external source by invoking an external process through a single HTTP POST request
- **Runbook**: Use this action to start an Azure Automation runbook
- **ITSM Actions**: Through integration between Log Analytics and your ITSM platform, use this action to create work items (events, alerts, and incidents) in ITSM from OMS alerts

Email actions

When configured in alert rules, email actions send emails with the details of the alert to one or more recipients. Email notifications will include summary information about the alert, including the name of the alert, severity, Log Analytics workspace name, information about the search query, and details of up to 10 records returned by the search query.

The email notification also includes a link to a log search in Log Analytics that will return all the records referenced in the alert that triggered the email notification:

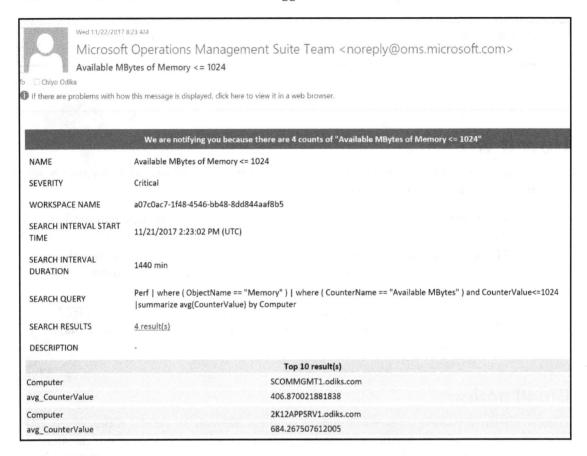

Figure 3.18

Log Analytics notification emails show sender information as Microsoft OMS team noreply@oms.microsoft.com.

Webhook actions

When configured in alert rules, these enable you to invoke an external process through a single HTTP POST request. When used with alert rules, a webhook can send a message to an external service, such as Mockbin or Slack, which supports webhooks and accepts JSON payloads. Webhooks can also be used to start runbooks in Azure Automation through a single HTTP request.

Webhooks include a URL and a custom JSON payload that includes the message text and some options. Message attachments can also be used with webhooks to display richly-formatted messages in certain external services such as Slack.

> You can replace the default JSON payload with a custom payload of your own, using supported parameters and variables.

This table shows some supported parameters and variable values that you can use in a custom payload:

Parameter	Variable	Description
AlertRuleName	#alertrulename	The name of the alert rule generating the alert.
AlertThresholdOperator	#thresholdoperator	Greater than or less than threshold operator for the alert rule.
AlertThresholdValue	#thresholdvalue	Alert rule threshold value used with the threshold operator.
LinkToSearchResults	#linktosearchresults	Link to the log search query that returns records that the alert is based on.
ResultCount	#searchresultcount	Number of records returned by the search.
SearchIntervalStartTimeUtc	#searchintervalstarttimeutc	Query start time in UTC format.

SearchIntervalEndtimeUtc	`#searchintervalendtimeutc`	Query end time in UTC format.
SearchIntervalInSeconds	`#searchinterval`	The time window for the alert rule.
SearchQuery	`#searchquery`	Log search query in the alert rule.
SearchResults	N.A.	First 5,000 records returned by the log search query in JSON format.
WorkspaceID	`#workspaceid`	OMS workspace ID.

Table 3.1

For external services that don't support webhooks specifically, you can still call a REST API using a HTTP request formatted for the service API.

Using automation with alert rules

Automation plays an important part in the fabric of OMS and enables much of the functionality in the service. One use case is the application of automation for alert management and issue remediation. In addition to the email and webhook actions reviewed in the previous section, you can also configure Runbook actions within OMS alert rules to start a Runbook in Azure Automation. Alert rules can be configured to automatically run an automation Runbook to remediate an issue identified by the alert rule. Alert configurations provide two options for calling Runbooks:

- Directly selecting a Runbook
- Using a webhook

While you can use a webhook without linking your OMS workspace to an Automation account, you will need to link your OMS workspace to an Automation account in order to directly select a runbook for use with an alert rule.

Getting ready

You can link an automation account to your OMS workspace from the Azure portal.

Installing automation solution in OMS workspace

To add the **Automation & Control** solution offering, you must create an automation account or select an existing automation account. An automation account is an Azure resource, through which you can manage all of your Azure, cloud, and on-premises resources:

1. Navigate to the Azure portal and click the **New** button. Type **Automation & Control** into the marketplace search field and press *Enter*.
2. Select **Automation & Control** in the **Everything** blade and click **Create**.
3. In the create new solution blade, click the **OMS Workspace**, select your **OMS Workspace**, check the **Automation Hybrid Worker** and any other solutions you would like to install, and click the **OMS Workspace Settings** tab.
4. In the resulting blade, confirm your workspace, Azure subscription, location, resource group, and pricing tier information, and click **Automation account.**
5. In the **Automation Account** blade, select an existing automation account or click on the **Create an Automation account** option.

Creating the Automation account when you add the Automation & Control solution offering to your workspace establishes the integration with your OMS workspace and enables you to install related management solutions into your workspace.

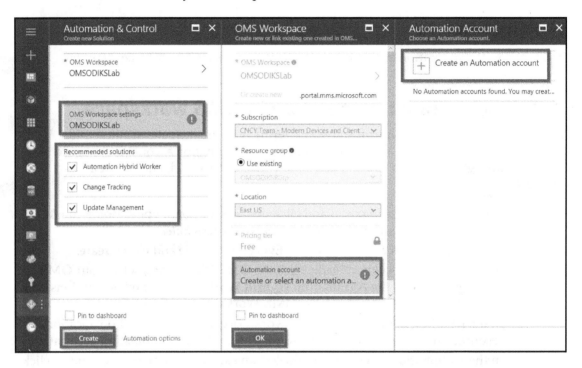

Figure 3.19

6. In the **Add Automation Account** blade, enter the name of your Azure automation account in the **Name** field, review the subscription, resource group, location, and Azure Run As account creation options, and click **OK** as shown in the following screenshot:

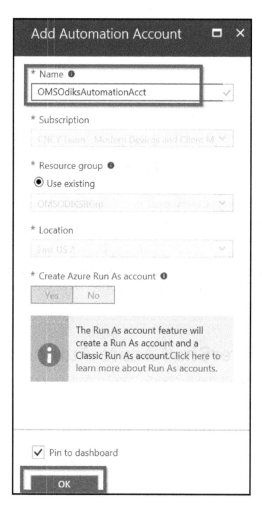

Figure 3.20

7. After the deployments are complete, click **OK** in the **OMS Workspace** blade and upon completion of the deployment, click **Create** in the **Automation & Control** blade to finish adding the Automation & Control solution offering to your workspace.

After completing this exercise, you will now be able to perform Runbook actions and call Runbooks in alert rules.

How to do it...

Configuring a Runbook action in OMS consists of the following steps:

1. Create a new Azure Automation Runbook in the Azure portal
2. Define any necessary credential assets if the Runbook will run on a hybrid worker group
3. Create an OMS search query and use the query in an alert rule
4. Use the automation solution and invoke the Runbook in the OMS alert rule

For illustration, we will create an alert rule that is based on a search query which looks for Nagios alert records indicating that an on-premises server is down. The alert rule will then make use of a runbook action run on a hybrid worker to determine the state of the virtual machine and restart it if necessary.

Create a new PowerShell Azure Automation runbook

In this scenario, we will import the runbook into an Automation account that is linked to the Log Analytics workspace, so that we can invoke the runbook from the Log Analytics alert rule described above:

```
workflow Start-OnPremVM
{
    param (
        [object]$WebhookData
        )
    $RequestBody = ConvertFrom-JSON -InputObject $WebhookData.RequestBody
    # Get all metadata properties
    $AlertRuleName = $RequestBody.AlertRuleName
    $ResultCount =$RequestBody.ResultCount
    $SearchQuery = $RequestBody.SearchQuery
    $WorkspaceID = $RequestBody.WorkspaceId
    # Get detailed search results
    if($RequestBody.SearchResult -ne $null)
```

```
    {
      $SearchResultRows   =
      $RequestBody.SearchResult.tables[0].rows
      $SearchResultColumns =
      $RequestBody.SearchResult.tables[0].columns;
  #Get Azure Automation VMHost Variable
      If (!$VMHost)
      {
          $VMHost = Get-AutomationVariable
          StartComputerDefaultHostName
      }
Write-Output "VM Host automation asset is $VMHost"
Write-Output "Workspace ID: '$WorkspaceID'."
Write-Output "Alert Rule Name: '$AlertRuleName'."
Write-Output "Search Query: '$SearchQuery'."
Write-Output "Result Count: '$ResultCount'."
foreach ($SearchResultRow in $SearchResultRows)
{
        $Column = 0
        $Record=New-Object-TypeNamePSObject
foreach ($SearchResultColumn in $SearchResultColumns)
  {
    $Name = $SearchResultColumn.name
    $ColumnValue = $SearchResultRow[$Column]
    $Record | Add-Member -MemberType NoteProperty -Name
    $name -Value $ColumnValue -Force
    $Column++
  }
    #Retrieve VM target from OMS Alert Record
    $GetVM=$Record.HostName
    Write-Output "OMS Reports Computer '$GetVM' is
    down. Checking VM State..."
    $Computer= Get-WmiObject -Namespace
              root\virtualization\v2 -Class
              Msvm_ComputerSystem |
              Where{$_.ElementName -ieq $GetVM}
    $VM=$Computer.ElementName
    If ($Computer.EnabledState -ieq 3)
    {
    Write-Output "VM State is stopped. Will start VM"
    Start-VM -ComputerName $VMHost -Name $VM
    Write-output "VM Host is $VMHost"
    Write-Output "Attempting to Start '$VM'"
    Start-Sleep-s20
    $Computer= Get-WmiObject -Namespace
              root\virtualization\v2 -Class
              Msvm_ComputerSystem |
              Where{$_.ElementName -ieq $GetVM}
```

```
      $VM=$Computer.ElementName
      If ($Computer.EnabledState -ieq 3)
      {
         Write-Output "Failed to Start $VM"
      }
      else
      {
         Write-Output "Successfully started $VM"
      }
  }
  else
  {
     Write-Output "VM State is not stopped. Will now
     exit."
  }
 }
}
}
```

Perform the following steps:

1. Download this PowerShell Workflow runbook from the GitHub at `https://github.com/MSOMSBook/BookChapters`. The file is named **Start-OnPremVM.ps1**.

2. Navigate to the Azure Portal (`http://portal.azure.com`) and sign in

3. In the Azure Portal, type Automation Accounts and select and open your Automation account.

4. In Automation Account, select Runbooks, click Add a runbook at the top of the page and select Import an existing runbook.

5. In the Import blade, for the **Runbook file**, click the browse button, and select the runbook you downloaded from GitHub in step 1. This will automatically fill in the **Runbook type** and **Name** fields.

6. Click Create to finish importing the runbook.

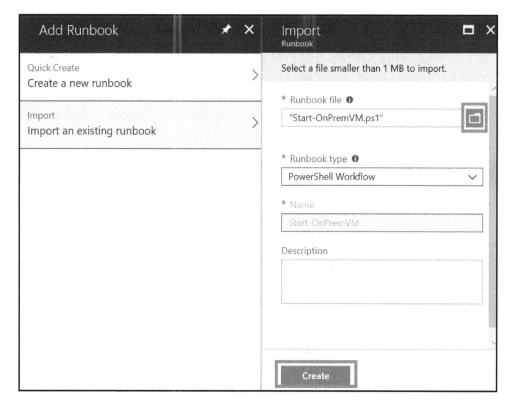

Figure 3.21

7. After importing the runbook, select the runbook, and click Edit at the top of the menu.
8. Once in the **Edit** menu, click Publish to make the runbook available for execution, and click **Yes** at the prompt. While you can address this in the code, we will create the variable for the host computer on which the VM is running.

Creating an automation variable

1. From your automation account, click the **Assets** tile and **Assets** blade, and select **Variables**.
2. On the **Variables** tile, select **Add a variable**.
3. Complete the options on the **New Variable** blade and click **Create** to save the new variable. We named the automation variable StartComputerDefaultHostName in the preceding code.

Defining a search query and creating an alert rule

1. Navigate to the Azure portal at `http://portal.azure.com` and sign in.
2. In the Azure portal, type **Log Analytics** in the **Search resources** search field and select your workspace.
3. In the **Log Analytics** blade for your workspace, click the **Log Search** button to take you to the search field:

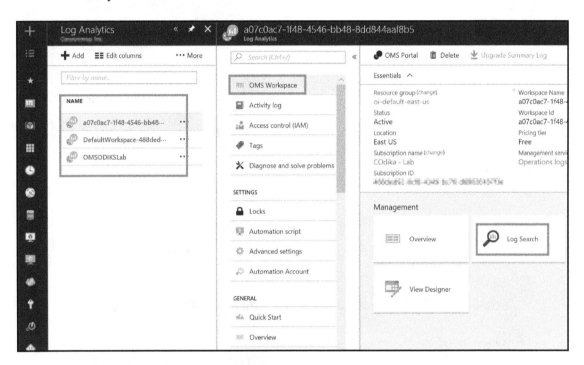

Figure 3.22

4. In the log search editor, conduct a search by typing in this table-based query and clicking the search button:

```
Alert
| where SourceSystem == "Nagios" and AlertName == "HOST ALERT"
and AlertState == "DOWN" and StateType == "HARD"
```

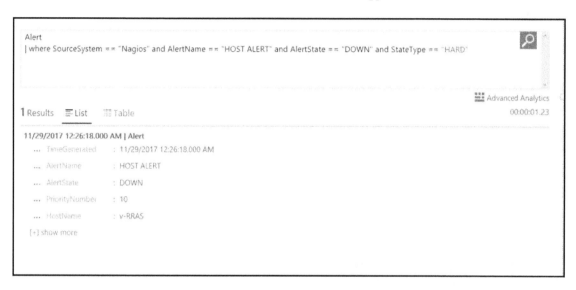

Figure 3.23

5. After the results are displayed in the results field, click the **Alert** button at the top of the **Log Search** page to open the alert rule page:

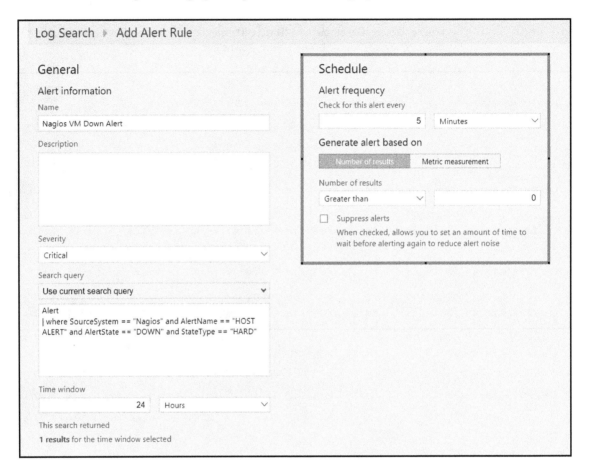

Figure 3.24

6. In the **Add Alert Rule** page, enter a rule name in the **Name** field, such as `Nagios VM Down Alert`, and optionally, fill in the **Description** field.

7. Click the drop-down under **Severity** to select an alert severity, review the query in the **Search query** field, and enter a time range in the **Time window** field.

8. In the **Schedule** section of the alert rule page, enter a time frequency in the **Alert frequency** field to indicate how often the query should be run.

You can specify a time range and alert frequency of between 5 minutes and 24 hours in both the **Time window** and **Alert frequency** fields.

9. Next, select **Number of results** and **Greater than 0** in the **Number of results** field. Click **Save**:

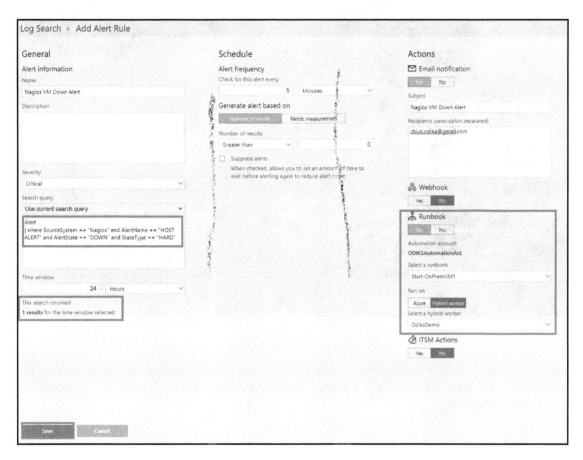

Figure 3.25

10. Under **Actions**, Select **Yes** for Runbook, and from the **Select a runbook** drop-down, select the `Start-OnPremVM1` Runbook imported earlier, select run on **Hybrid worker** , and select your hybrid worker from the drop-down menu. Click **Save.**

How it works...

Once the alert rule generates an alert, it triggers the Runbook action, which starts the Runbook in Azure Automation but executes it on the hybrid worker as defined within the alert rule. The following screenshot shows what the output will look like when the Runbook runs:

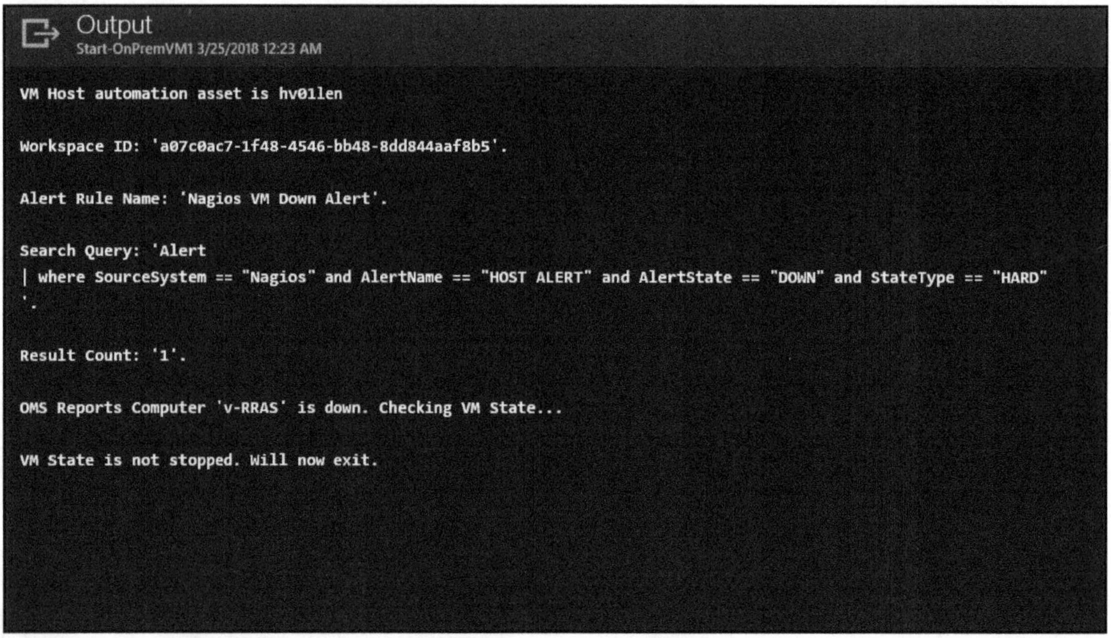

```
Output
Start-OnPremVM1 3/25/2018 12:23 AM

VM Host automation asset is hv01len


Workspace ID: 'a07c0ac7-1f48-4546-bb48-8dd844aaf8b5'.


Alert Rule Name: 'Nagios VM Down Alert'.


Search Query: 'Alert
| where SourceSystem == "Nagios" and AlertName == "HOST ALERT" and AlertState == "DOWN" and StateType == "HARD"
'.


Result Count: '1'.


OMS Reports Computer 'v-RRAS' is down. Checking VM State...


VM State is not stopped. Will now exit.
```

Figure 3.26

Runbook actions start a Runbook in Azure Automation, and in order to use this action type within an OMS alert rule, you will need to install and configure the automation solution in your OMS workspace.

Once this solution is installed, and when configuring the Runbook action for the alert rule, you can view all Runbooks available for the linked Azure Automation account, and from the drop-down menu, select a Runbook that can be called by the alert rule:

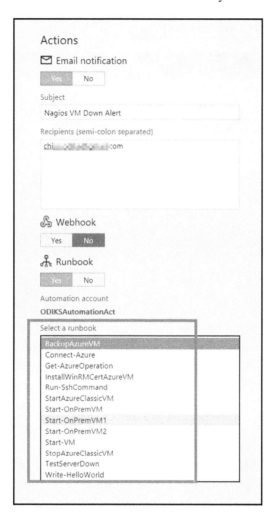

Figure 3.27

After selecting the Runbook, you can choose to run it in Azure or on a hybrid Runbook worker. When you create the alert rule, it will automatically create a new webhook for the Runbook. This is because Runbook actions start the Runbook using a webhook. The webhook will have the name OMS alert remediation with a GUID. You can see this as the input for the Runbook in the Azure portal:

Figure 3.28

You cannot populate any parameters in the Runbook directly. The `$WebhookData` parameter will include details of the alert generated by the alert rule. For this to happen, you must have an input parameter of type `Object` called `WebhookData` defined as either mandatory or optional:

```
param (
    [object]$WebhookData
    )
```

The **Log Analytics** alert will then use this input parameter to pass the search results to the Runbook. Additionally, you must have code to convert the `WebhookData` to a PowerShell object:

```
$SearchRecords = (ConvertFrom-JSON -InputObject
$WebhookData.RequestBody).SearchResult.value
```

The alert data is made available in JSON format in a single property called `SearchResult` in the `RequestBody` property of `$WebhookData` parameter.

When you use Runbook actions and webhook actions with a standard payload, the alert data will be available in a single JSON format property called `SearchResult`. If, however, you use webhook actions with a custom payload, the alert data property will be called `SearchResults`.

Because the Runbook converts the `RequestBody` from JSON, it can be worked with as a PowerShell object. You can therefore reference the properties of the alert once you are able to work with `RequestBody` as a PowerShell object. For instance, you can get the search query that generated the alert using the following code:

```
param (
    [object]$WebhookData
    )
$RequestBody = ConvertFrom-JSON -InputObject $WebhookData.RequestBody
$SearchQuery = $RequestBody.SearchQuery
Write-Output "Search Query: '$SearchQuery'."
```

There's more...

You can also call a Runbook in the **Log Analytics** alert rule configuration using a webhook. This can be particularly useful if you have not linked your OMS workspace to an Azure Automation account. With a webhook action, you will be able to start an Azure Automation Runbook using a single HTTP request.

Creating a webhook for a Runbook

Perform the following steps:

1. Navigate to the Azure portal at `http://portal.azure.com` and sign in.
2. In the Azure portal, type **Automation Accounts** and select and open your automation account.
3. From the hub, select **Runbooks** and open the list of Runbooks.
4. From the **Runbooks blade** in the Azure portal, click the Runbook that the webhook will start.
5. Click **Webhook** at the top of the blade to open the **Add Webhook** blade.
6. Specify a name, enabled status (yes or no), and an expiration date.
7. Copy and record the URL.
8. Click **Parameters** to specify the webhook parameters, and click **Create** to finish.

See also

The following are useful links to additional resources on actions for OMS alert rules:

- **Starting an Azure Automation runbook with a webhook**: `https://docs.microsoft.com/en-us/azure/automation/automation-webhooks#creating-a-webhook`.
- **Add actions to alert rules in Log Analytics**: `https://docs.microsoft.com/en-us/azure/log-analytics/log-analytics-alerts-actions`.

Using ITSM Actions

In addition to the email, webhook, and Runbook actions that are supported for Log Analytics alert rules, OMS also provides support for ITSM actions, and through integration between Log Analytics and your ITSM platform, you can use these actions to create work items (events, alerts, incidents) in ITSM from OMS alerts.

How to do it...

To centrally manage ITSM work items in Log Analytics, you will need to add the ITSM Connector solution to your OMS workspace.

Adding the ITSM Connector solution in OMS

1. Navigate to the Azure portal at `http://portal.azure.com` and sign in.
2. In the Azure portal, type **Log Analytics** in the **Search resources** search field and select your workspace.
3. In the **Log Analytics** blade for your workspace, click the **OMS Portal** button to take you to the OMS portal.

4. In the OMS portal, navigate to the **Solutions gallery**, select **the IT Service Management Connector** solution and click **Add** to add the solution to your workspace:

Figure 3.29

5. Navigate to the **Settings** page, and click on the **Connected Sources** option and the **ITSM Connector** to view configuration options:

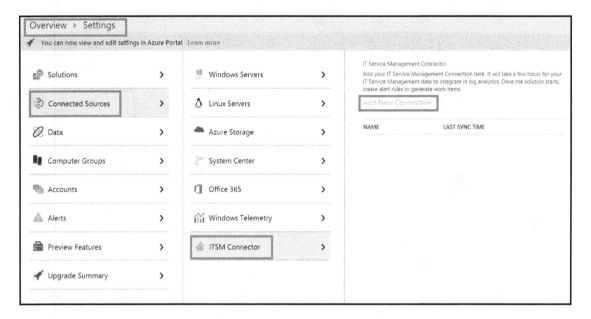

Figure 3.30

6. In the **IT Service Management Connector** blade, click on **Add New Connection**.

7. Provide the information for all the mandatory connection parameters, and click **Save** to create the connection:

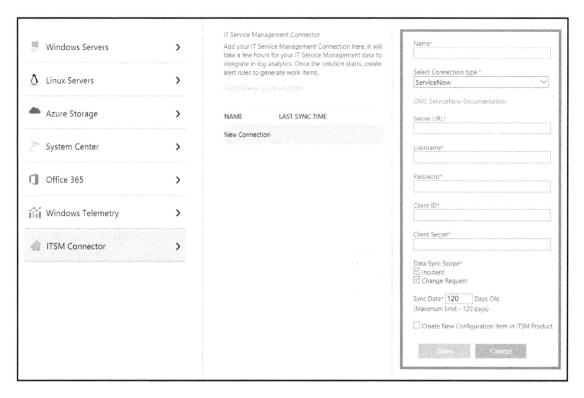

Figure 3.31

ITSM Connector connection parameters.

Field	Description
Name	Type the name of the supported ITSM product that you want to connect with the ITSM connector
Select Connection Type	Select **System Center Service Manager** (**SCSM**), ServiceNow, Provance, or Cherwell from the drop-down menu
Server URL	Type the URL of the ITSM product selected previously
Client ID	Enter the client ID for authenticating to the ITSM product
Client Secret	Enter the client secret generated for the ID
Data Sync Scope	Select the work items that you want to sync through the ITSM connector
Sync Data	Enter the number of past days of data you would like, up to 120 days
Create new configuration item in ITSM product	Select this option if you want to create the configuration items in the ITSM product

Table 3.2

How it works...

The ITSM Connector provides a bi-directional integration between Log Analytics and a supported ITSM product. This connection enables the creation of alerts, incidents, or events in the ITSM product based on Log Analytics alerts generated by the alert rules, and through the bi-directional connection, the connector can also import ITSM product data such as change requests and incidents into Log Analytics.

After setting up the integration between the ITSM product and Log Analytics, the work items selected during the connector configuration are imported into OMS Log Analytics and can be viewed in the **IT Service Management Connector** solution tile:

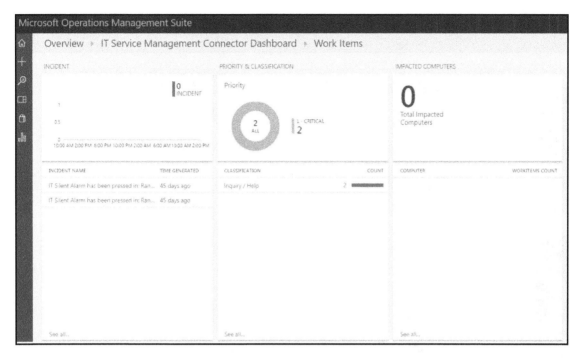

Figure 3.32

Once the ITSM product is configured in the OMS IT Service Management Connector configuration, you can now make use of the ITSM action in an OMS Log Analytics alert rule.

Using ITSM action in a Log Analytics alert rule

1. Navigate to the Azure portal at `http://portal.azure.com` and sign in
2. In the Azure portal, type **Log Analytics** in the **Search resources** search field and select your workspace

3. In the **Log Analytics** blade for your workspace, click the **Log Search** button to take you to the search field:

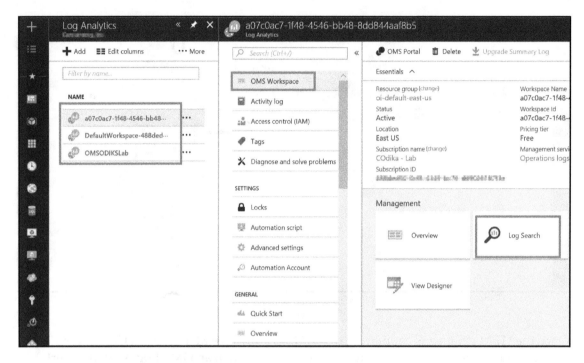

Figure 3.33

4. In the log search editor, conduct a search by typing in the following table-based query and clicking the search button:

```
Alert
| where SourceSystem == "Nagios" and AlertName == "HOST ALERT"
and AlertState == "DOWN" and StateType == "HARD"
```

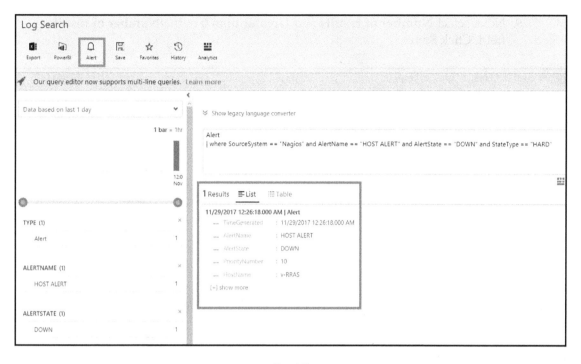

Figure 3.34

5. After results are displayed in the results field, click the **Alert** button at the top of the **Log Search** page to open the alert rule page

6. In the **Add Alert Rule** page, enter a rule name in the **Name** field, such as `Nagios VM Down Alert` and optionally, fill in the **Description** field

7. Click the drop-down under **Severity** to select an alert severity, review the query in the **Search query** field, and enter a time range in the **Time window** field

8. In the **Schedule** section of the alert rule page, enter a time frequency in the **Alert frequency** field to indicate how often the query should be run

You can specify a time range and alert frequency of between 5 minutes and 24 hours in both the **Time window** and **Alert frequency** fields.

9. Next, select **Number of results** and **Greater than 0** in the **Number of results** field. Click **Save**:

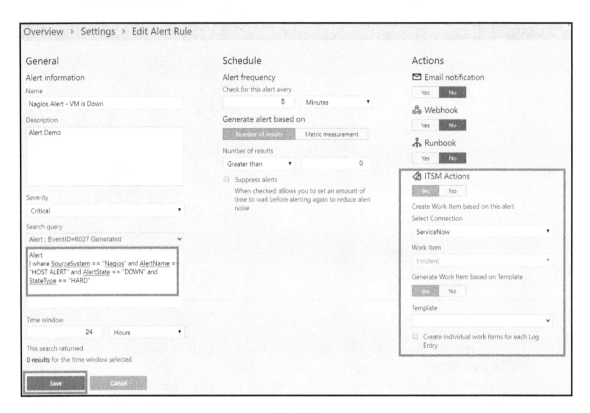

Figure 3.35

10. Under **Actions**, Select **Yes** for ITSM Actions, and from the **Select Connection** drop-down, select the ITSM product you have configured, fill in the other ITSM action fields, and click **Save**.

There's more...

When the ITSM connector successfully connects and syncs Log Analytics to the configured ITSM product or service, selected work items are imported into OMS Log Analytics, and incidents can be created in the ITSM product or service based on Log Analytics alerts.

Data imported from the connected ITSM product will appear in OMS Log Analytics as records of type `ServiceDesk_CL`. ITSM work item records in Log Analytics are either of type change request or incident. The `ServiceDeskWorkItemType_s` field of the log record shows what work item type a record is. Use the following query to aggregate the ITSM data by count of work item types:

```
ServiceDesk_CL
| summarize count() by ServiceDeskWorkItemType_s
```

Furthermore, ITSM records will have the following fields, depending on the work item type indicated by the `ServiceDeskWorkItemType_s` field:

```
ServiceDeskWorkItemType_s="Incident"
```

Fields:

Fields below are for work items for `ServiceDeskWorkItemType_s="Incident"`

- ServiceDeskConnectionName
- Service Desk ID
- State
- Urgency
- Impact
- Priority
- Escalation
- Created By
- Resolved By
- Closed By
- Source
- Assigned To
- Category
- Title
- Description
- Created Date
- Closed Date
- Resolved Date
- Last Modified Date
- Computer

```
ServiceDeskWorkItemType_s="ChangeRequest"
```

Fields:

Fields below are for work items:

```
ServiceDeskWorkItemType_s="ChangeRequest"
```

- ServiceDeskConnectionName
- Service Desk ID
- Created By
- Closed By
- Source
- Assigned To
- Title
- Type
- Category
- State
- Escalation
- Conflict Status
- Urgency
- Priority
- Risk
- Impact
- Assigned To
- Created Date
- Closed Date
- Last Modified Date
- Requested Date
- Planned Start Date
- Planned End Date
- Work Start Date
- Work End Date
- Description
- Computer

See also

For more information, visit the following links:

- **OMS Cherwell ITSM Integration**: http://www.buchatech.com/2017/05/oms-and-cherwell-itsm-integration/.

Working with the Alert Management solution

The OMS Alert Management solution helps you analyze alerts in the OMS Log Analytics repository. The alerts can come from multiple sources, including:

- Alert records created by Log Analytics alert rules
- Nagios and Zabbix alerts
- Alerts from SCOM

Getting ready

The solution works with any records in the OMS Log Analytics repository that are of type Alert. To analyze alerts in the Alert Management solution, you will need to follow the steps in the preceding sections for creating alert rules in Log Analytics, configuring Zabbix, and Nagios servers to send alerts to Log Analytics, and integrating SCOM with OMS.

How to do it...

Once these sources and data sources are connected to OMS Log Analytics, you are now ready to install and work with the Alert Management solution.

Adding the Alert Management solution in OMS

1. Navigate to the Azure portal at http://portal.azure.com and sign in.
2. In the Azure portal, type **Log Analytics** in the **Search resources** search field and select your workspace.

3. In the **Log Analytics** blade for your workspace, click the **OMS Portal** button to take you to the OMS portal.
4. In the OMS portal, navigate to the **Solutions gallery**, select the **Alert Management** solution, and click **Add** to add the solution to your workspace.

How it works...

The Alert Management solution supports Windows and Linux agents, and SCOM management groups, as connected sources.

For both Windows and Linux agents, Log Analytics alerts can be created from performance and event data. Direct Windows and Linux agents, however, do not generate alerts. Alerts from Nagios and Zabbix are collected through the Linux agents on the application servers.

Through SCOM integration with OMS, SCOM alerts are relayed to the management group and then forwarded to OMS Log Analytics every three minutes. The Alert Management solution is able to analyze alerts as soon as they are stored in the OMS repository.

Working with the Alert Management solution

The **Alert Management** tile is added to your OMS dashboard after you add the solution to your OMS workspace. The tile shows a count of the number of currently active alerts generated over the last 24 hours:

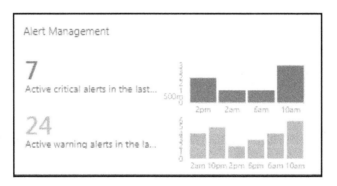

Figure 3.36

When you click on the **Alert Management** tile from the OMS portal overview page, it will take you to the **Alert Management Dashboard**. The dashboard shows a grouping of the top 10 alerts grouped by critical, warning, active SCOM, and all active alerts:

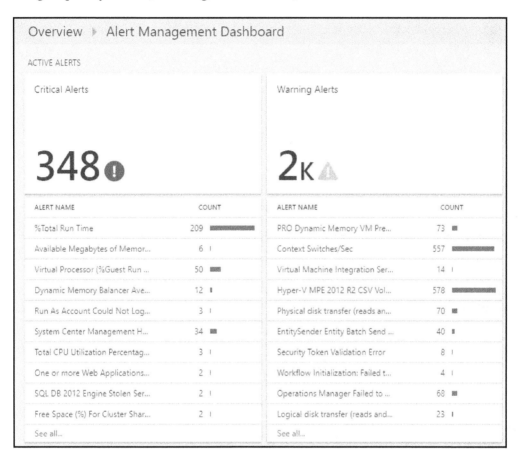

Figure 3.37

There's more...

Alert records created by alert rules in Log Analytics have a **SourceSystem** property value of **OMS**. This can be used to distinguish them from alert records from other sources, such as SCOM, and from alerts from Nagios and Zabbix.

You can use this query to find alert records in your workspace:

```
Alert
| summarize count () by SourceSystem
```

This query aggregates the content of the `Alert` table and returns the count of alert records by the **SourceSystem** field property:

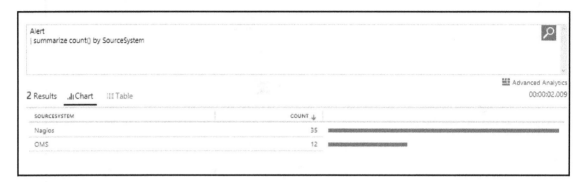

Figure 3.38

You can also use the **SourceSystem** field to specify alerts generated from a certain connected source. For instance, this query finds alert records for alerts generated in SCOM:

```
Alert
| where SourceSystem == "OpsManager"
```

Alert records generated by the SCOM alerts in Log Analytics, for instance, will have a type of `Alert`, and a `SourceSystem` of `OpsManager`. The properties for these records will differ slightly from those of alert records created by alert rules in Log Analytics. This is because alerts in SCOM are generated by monitors or SCOM rules, and with integrated alert management in SCOM, monitors in SCOM for instance the state of alerts in SCOM can be updated manually, or automatically if the alert is generated by a monitor.

To view the properties of an alert record created from a SCOM alert, from the results of the preceding query, click the [+] **show more** button to expand the result view for one of the alert records.

This will display all of the alert record properties and corresponding property values:

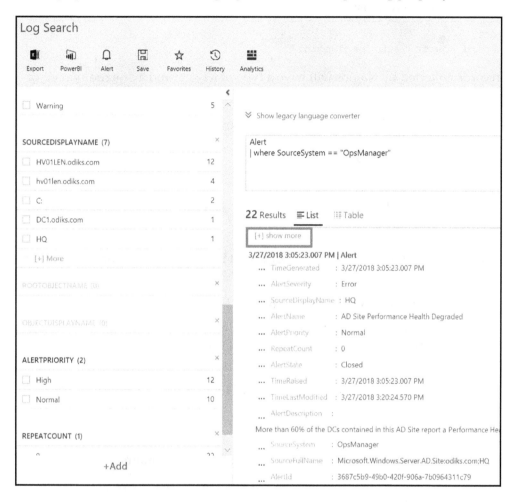

Figure 3.39

Once you start collecting Nagios alerts in OMS, you can use this query to find alert records for alerts generated in Nagios:

```
Alert
| where SourceSystem == "Nagios"
```

Alert records collected by Nagios will have a type of Alert, and a SourceSystem of Nagios.

And for Zabbix alerts in OMS, you can use the following query to find alert records for alerts generated in Zabbix:

```
Alert
| where SourceSystem == "Zabbix"
```

Alert records collected by Nagios will have a type of Alert, and a SourceSystem of Zabbix.

Some common alerts for this solution, as contained in the solution dashboard, are shown here:

- **Critical alerts raised during the past 24 hours**:

  ```
  search in (Alert) (AlertSeverity == "error" or AlertSeverity ==
  "critical") and TimeGenerated > ago(24h) | sort by
  TimeGenerated desc
  ```

- **Warning alerts raised during the past 24 hours**:

  ```
  search in (Alert) AlertSeverity == "warning" and TimeGenerated
  > ago(24h) | sort by TimeGenerated desc
  ```

- **Sources with active alerts raised during the past 24 hours**:

  ```
  search in (Alert) AlertState != "Closed" and TimeGenerated >
  ago(24h) | summarize Count = count() by SourceDisplayName
  ```

- **Critical alerts raised during the past 24 hours that are still active**:

  ```
  search in (Alert) (AlertSeverity == "error" or AlertSeverity ==
  "critical") and TimeGenerated > ago(24h) and AlertState !=
  "Closed" | sort by TimeGenerated desc
  ```

- **Alerts raised during the past 24 hours that are now closed**:

  ```
  search in (Alert) TimeGenerated > ago(24h) and AlertState ==
  "Closed" | sort by TimeGenerated desc
  ```

- **Alerts raised during the past 1 day grouped by their severity**:

```
search in (Alert) TimeGenerated > ago(1d) | summarize Count =
count() by AlertSeverity
```

- **Alerts raised during the past 1 day sorted by their repeat count value**:

```
search in (Alert) TimeGenerated > ago(1d) | sort by RepeatCount
desc
```

- **Alerts raised by Nagios servers**:

```
search in (Alert) SourceSystem == "Nagios" | sort by
TimeGenerated desc
```

- **Alerts raised by Zabbix server**:

```
search in (Alert) SourceSystem == "Zabbix" | sort by
TimeGenerated
```

See also

For more information, visit the following URL:

- **Understanding alerts in Log Analytics**:https://docs.microsoft.com/en-us/ azure/log-analytics/log-analytics-alerts.

4
Protecting and Recovering Data with OMS

IT organizations are tasked with ensuring the availability of mission critical business services, and a key component of this service delivery is ensuring that there is a plan in place to mitigate the impact of a disaster if and when it occurs. A disaster recovery strategy and plan is only as good as the solution that underlies it. As organizations increasingly migrate workloads to the cloud, disaster recovery solutions must evolve to support evolving disaster recovery needs, such as multi-site workloads availability, support for workloads across on-premises and cloud environments, and fast and reliable recovery while ensuring cost effectiveness. The OMS business continuity and disaster recovery service offerings comprise cloud-based services for comprehensive backup and workload recovery management. In this chapter, we will explore the data protection and recovery capabilities in OMS and review the features in OMS that provide you with cloud-first enterprise backup capabilities and the ability to customize and automate your disaster recovery strategy.

In this chapter, we will cover the following recipes:

- Understanding Backup and Recovery with OMS
- Understanding Azure Backup Components and Options
- Working with Azure Backup
- Working with **Azure Site Recovery** (**ASR**)
- Protect and Replicate Hyper-V VMs in Azure
- Replicate Physical Servers and VMWare VMs
- Configure Recovery Plans
- Configure Failover and Failback Actions

Understanding Backup and Recovery with OMS

A disaster recovery and business continuity strategy keeps your business running when unexpected events happen. OMS provides a protection and recovery management capability that includes integrated cloud backup and disaster recovery capabilities that enable you to protect data and enterprise applications, wherever they may reside. OMS Backup and Site Recovery are components of the Protection and Recovery solution offerings in OMS and are based on the Azure Backup and ASR services. Azure Backup is a service based in Azure that enables you to protect and restore your data from the Microsoft cloud and includes support for the protection and recovery for files, folders, application workloads, private clouds, Azure virtual machines, and Microsoft workloads such as SQL and Exchange. Some key benefits of the Backup service include:

- Simple and consistent management enables you to protect resources using a cloud-based wizard that provides a consistent management experience.
- It is secure and reliable. OMS provides a software-as-a-service offering that is backed by an enterprise-grade SLA, and that provides data encryption and little management overhead.
- Cloud scale. OMS supports the protection of unlimited data, and with over 9,000 recovery points and 99-year retention, you can leverage the benefits of scale in the cloud.
- It is a compelling on-premises alternative. Increased reliability, cost competitiveness, decades of retention, and the ability to intelligently protect to and restore workloads directly from Azure are some additional benefits OMS Backup.

ASR is a service in Microsoft Azure that facilitates your disaster recovery and business continuity strategy by enabling you to replicate, fail over, and recover your workloads in the event of a failure. With ASR, you can replicate on-premises VMware and Hyper-V VMs and Windows and Linux physical servers to either Azure storage or to a secondary datacenter. Some key benefits of the ASR service include:

- Protecting Windows and cross-platform workloads regardless of Hypervisor solutions in use
- Migrating workloads seamlessly to Azure with minimal impact to the business
- Cost savings and operating expenditure reduction through use of Azure as a secondary data center

- Disaster recovery simplification through use of failover and failback testing, ample compute resources and recovery task streamlining using automation

The Azure Backup and Site Recovery solutions in OMS are now deprecated. If you still have these solutions installed in your Log Analytics workspace, they will simply link to your recovery services vault in Azure. As an alternative to these legacy solutions, consider the OMS monitoring solution for Azure Backup, which you can install through using an Azure Resource Manager (ARM) template. Additionally, consider visualizing your backup metrics and parameters with Power BI using the Azure Backup Reports feature in your Recovery Services vault.

Working with Azure Backup

Azure backup is a secure, reliable, and cost-effective cloud-based service that you can use to protect and restore your data in the Microsoft cloud. For ease of use, Azure Backup has various components that you can deploy to facilitate data protection wherever your workloads may reside.

Getting ready

To get started with Azure Backup, you will need to set up a Recovery Services vault in the Azure portal. A Recovery Services vault is a storage entity in Azure that is used to hold protection and recovery data, such as backup copies, policies, and recovery points. Recovery Services vaults can be used to hold data for on-premises systems and for Azure services.

Creating a Recovery Services vault

To create a Recovery Services vault, take the following steps:

1. Navigate to the **Azure Portal** (`https://portal.azure.com`) and sign in
2. In the Azure Portal, type **Recovery Services** in the **Search resources** search field and select **Recovery Services vaults**
3. On the **Recovery services vaults** menu, click **Add**

4. In the **Recovery Services** vault blade, provide a Name for the vault:

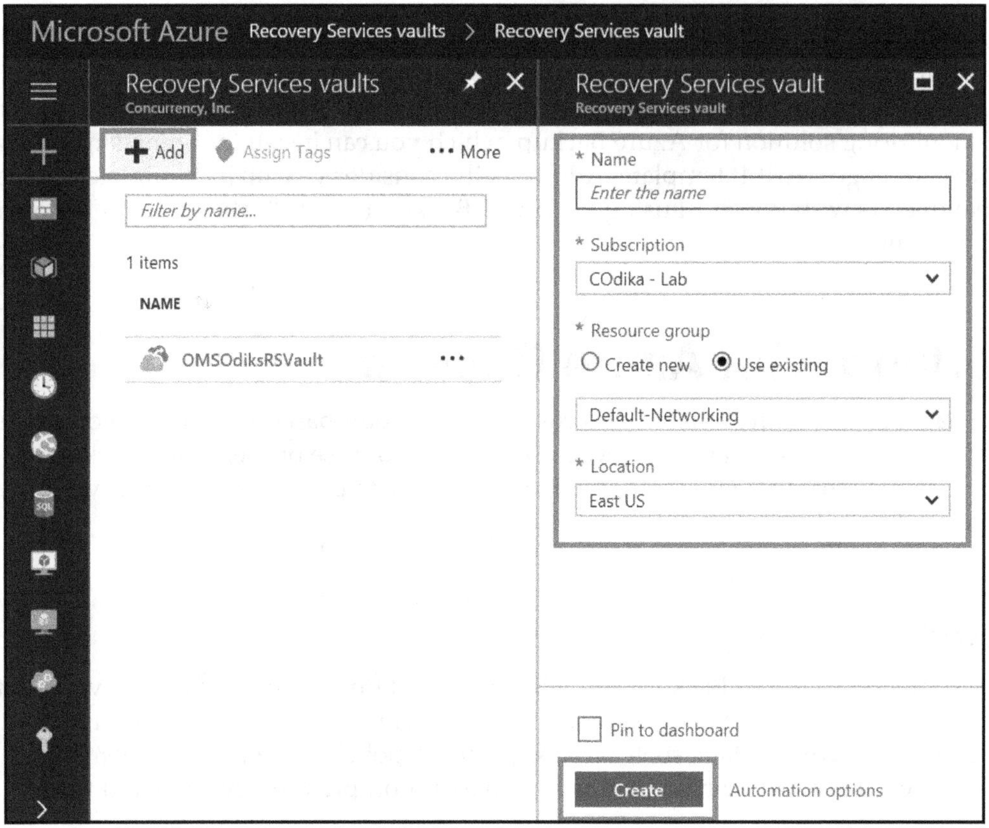

Figure 4.1: Create Recovery Services vault

5. In the **Subscription** field, select the subscription or choose from the drop down if you have multiple subscriptions
6. In the **Resource group** field, choose to use existing resource group or create a new resource group
7. In the **Location** field, select the geographic region for the vault
8. Click **Create** to create the Recovery Services vault

Once the Recovery Services vault is created, you can now register the Azure Backup components with the vault.

How to do it...

In this section, we will look at various methods for protecting data in and restoring data from Azure Backup. This will review protection steps using various Azure Backup components.

Backing up a Virtual Machine in Azure

This tutorial will review the steps for backing up a single VM in Azure:

1. Navigate to the **Azure Portal** (`https://portal.azure.com`) and sign in.
2. In the Azure Portal, type **Virtual machines** in the **Search resources** search field and select **Virtual machines**.
3. From the list of Virtual machines, choose a VM to back up:

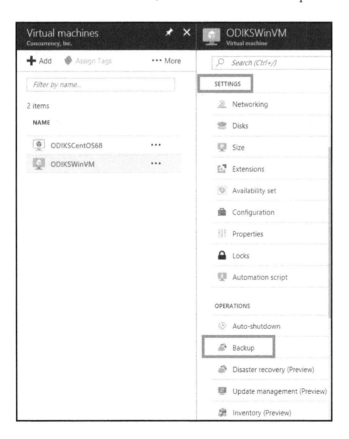

Figure 4.2: Backup an Azure VM

4. In the Settings section of the VM blade, click **Backup**
5. In the **Enable backup** window, under **Recovery Services** vault, leave the **Select existing** option and, from the drop down, select the vault created in the *Getting ready* section of this recipe
6. Under **Backup policy**, leave the **DefaultPolicy** option and select **Enable Backup**

You can use the Default policy to quickly protect your VM or choose to create a custom backup policy. The default protection policy backs up the VM daily and retains recovery points for 30 days.

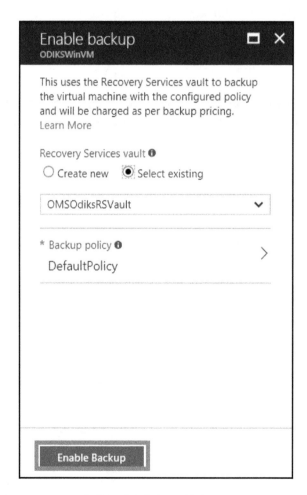

Figure 4.3: Enable Azure VM backup

Once created, the policy is deployed to the resource group to which the protected VM belongs. You can now manually initiate backups for the VM, without waiting for the default policy to run the backup job at the scheduled time.

Manually starting a backup job

This tutorial will review the steps for manually starting a backup job in Azure:

1. Navigate to the **Azure Portal** (`https://portal.azure.com`) and sign in
2. In the Azure Portal, type **Virtual machines** in the **Search resources** search field and select **Virtual machines**
3. From the list of Virtual machines, choose a VM to backup
4. In the **Settings** section of the VM blade, click **Backup**
5. On the **Backup** window of the VM, select **Backup now**:

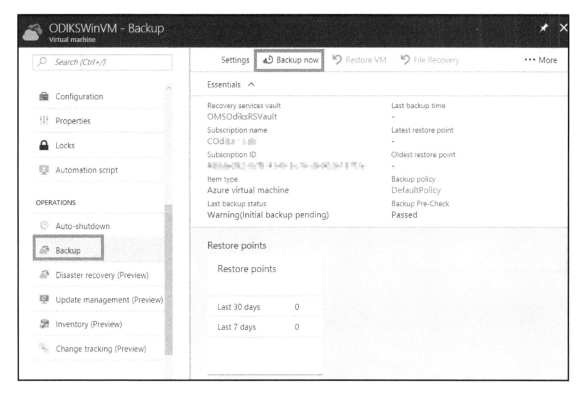

Figure 4.4: Manually start backup job

6. Leave the default date in the **Retain Backup Till** field, to accept the backup retention policy of 30 days, and click **Backup**

Backup multiple virtual machines

This tutorial will review the steps for creating and applying a backup policy to multiple virtual machines. A backup policy can be applied to VMs both on-premises and in Azure:

1. Navigate to the **Azure Portal** (`https://portal.azure.com`) and sign in
2. In the Azure Portal, type **Recovery Services** in the **Search resources** search field and select **Recovery Services vaults**
3. From the list of **Recovery Services vaults**, select the vault created in the *Getting ready* section of this recipe
4. On the vault dashboard menu, click **Backup** to open the **Backup** menu:

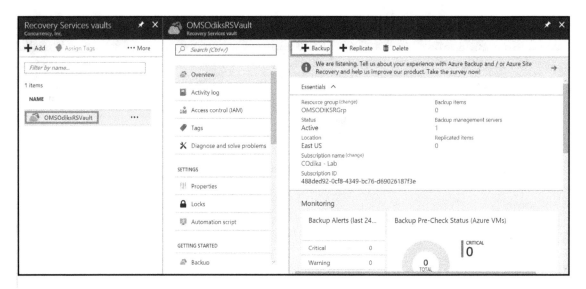

Figure 4.5: Create a Backup Policy

5. On the **Backup Goal** menu, click the drop down under the **Where is your workload running?** field and select **Azure**

6. Choose virtual machine in the **What do you want to backup?** field and click **Backup**

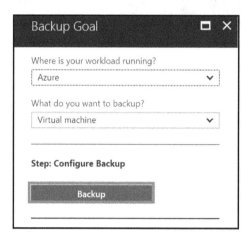

Figure 4.6: Backup multiple VMs

7. On the resulting **Backup policy** menu, click the drop down under the **Choose backup policy** field and select **Create New**
8. In the **Backup Policy** menu, enter a friendly name for the policy in the **Policy name** field
9. In the **Backup frequency** menu, select between **Daily** and **weekly**, select a time, and select the time zone (UTC is default) from the drop down
10. In the **Retention range** menu, under the **Retention of daily backup point** menu, select the number of daily backup points you would like (**180 days** is default)
11. If interested in weekly backup points, check the box for **Retention of weekly backup point** and select a day for restore points and a number of weeks of retention. (Sunday and 104 weeks are the defaults.)
12. If interested in monthly retention, check the box for **Retention of monthly backup point**, select between **Week-based** and **Day-based** retention, and select day of the month and number of months. (**Week-based** retention and **First Sunday** for **60 months** are the defaults.)
13. If interested in yearly retention, check the box for **Retention of yearly backup point**, select between **Week-based**, and **Day-based** retention, and select month, day of the month, and number of years. (**Week-based**, first **Sunday** of **January**, and **10** years are the defaults.)

14. Click **OK** to create the backup policy:

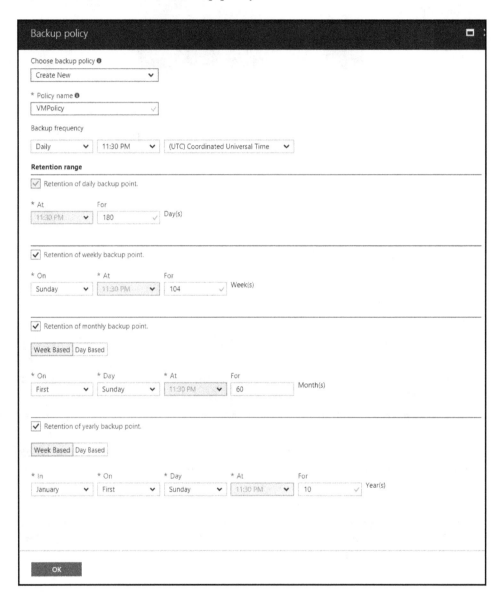

Figure 4.7: Configure Backup Policy

15. In the **Select virtual machines** dialog, select the virtual machines from the list to which you would like to deploy the backup policy and click **OK** to deploy the policy:

Figure 4.8: Apply Policy to VMs

How it works...

When storing backups in Azure and depending on the backup component you utilize, once the data is backed up at the protection point, it is compressed and stored in an Azure-based online storage entity called a Recovery Services vault and, based on your storage needs, you can enable high availability through locally-redundant or geographically-redundant storage replication.

Azure Backup provides unlimited scaling by leveraging the Azure cloud to deliver high-availability. Azure Backup provides additional high availability through locally-redundant and geo-redundant storage replication options:

- **Locally-redundant storage** (**LRS**) is a low-cost storage replication option that creates three copies of protected data in a paired data center in the same region to protect your data from local hardware failures:

- **Geo-redundant storage** (**GRS**) is a higher-cost storage replication option, that replicates your protected data to a secondary region (hundreds of miles away from the primary location of the protected data), thereby protecting your data in the event of a regional outage.

The following figure depicts the Azure Backup data flow, backed up data relay to Azure Recovery Services vault, storage replication of protected data, and monitoring backup statistics and viewing backup reports with Power BI, as well as monitoring backup parameters with the OMS monitoring solution:

The legacy OMS solutions for Azure Site Recovery and Azure Backup are deprecated. Any tiles for these solutions in your OMS workspace will simply link to your Recovery Services vaults in Azure. As an alternative to the legacy Backup solution, you can use the OMS Monitoring solution for Azure Backup to monitor key backup parameters. See `https://azure.microsoft.com/en-gb/resources/templates/101-backup-oms-monitoring/` for more information. You can use Power BI to view backup report dashboards, download backup reports, and create custom backup visualizations.

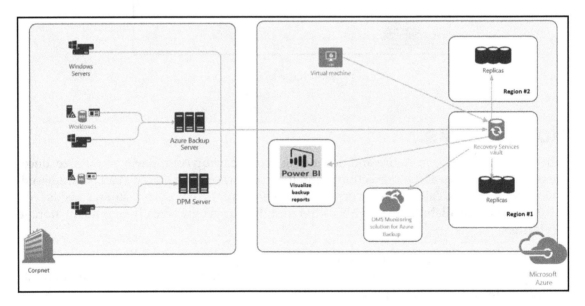

Figure 4.9: Azure Backup workflows

Some other features and capabilities of Azure Backup include:

- **Managed disk VMs**: You can protect managed disk VMs with Azure Backup. Managed disks simplify the provisioning of VMs by obviating the need for managing storage accounts of VM disks. Azure Backup also supports the protection of managed disk VMs encrypted using Azure Disk encryption (ADE).
- **Premium Storage VM Protection:** Azure Backup can protect Premium Storage VMs. Azure Premium Storage is a solid-state, drive-based storage solution that delivers low-latency, high performance disk support for VMs with I/O intensive workloads.
- **Linux Support**: Various Azure Backup components support the protection of Azure-endorsed Linux systems. Both the Azure Backup Server and System Center DPM provide file-consistent backup of VMWare and Hyper-V Linux guest VMs and VM restore of Hyper-V and VMWare Linux guest VMs. Azure IaaS VM Backup component supports application-consistent backup of Azure Linux VMs, using pre-script and post-script framework, VM restore, granular recovery of files, and restoration of all VM disks.

There's more...

Azure Backup offers various components that can be used to back up data to a Recovery Services vault in Azure.

Understanding Azure Backup Components and Options

The choice of component depends on the nature of the workload(s) you would like to protect. A Recovery Services vault is the storage entity in Azure that houses the protected data.

While various Backup components can also be used on premises, all of the Azure Backup components can be used to protect data in Azure. The Azure Backup components include:

- **Azure Backup (MARS) agent**: This is a service installed on the Windows systems that enables you to backup files and folders to a Recovery Services vault. This agent creates an association between the Windows system and the Recovery Services vault.

- **Azure Backup Server**: Azure Backup Server inherits much of the functionality of System Center **Data Protection Manager** (**DPM**) without support for tape storage. It provides cloud protection capabilities and much of the functionality of DPM without requiring a System Center license. Data protected with the Azure Backup server can be stored locally on an attached disk or in an Azure Recovery Services vault.
- **Azure IaaS VM Backup**: This uses a backup extension for backing up Windows and cross-platform VMs in Azure. Resources protected with this component are stored in a Recovery Services vault.
- **System Center DPM**: This is an enterprise backup system that is part of the System Center suite of tools. It provides data backup, storage, and recovery capabilities and enables the backup of data from a source location to disk, tape, or Azure Recovery Services Vault.

Comparing Azure Backup components

The following table outlines the various Azure Backup components and outlines the benefits, capabilities, and limitations of each component, as well as where components can be used and where backups are stored:

Component	Azure/On-premise	Benefits	Limitations	Protection Capabilities	Backup Target
Azure Backup (MARS) agent	Both	• Backs up files and folders on Windows systems anywhere • No need for separate backup server.	• No support for Linux • Not application aware • Backs up three times daily	• System state • Files • Folders	Recovery Services vault

Azure Backup Server	Both	• No System Center license required • Backup and restore VMWare VMs • Support for Linux on Hyper-V and VMWare • App aware snapshots (VSS)	• Cannot backup Oracle workload • Always requires live Azure subscription • No tape backup support	• VMs • Volumes • Applications • Workloads • Files • folders	• Locally attached disk • Recovery Services vault
Azure IaaS VM Backup	Azure only. Part of the Azure fabric	• Fabric-level backup with no backup infrastructure needed • No specific agent installation required • Native backups for Linux and Windows	• No on-premise backup support • Only restores VMs at disk level • Backs up VMs once daily	• VMs • All disks (using PowerShell)	Recovery Services vault
System Center DPM	Both	• Backs up and restores VMWare VMs • Support for Linux on Hyper-V and VMWare • App aware snapshots (VSS)	Cannot backup Oracle workload	• VMs • Volumes • Applications • Workloads • Files • Folders	• Locally attached disk • On-premise • Recovery Services vault

Table 4.1: Azure Backup Components

As outlined in the preceding table, all of the backup components support the Recovery Services vault as a storage target, while System Center DPM and Azure Backup Server also support the use of local disk as a target. System Center DPM is the only component that supports data writes to tape storage.

For more information on the Azure Backup Server protection matrix, visit the following URL: `https://docs.microsoft.com/en-us/azure/backup/backup-mabs-protection-matrix`.

See also

Visit the following links for more information:

- **Use Power BI Reports for Azure Backup**: `https://azure.microsoft.com/en-us/blog/azure-backup-reports/`
- **OMS Monitoring Solution for Azure Backup using Azure Log analytics**: `https://azure.microsoft.com/en-us/blog/oms-monitoring-solution-for-azure-backup-using-azure-log-analytics/`
- **Preparing to back up workloads to Azure with DPM**: `https://docs.microsoft.com/en-us/azure/backup/backup-azure-dpm-introduction`
- **Using Azure Backup Server**: `https://docs.microsoft.com/en-us/azure/backup/backup-azure-microsoft-azure-backup`
- **Working with Offline-backup**: `https://docs.microsoft.com/en-us/azure/backup/backup-azure-backup-import-export`
- **Backup Pricing**: `https://azure.microsoft.com/en-us/pricing/details/backup/`

Working with ASR

Any review of ASR would be incomplete without a review of disaster recovery and the need for a disaster recovery solution. Let's review some terms that will be used throughout this section:

- **Disaster Recovery (DR):** This is an area of security and organizational planning that involves a set of policies, procedures, and tools to enable the continuation and/or recovery of critical infrastructure and systems in the aftermath of a natural or other disaster
- **Business Continuity Plan:** This refers to the preparation and planning guidelines that ensure that an organization can continue to operate in the event of a disaster and, importantly, that the organization is, within a predetermined period of time, able to recover to an acceptable operational state

- **Recovery Time Objective (RTO)**: This is the amount of time after a disaster within which a business process must be restored to an acceptable operational state
- **Recovery Point Objective (RPO)**: This is the maximum amount of data loss that is acceptable or allowed for an IT service due to a disaster

There are numerous metrics out there for how enterprises encounter disasters and the impact such disasters have on businesses. Some noteworthy facts and figures from Gartner and the like indicate that:

- Disasters will inevitably occur in organizations and downtime is very costly; losses per hour of downtime could run into tens or hundreds of thousands of dollars
- In the past five years, more than 50% of organizations experienced downtime events that lasted more than eight hours
- Some of the more common causes of downtime include power outages, hardware and human errors, virus/ malware attacks, natural disasters, and onsite disasters
- Two in five companies surveyed don't have a well-defined and documented DR plan
- 40% of surveyed companies only test DR plans once a year, due to complexity of testing or other factors
- 80% of business critical applications are not capable of meeting the required RPO/RTO

As a **Disaster Recovery as a Service (DRaaS)** solution, ASR facilitates the recovery management capabilities for OMS. ASR is a service in Microsoft Azure that facilitates your disaster recovery and business continuity strategy by enabling you to replicate, failover, and recover your workloads in the event of a failure. With ASR, you can replicate on-premise VMWare and Hyper-V VMs, and Windows and Linux physical servers to either Azure storage or to a secondary datacenter. You can also use ASR to replicate Azure VMs to another Azure region.

ASR can be used in the following scenarios:

- **Hyper-V virtual machines**: ASR can protect workloads that are running on Hyper-V virtual machines. Furthermore, ASR supports scenarios where the Hyper-V hosts are managed with or without System Center **Virtual Machine Manager (VMM)**. You can replicate on-premise Hyper-V VMs to Azure or to a secondary site.

- **Physical servers**: ASR can protect physical servers running either Windows or Linux. ASR supports the replication of physical servers to Azure or to a secondary site.
- **Azure VMs**: ASR can replicate workloads running on supported Azure VMs. You can use ASR to replicate Azure VMs from one Azure region to another.
- **VMware virtual machines**: ASR can protect workloads running in VMware VMs. You can replicate VMware VMs to Azure or to a secondary site.

Getting ready

To get started with ASR, the first thing to do is to plan your DR strategy and understand the various requirements for replicating and failing resources over to Azure or a secondary site with ASR. Some important considerations include:

- Connectivity to and from on-premises.
- Network and IP addressing for replica machines for access to machines after failover.
- What, if any, endpoints will need to be exposed publicly once failed over to the target site?
- What workloads (AD, IIS, SQL, SharePoint, and so on) need to be migrated to the target location?
- Application dependency modeling to failover and bring up an application in a specific manner using a recovery plan.
- Source machines must be compliant with Azure requirements for replicating to Azure and for using ASR for DR.
- Capacity planning for replicating workloads to a target location with ASR.

Once you've sorted out these and other details of your failover plan, you will be ready to start using ASR. You will need to create a Recovery Services vault in the Azure portal. A Recovery Services vault is a storage entity in Azure that is used to hold protection and recovery data, such as backup copies, policies, and recovery points. This vault will be necessary for some of the scenarios described above. Recovery Services vaults can be used to hold data for on-premises systems and for Azure services.

Creating a Recovery Services vault

Take the following steps to create a Recovery Services vault:

1. Navigate to the **Azure Portal** (`https://portal.azure.com`) and sign in.
2. In the Azure Portal, type **Recovery Services** in the **Search resources** search field and select **Recovery Services vaults**.
3. On the **Recovery services vaults** menu, click **Add**.
4. In the **Recovery Services vaults** blade, provide a **Name** for the vault:

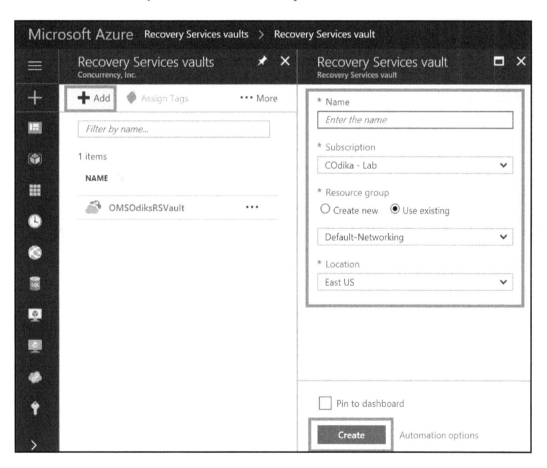

Figure 4.10: Create a Recovery Services vault

5. In the **Subscription** field, select the subscription or choose from the drop down if you have multiple subscriptions.

6. In the **Resource group** field, choose to use the existing resource group or create a new resource group.

7. In the **Location** field, select the geographic region for the vault.

8. Click **Create** to create the Recovery Services vault.

Once the Recovery Services vault is created, you can now proceed to configure DR for Azure VMs.

How to do it...

In this section, we will look at how to set up **disaster recovery** (**DR**) for Azure VMs to a secondary Azure region. Note that, at this time, Azure VM replication with ASR is in preview. This means that the underlying functionality and replication steps are subject to change. For this reason, we will only cover relevant concepts in this section. Ensure that you are a member of the correct site recovery-related built-in roles to perform Site Recovery management operations. The Site Recovery contributor role or higher role is required to follow along in this section.

Replicate Azure VMs to a Secondary Azure Region

Once you have a recovery services vault, the following additional steps are required:

- Configure outbound network connectivity
- Verify Azure VM certificates
- Enable replication for Azure VMs

Configure outbound network connectivity

ASR does not support the use of authentication proxies for network connectivity control. Additionally, if you control outbound network connectivity with firewall proxies, you will need to allow access to various URLs that are used by ASR:

URL	Purpose
`Login.microsoftonline.com`	This provides authentication and authorization to ASR service URLs.
`*.blob.core.windows.net`	This allows data to be written to the cache storage account in the source region from the VM.
`*servicebus.windows.net`	This allows the VM to write diagnostics and ASR monitoring data.
`*.hypervrecoverymanager.windowsazure.com`	This allows the VM to communicate with the ASR service.

Table 4.2: Configure Outbound Network Connectivity

Additionally, you will need to configure outbound connectivity for IP address ranges if you use NSG or other restrictions to control outbound connectivity. You can use the script at the following link to create required NSG rules: `https://gallery.technet.microsoft.com/Azure-Recovery-script-to-0c950702`

Verify Azure VM Certificates

For security reasons, Azure VMs will require the latest root certificates to be present in order to be registered to ASR and replicated. Verify that certificates are properly installed and configured on any Windows and cross-platform VMs that you would like to replicate with ASR:

Enable Replication

To replicate an Azure VM:

1. Navigate to the **Azure Portal** (`https://portal.azure.com`) and sign in.
2. In the Azure portal, type **Recovery Services** in the **Search resources** search field and select **Recovery Services vaults**.

3. Select and click the vault name and click the **+Replicate** button.

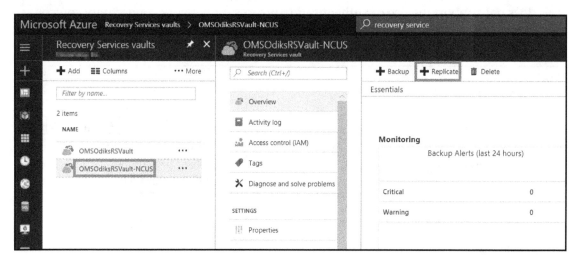

Figure 4.11: Azure VM Replication

4. In the **Source Configure** menu, select **Azure - PREVIEW** as the source and, under **Source location**, select the source Azure region where the Azure VMs are currently running.

You cannot protect VMs from the same region as the vault or the vault's resource group.

5. For the Azure virtual machine deployment model, select **Resource Manager**, and select your resource group from the **Source resource group** dropdown:

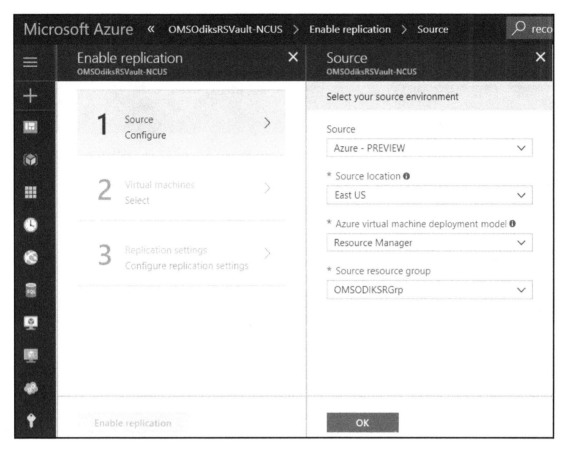

Figure 4.12: Replicate Azure VMs

6. Click **OK** to save your settings.
7. In the **Virtual Machines** menu, select the VMs you would like to replicate, and click **OK**.

ASR will now create default settings and replication policy for the target region. You can modify the settings where necessary:

1. Click **Settings** to view and configure the target and replication settings.
2. Click the **Target location** dropdown to select the target location to which the VMs will be replicated.

3. Review the default settings for resource group, storage, availability sets and replication policy. To override and modify the default settings, click the **Customize** option next to each setting:

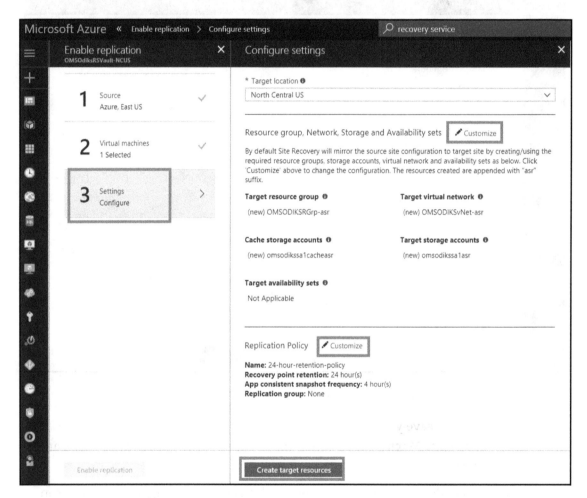

Figure 4.13: Configure Azure VM Replication Settings

4. Click **Create target resources** to finish.

How it works...

When you configure replication for an Azure VM or VMs, ASR will create various resources in the target Azure region, based on source region settings. The following resources are created:

- **Target resource group**: This is the resource group to which the replicated Azure VMs will belong after failover.
- **Target virtual network**: This is the virtual network that the replicated VMs will be located in after failover. ASR creates a network mapping between source and target virtual networks and between target and source networks.
- **Cache storage accounts**: This is where source VM changes, such as data writes, are tracked and sent to before they are replicated to the target storage account. This is done to minimize and mitigate impact on production applications running on the VM(s).
- **Target storage accounts**: These are storage accounts in the target region to which the VM data is replicated.
- **Target availability sets**: These are the availability sets in which the VMs are located after failover.
- **Replication Policy**: This contains configurations for such settings as recovery point retention, frequency of app-consistent snapshot, and replication group.

When replication is enabled, ASR automatically installs the ASR extension Mobility service on the VM(s). The VM is then registered with ASR and continuous replication is configured for the VM. Data writes on the VM disks will then be continuously written to the cache storage account. Site recovery then processes the data and sends it to the target storage account and, after the data is processed, recovery points are generated in the target storage account every few minutes.

There's more...

The default replication policy setting for Azure VMs does not enable multi-VM consistency. Multi-VM consistency replicates machines together. If this is enabled, all machines in the replication group would need to communicate with each other over port 20004. This port applies to both Windows and Linux computers. It is therefore important to ensure that there are no restrictions to internal communication between the VMs over port 20004 if you desire multi-VM consistency.

Additionally, when machines in a replication group are failed over, they will all have shared app-consistent and crash-consistent recovery points. It is recommended, therefore, to use multi-VM consistency if machines are running the same workload and you need consistency across multiple machines; otherwise, multi-VM consistency can impact workload performance.

Network Infrastructure Considerations

When protecting workloads with ASR an important consideration is that of network mapping to ensure that when you failover a VM or workload to Azure or a secondary site, the replicated VM is created on the network that is mapped to the network of the source VM. There are various mapping strategies that can be employed for the various ASR scenarios, including mapping between Azure regions, mapping for Hyper-V VM replication, and other on-premises to Azure scenarios. Consult the relevant guides in the following links for further details on each scenario.

See also

Visit the following links for more information:

- **Support Requirements for ASR Components:** https://docs.microsoft.com/en-us/azure/site-recovery/site-recovery-support-matrix-azure-to-azure
- **Mapping networks between two Azure regions:** https://docs.microsoft.com/en-us/azure/site-recovery/site-recovery-network-mapping-azure-to-azure
- **Network mapping for Hyper-V VM replication with ASR:** https://docs.microsoft.com/en-us/azure/site-recovery/site-recovery-network-mapping
- **VM network interfaces for on-premises to Azure scenarios:** https://docs.microsoft.com/en-us/azure/site-recovery/site-recovery-manage-network-interfaces-on-premises-to-azure

Protect and Replicate Hyper-V VMs

ASR supports the protection of Hyper-V VMs in scenarios where Hyper-V is used with System Center VMM and without VMM. In the scenario where the Hyper-V host(s) are not managed with VMM, you can perform disaster recovery of the VMs on the hosts to Azure.

In the scenario where Hyper-V hosts are managed with VMM fabric, you can perform disaster recovery of VMs on the Hyper-V hosts to Azure or to a secondary on-premises site.

Getting ready

For both scenarios where Hyper-V is managed with or without VMM, you will need to have an Azure subscription, Azure storage account, and Azure network. Review up-to-date steps here: `https://docs.microsoft.com/en-us/azure/site-recovery/tutorial-prepare-azure`.

> Site recovery performs best when storage and network bandwidth are sufficiently provisioned. Use the deployment planner to accurately estimate requirements to meet your replication needs. Deployment planning guidance can be found at this link: `https://docs.microsoft.com/en-us/azure/site-recovery/site-recovery-hyper-v-deployment-planner`.

Additionally, review and complete the following tasks:

Where Hyper-V is not managed with VMM do the following:

- Ensure that Hyper-V host(s) is running a supported version of Windows Server - Server 2012 R2 or above
- Configure proxy settings and ensure that hosts can access the service URLs
- Configure Hyper-V hosts and clusters into Hyper-V sites
- Install the ASR provider and Recovery Services agent on each Hyper-V machine
- Download the vault registration key to register the host in the vault

Where Hyper-V is managed with VMM do the following:

- Configure VMM cloud(s) with Hyper-V hosts/clusters.
- Configure required proxy settings so that the VMM service can access the service URLs.

- Set up logical and VM networks on the VMM server. VM networks are mapped to Azure virtual networks for failover.
- Download the vault registration key and the installer for the ASR Provider.
- Install the Provider on the VMM server and use the registration key to register the server in the vault.
- Ensure that Hyper-V host(s) is running the supported version of Windows Server - Server 2012 R2 or above.
- Confirm that Hyper-V hosts are assigned to the correct VMM cloud.
- Configure proxy settings and ensure that hosts can access the service URLs.
- Download and install the Recovery Services agent on each Hyper-V host or cluster member.

How to do it...

Prepare the on-premise Hyper-V infrastructure for replication of Hyper-V VMs to Azure. This applies to both scenarios where Hyper-V hosts are managed with VMM and scenarios where Hyper-V hosts are not managed with VMM.

Review the most up-to-date list of requirements to prepare Hyper-V for DR to Azure here: `https://docs.microsoft.com/en-us/azure/site-recovery/tutorial-prepare-on-premises-hyper-v`

Hyper-V (without VMM) replication to Azure

Once the preceding steps for preparing the Azure fabric and on-premise Hyper-V infrastructure are complete, continue with the following steps in Azure:

1. Navigate to the **Azure Portal** (`https://portal.azure.com`) and sign in
2. In the Azure Portal, type **Recovery Services** in the **Search resources** search field and select **Recovery Services vaults**
3. Select and click the vault name to work in
4. In **Getting Started**, click **Site Recovery** and then click **Prepare Infrastructure**

Prepare Infrastructure – Protection Goal

5. In **Protection goal**, for **Where are your machines located?**, select **On-premises**
6. In **Where do you want to replicate your machines to?**, select **To Azure**
7. In **Are your machines virtualized?**, select **Yes, with Hyper-V**

8. In **Are you using System Center VMM to manage your Hyper-V hosts?** Select **No**. Click **OK**:

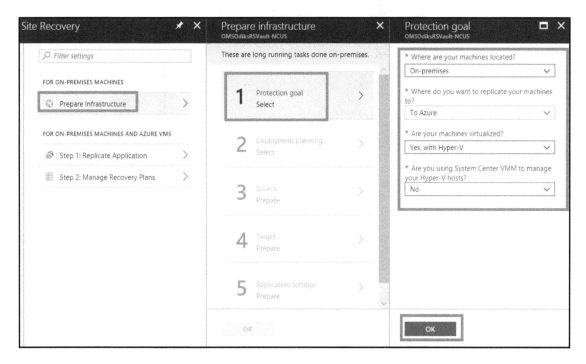

Figure 4.14: Hyper-V Replication to Azure

9. In **Deployment planning**, for **Have you completed deployment planning?**, select **Yes, I have done it**. Click **OK**.

Prepare Infrastructure - Source environment

10. In **Source**, click **+Hyper-V Site** and specify the name of your Hyper-V site
11. Click **+Hyper-V server**, download the installer for the ASR provider

12. Download the vault registration key:

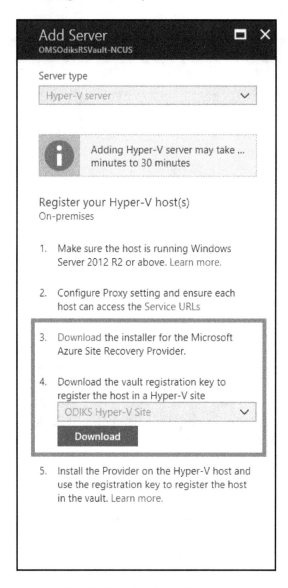

Figure 4.15: Prepare Hyper-V Source Environment

Run the ASR Provider setup file (`AzureSiteRecoveryProvider.exe`) on each Hyper-V host that you added to the Hyper-V site that you created earlier. This installs the ASR Provider and Recovery Services agent on the Hyper-V host(s):

13. In **Installation**, accept the default installation settings for the agent and provider and click **Install**:

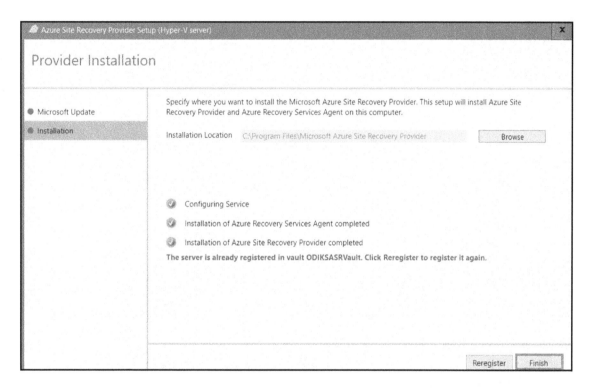

Figure 4.16: Set up ASR provider

14. In the **Microsoft Azure Site Recovery Registration Wizard**, under **Vault Settings**, click **Browse**, and select the vault key that you downloaded in the Azure Portal

15. Enter information for the **Azure subscription**, **vault name**, and **Hyper-V site name** to which Hyper-V belongs:

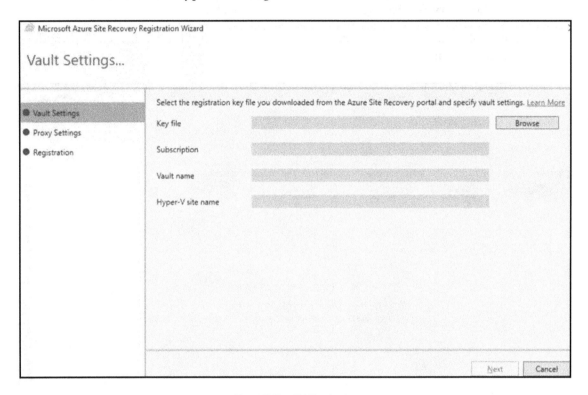

Figure 4.17: Hyper-V ASR registration

16. In Proxy Settings, select **Connect directly to Azure Site Recovery without a proxy**
17. In **Registration**, click **Finish** after the server is registered in the vault

ASR then retrieves information from the Hyper-V server(s). This can take up to 30 minutes.

Prepare Infrastructure — Target environment

18. In the Azure Portal, back in the **prepare Infrastructure** wizard, click **Target.**
19. Select the **Subscription** and **Resource group** in which the Azure VMs will be created after failover on Hyper-V VMs.

20. Select the **Resource Manager** deployment model for use after failover. ASR will then validate that you have a compatible network and storage accounts.

Prepare Infrastructure - Replication Policy

21. Click **Replication Settings** and click **+Create and associate.**
22. In **Create and associate policy**, enter a policy name, leave the default settings, and click **OK.**
23. Click **OK** after the policy is created.

To Enable Replication

Perform the following steps:

1. In **Replicate Application**, click **Source.**
2. In **Source**, select the name of your Hyper-V site. Click **OK.**
3. In **Target**, select **Azure** as the target, the vault subscription, and the **Resource Manager** deployment model.
4. Select the storage account and network in which the Azure VMs will be located after failover. These should have been created in the preceding **Getting ready** section.
5. In **Virtual machines**, select the VM(s) you want to replicate. Click **OK:**

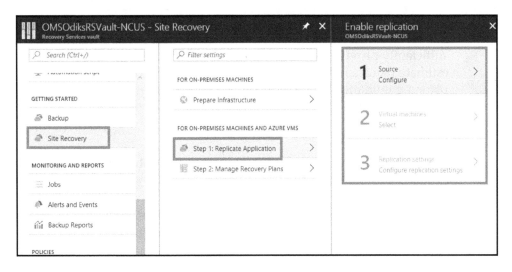

Figure 4.18: Enable Replication

See also

For more information, visit the following links:

- **For the most up-to-date, step-by-step guidance on setting up DR for Hyper-V (with VMM) replication to Azure, use the following tutorial**: `https://docs.microsoft.com/en-us/azure/site-recovery/tutorial-hyper-v-vmm-to-azure`.
- **For the most up-to-date, step-by-step guidance on setting up DR Hyper-V (managed in VMM clouds) replication to secondary site, use the following tutorial**: `https://docs.microsoft.com/en-us/azure/site-recovery/tutorial-vmm-to-vmm`.

Replicate Physical Servers and VMWare VMs

ASR supports the replication of VMware VMs and physical servers to Azure and to a secondary VMware site.

Getting ready

To begin, you will need to prepare Azure. You will need an Azure subscription, an Azure storage account, and an Azure network. Review up-to-date steps here: `https://docs.microsoft.com/en-us/azure/site-recovery/tutorial-prepare-azure`.

Site recovery performs best when storage and network bandwidth are sufficiently provisioned. Use the deployment planner to accurately estimate requirements to meet your replication needs. A deployment planning guidance can be found at this link: `https://docs.microsoft.com/en-us/azure/site-recovery/site-recovery-deployment-planner`

Additionally, review and complete the following tasks:

- Review the supported components and settings for VMware VM DR to Azure: `https://docs.microsoft.com/en-us/azure/site-recovery/support-matrix-vmware-to-azure`.
- Review your Azure subscription limits and quotas. Further guidance can he found at: `https://docs.microsoft.com/en-us/azure/azure-subscription-service-limits`.

- Set up the management server, which holds the Configuration server role. The Configuration server coordinates communications between on-premises and Azure and manages data replication. You can configure a single on premise machine with this role and, by default, the Process server and master target server roles are also installed on this machine. More information can be found at: `https://docs.microsoft.com/en-us/azure/site-recovery/site-recovery-vmware-to-azure-manage-configuration-server`.

How to do it...

Prepare the on-premise Hyper-V infrastructure for replication of Hyper-V VMs to Azure. This applies to both scenarios where Hyper-V hosts are managed with VMM and scenarios where Hyper-V hosts are not managed with VMM.

STEP-BY-STEP: Review the most up-to-date list of requirements to prepare Hyper-V for DR to Azure here: `https://docs.microsoft.com/en-us/azure/site-recovery/tutorial-prepare-on-premises-vmware`. STEP-BY-STEP: To configure DR to Azure for on-premises VMware VMs, follow the detailed up-to-date guide: `https://docs.microsoft.com/en-us/azure/site-recovery/tutorial-vmware-to-azure`.

How it works...

ASR supports the replication of VMware VMs and physical servers to Azure and to a secondary VMware site.

For DR to Azure of VMware VMs, when you configure the replication settings in the ASR vault, you are also able to set up and configure the on-premises configuration server. To set up the configuration server as a VMware VM, you download the OVF template and create the VM by importing it into VMware. When you register the Configuration server with the ASR vault, ASR discovers the on-premises VMware VMs.

Once you configure replication settings, machines will replicate based on the configured replication policy and an initial copy of the VMware VM data is replicated to Azure storage. Once the initial replication finishes, delta changes begin to replicate to Azure.

There's more...

For DR to a secondary VMware site, ASR includes InMage Scout, which provides real-time replication between on-premises VMware sites. You can download the InMage Scout software from the ASR vault:

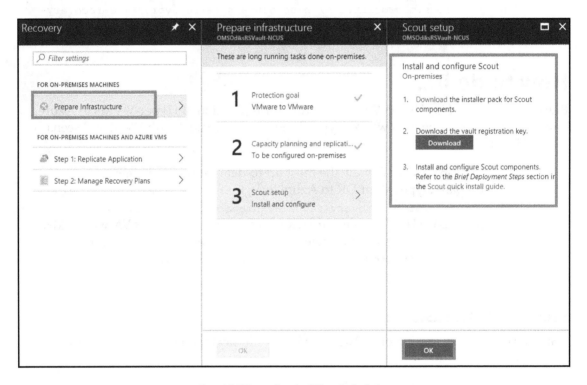

Figure 4.19: VMware to Secondary VMware Site Replication

To configure DR to a secondary VMware site for on-premises VMware VMs, follow the detailed up-to-date, step-by-step guide: https://docs.microsoft.com/en-us/azure/site-recovery/tutorial-vmware-to-vmware.

See also

Visit the following link for more information:

- **For the most up-to-date, step-by-step guidance on setting up DR for replicating Physical servers to Azure, use the following tutorial**: `https://docs.microsoft.com/en-us/azure/site-recovery/tutorial-physical-to-azure`.

Configure Recovery plans

With the failover capability in ASR, you can failover a single machine to Azure or to a secondary site, or use a recovery plan to failover multiple machines to a target location. With recovery plans, you can sequence and customize the failover and recovery of multi-tier applications that run on multiple VMs. Recovery plans in ASR are used to determine which machines fail over and the manner in which they failover and start up together. Scripts for automation, runbooks, and manual actions can be added to a recovery plan. With this said, it is quite evident that recovery plans are a very important aspect of the failover process in ASR because they enable you to effectively build in or define a failover strategy for your applications. Additionally, ASR recovery plans enable you to achieve one-click failover through the automation of recovery tasks using automation runbooks. This results in a significantly reduced RTO.

Getting ready

To create a recovery plan, you must have machines that are configured for protection.

How to do it...

To create a recovery plan:

1. Navigate to the **Azure Portal** (`https://portal.azure.com`) and sign in.
2. In the Azure Portal, type **Recovery Services** in the **Search resources** search field and select **Recovery Services vaults**.
3. Select and click the vault name to work in.

4. Under **Manage**, click **Recovery Plans (Site Recovery)** and then click **+Recovery plan**. Enter a name for the plan and specify a source and target based on the following scenarios:

ASR Scenario	Source	Target
Azure VMs to Azure	Azure region	Azure region
Hyper-V (without VMM) to Azure	Hyper-V site	Azure
VMM to Azure	VMM server	Azure
VMware/ Physical server to Azure	Configuration server	Azure
VMM to secondary VMM	VMM servers	VMM servers

Table 4.3: Recovery Plan ASR Scenarios

5. In **Select virtual machines**, select the replication group (or VMs) to add to the default group in the recovery plan:

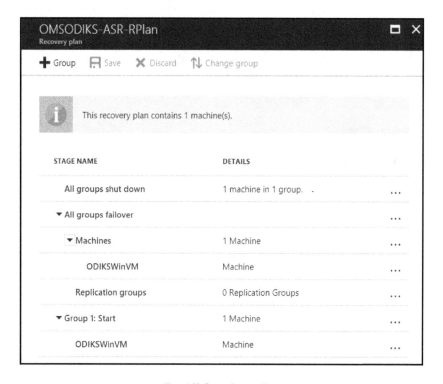

Figure 4.20: Create a Recovery Plan

How it works...

Recovery plans are used to determine which machines failover and the manner in which they failover and start up together. Plans are also used to define the dependencies between machines through groupings. Additionally, plans can be used to run test planned or unplanned failovers for workloads.

For example, consider a recovery plan that replicates and protects the application servers (VMs) for a three-tier web application comprised of a database tier running on SQL server, a logic tier for the application, and a web front end in IIS. The applications servers are grouped logically in the recovery plan, based on the desired start-up behavior. If there are multiple VMs in any group, they are generally all started up together. The general format of the recovery plan would be as follows:

Plan Stage Name	Stage Details
All groups shutdown	This step in the recovery plan performs a shutdown of all the on-premises VMs that are members of the group.
All groups failover	This step then triggers a failover of all members of the recovery plan in parallel.
Group 1: Start	This step will start the SQL Server VM(s).
Group 2: Start	This step will start the application VM(s).
Group 3: Start	This step will start the web frontend VM(s).

Table 4.4: Recovery Plan Format

There's more...

ASR has provisions for extending recovery plans, enabling the addition of new groups to an existing plan, scripts, and manual actions that can be executed before or after a recovery plan group. You can also add Azure runbooks to recovery plans to automate tasks.

To add a manual action or script to a recovery plan

Take the following steps to add a manual action or script to your recovery plan:

1. Navigate to the **Azure Portal** (`https://portal.azure.com`) and sign in.
2. In the Azure Portal, type **Recovery Services** in the **Search resources** search field and select **Recovery Services vaults**.
3. Select and click the vault name to work in.
4. Under **Manage**, click **Recovery Plans (Site Recovery)** and select and open your recovery plan.
5. Click an item in the **Step** list and then click **Script** or **Manual Action**.
6. Use the **Move Up** and **Move Down** buttons to move script position accordingly and specify whether to add the script or action before the selected item.
7. After adding desired manual action or script, perform a failover of the recovery plan to ensure the added task or script works as desired.

See also

Visit the following website for more information:

- **Add Azure Automation runbooks to recovery plans**: `https://docs.microsoft.com/en-us/azure/site-recovery/site-recovery-runbook-automation`.

Configure failover and failback

ASR provides flexible failover and failback capabilities, enabling you to failover applications to Azure or to a secondary site, and failback the application to the primary site once connectivity is restored. As part of your DR plan and testing, you can run test failovers to review and validate your DR strategy and plan, with no loss of data or downtime. You can also run planned failovers for planned outages with no data loss, or unplanned failovers with minimal data loss for unexpected disasters.

Getting ready

Before performing a failover, test your failover plan to validate your DR strategy without any downtime. ASR enables you to run a test failover without any data loss. You can run a test failover for a single VM or for a recovery plan.

In order to test your failover plan, you will need to determine the network settings to use for the replica VM(s). When performing a test failover, you have the option of testing to a non-production network on a recovery site (recommended) or testing to a production network on a recovery site. You can run a test failover to a secondary site:

STEP-BY-STEP: The following detailed Microsoft article provides detailed guidance on planning your infrastructure for failover testing, using an on-premises site managed by VMM as the recovery site: `https://docs.microsoft.com/en-us/azure/site-recovery/site-recovery-test-failover-vmm-to-vmm#prepare-the-infrastructure-for-test-failover`.

ASR also supports running a test failover of on-premises resources to Azure and Azure VMs to another **Azure region (Preview)**:

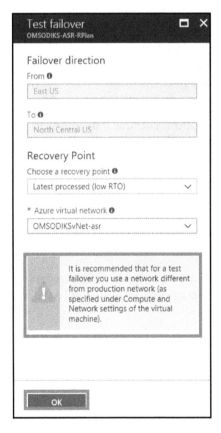

Figure 4.21: Configure Test Failover

As shown in the previous image, it is recommended to use a non-production network for a test failover.

 STEP-BY-STEP: The following detailed Microsoft article provides detailed guidance on testing your DR plan to Azure. `https://docs.microsoft.com/en-us/azure/site-recovery/site-recovery-test-failover-to-azure#run-a-test-failover`.

Another important consideration for your DR plan is that of how to connect to the replica machine(s) in Azure or the secondary site after failover. It is therefore important to prepare the network at your DR target location. This applies to both scenarios for failing over to Azure and to a secondary site. Generally, you have the option of keeping the same IP address for your replica machines in the target site after failover or using a different IP address. Use the table below to evaluate your options:

Network option	Details
Keep IP addresses	With this option, you can keep the same address range in the target location that you used on-premises. With this option you will need to update your network routes with the new location of the IP addresses after failover when replicating workloads to Azure.
Use different IP addresses	With this option, you use a different IP address range for the network of the replicated Azure VM(s). This will result in the VM(s) getting new IP addresses and so you will need to update DNS accordingly.

Table 4.5: Failover network options

How to do it...

In this section, we will review failover steps for various replication scenarios (Hyper-V, VMware, physical to Azure or secondary site), as well as failover scenarios (planned and unplanned failover) in ASR.

Failover an Azure VM(s) to secondary Azure region

The process will failover an Azure VM from one region to another:

1. Navigate to the **Azure Portal** (`https://portal.azure.com`) and sign in.
2. In the Azure Portal, type **Recovery Services** in the **Search resources** search field and select **Recovery Services vaults**.
3. Select and click the vault name to work in.
4. Under **Manage**, click **Recovery Plans (Site Recovery)**, click your recovery plan name, click **...More** and click **Failover**.
5. On the **Failover** screen, confirm the direction of failover and, from the drop down menu, select a **Recovery Point** to failover to.

 For the recovery point, you can select between **Latest**, which is the default and has the lowest RPO; **Latest processed**, which provides a low RTO, and **Latest app-consistent**. Also, the option to choose a recovery point is available only when you are failing over to Azure.

6. Under **Shut down machines**, if you want ASR to attempt a shutdown of the source VM(s) before starting the failover, select the option to **Shut down machines before beginning failover**. Click **OK**.
7. After the failover operation completes confirm that the VM(s) is running in the target Azure region.
8. Connect to the Azure VM to validate it, if you prepared to connect to it after failover.

9. After you verify the VM, click **...More** and click **Commit**. This deletes the available recovery points:

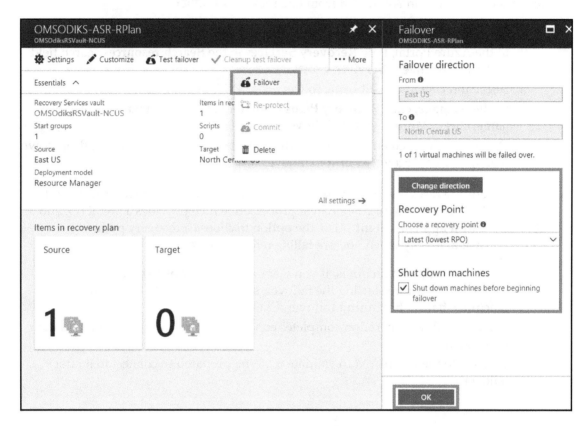

Figure 4.22: Configure ASR Failover

After the VM(s) failover, you can re-protect the replica machine(s) so that it replicates back to the primary region:

10. In the Recovery vault, under **Protected items**, click **Replicated items**. Confirm that status of VM(s) says **Failover committed**.

11. Right-click the VM(s) that have been failed over and select the option to **Re-protect**:

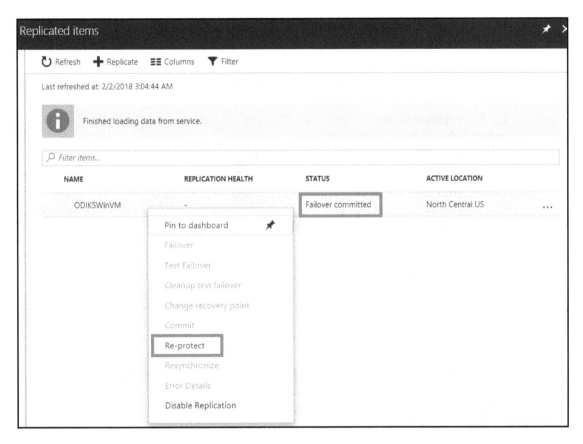

Figure 4.23: Re-protect VM

Failback an Azure VM(s) to primary region

After you re-protect VM(s), you can then failback the machine(s) to the primary Azure region. To do this, you will need to follow the exact steps (1 - 11) above. However in step 5, ensure that you click the button to **Change direction** from secondary region to primary region.

Failover on-premises Hyper-V VM(s) to Azure

The process will failover on-premises VM(s) to Azure:

1. Navigate to the **Azure Portal** (https://portal.azure.com) and sign in.

2. In the Azure Portal, type **Recovery Services** in the **Search resources** search field and select **Recovery Services vaults**.

3. Select and click the vault name to work in.

4. Under **Manage**, click **Recovery Plans (Site Recovery)**, click your recovery plan name, click **...More,** and click **Failover**.

5. On the **Failover** screen, confirm the direction of failover and, from the drop down menu, select a **Recovery Point** to failover to.

6. If data encryption is enabled for the VMM cloud, under **Encryption Key**, select the certificate issued when you set up data encryption on the VMM server.

7. Under **Shut down machines**, if you want ASR to attempt a shutdown of the source VM(s) before starting the failover, select option to **Shut down machines before beginning failover**. Click **OK**.

When you opt to shut down, ASR will attempt to synchronize the on-premises data to the service before it triggers the failover. Additionally, the failover operation will continue even if the shutdown operation is unsuccessful.

8. After the failover operation completes, confirm that the VM(s) is running in the target Azure region.

9. Connect to the Azure VM to validate it, if you prepared to connect to it after failover.

10. After you verify the VM, click **...More** and click **Commit**. This deletes the available recovery points.

After the VM(s) failover, you can re-protect the replica machine(s) so that it replicates back to the primary region:

11. In the Recovery vault, under **Protected items**, click **Replicated items**. Confirm that status of VM(s) says **Failover committed.**

12. Right-click the VM(s) that have been failed over and select the option to **Re-protect.**

Failback Hyper-V VM(s) from Azure to on-premises site

After you re-protect Hyper-V VM(s), you can use a planned failover to failback the machine(s) from Azure to the primary on-premises site. To do this, you will need to follow the same steps (1 - 12) above. However, note the following important steps:

- For step 4, run a **Planned Failover**

- For step 5, the direction of the job would be **from Azure to your on-premises site**

Failover on-premises Hyper-V VM(s) to secondary site

ASR supports replicating Hyper-V VMs to a secondary on-premises site. You can perform a regular or planned failover of Hyper-V VMs to a secondary site. Use the regular failover in the event of an unexpected disaster or outage. Follow the same steps above for failing over Hyper-V VMs to Azure. However, note the following important steps:

- **Skip step 6**: In this scenario, the encryption key doesn't apply.
- **Skip step 12**: Re-protection in this scenario will be done through reverse replication. See failback in the following section.

Failback Hyper-V VM(s) from secondary site to primary site

Once VMs are running in the secondary site, you can failback to the primary site. You'll need to ensure that the primary and secondary VMM servers are connected to ASR:

1. Navigate to the **Azure Portal** (`https://portal.azure.com`) and sign in.
2. In the Azure Portal, type **Recovery Services** in the **Search resources** search field and select **Recovery Services vaults**.
3. Select and click the vault name to work in.
4. Under **Settings | Replicated items**, right-click the VM(s) and enable **Reverse Replicate** to start replicating the VM back to the primary site.

> If the primary VM is not available, restore the VM from a backup before starting the reverse replication process.

5. Next, select the VM and click **Planned Failover**. Confirm the direction of failover (from secondary VMM cloud).
6. Under **Data Synchronization**, specify whether you want to synchronize data during failover only (full download) or synchronize data before failover (delta change synchronization). Proceed to start the failover.
7. After data synchronization, click **Jobs** and select **Complete Failover** to shut down the replica VM in the secondary site.
8. Verify that the VM is available in the primary site and in **Commit Pending** state. Click **Commit** to commit the failover.

9. To re-protect the VM back to the secondary VMM cloud, enable **Reverse Replicate** to replicate delta changes since replica VM was shutdown.

Failover on-premises VMware VM(s) and Physical servers to Azure

This process will fail over on-premises VMware VM(s) and physical servers to Azure:

1. Navigate to the **Azure Portal** (https://portal.azure.com) and sign in.
2. In the Azure Portal, type **Recovery Services** in the **Search resources** search field and select **Recovery Services vaults**.
3. Select and click the vault name to work in.
4. Under **Settings | Replicated items,** right-click the VM(s) and click **Failover**.
5. On the **Failover** screen, select a **Recovery Point** to fail over to.
6. Under **Shut down machines**, if you want ASR to attempt a shutdown of the source VM(s) before starting the failover, select option to **Shut down machines before beginning failover**. Click **OK**.

When you opt to shutdown, ASR will attempt to synchronize the on-premises data to the service before it triggers the failover. Additionally, the failover operation will continue even if the shutdown operation fails.

7. After the failover operation completes confirm that the VM(s) is running in the target Azure region.
8. Connect to the Azure VM to validate it, if you prepared to connect to it after failover.
9. After you verify the VM, click **...More** and click **Commit**. This deletes the available recovery points.

Failover processing time will vary and could take up to ten minutes to complete for Physical servers and some other VMware workloads such as Linux machines.

Failback VMware VM(s) and Physical servers to on-premises

For this exercise, you will make use of the process server and Master target server which are installed by default on the on-premise configuration server machine. Note that for this to be viable you will need a low-latency network connection between your on-premises infrastructure and Azure network. An ExpressRoute connection is recommended if you will be using on-premises process server. In a production environment, it is generally recommended to do so.

In a production environment, it is highly recommended to set up and configure an Azure VM as a process server for failback. As your deployment grows, you can add additional process servers to handle larger replication traffic volume.

After the VM(s) failover, you can re-protect the replica machine(s) so that it replicates back to the primary region:

1. In the **Recovery vault**, under **Settings | Replicated items**, right-click the VM that was failed over above and confirm that status of VM(s) says **Failover committed**.
2. Right-click the VM(s) that have been failed over and select the option to **Re-protect**. Verify that **Azure to On-premises** option is selected.
3. Choose the on-premises process server and master target server.
4. Under **Datastore**, select the master target datastore to which to recover the disks on-premises. This applies if the on-premises VM has been deleted, and you need to create new disks. Ignore if disks exist.
5. Select the master target retention drive. Click **OK** to start re-protection and replicate the VM to the on-premises site from Azure.
6. Under **Settings | Replicated items**, right-click the VM(s) and click **Unplanned Failover**.

You need a VMware infrastructure for failback, and must failback to an on-premises VMware VM, even when you replicate on-premises physical servers to Azure. Failback to a physical server is not supported at this time.

7. Confirm the direction of failover from the drop down menu (**From Azure**) and select a **Recovery Point** to failover to.
8. Right-click the machine, and click **Commit**. This deletes the available recovery points.

After the VM(s) failback, data will now be in your on-premises site. You can re-protect the data to Azure again:

1. In the Recovery vault, under **Protected items**, click **Replicated items**. Confirm that status of VM(s) says **Failover committed**.
2. Right-click the VM(s) that have been failed over and select the option to **Re-protect**.

How it works...

For the various ASR supported scenarios, you can run planned or unplanned failover operations, depending on the supported infrastructure.

In general, when you initiate a failover, ASR runs a prerequisite check to ensure that all conditions for failover are met:

- ASR creates the VMs in the target resource group, a target virtual network (for failover to Azure), target subnet, and target availability set.
- ASR then processes the data and makes it ready so that an Azure VM can be created from it. Based on the selected recovery point, ASR will either revert the VM to the latest recovery point or process all the data and provide the lowest RPO.
- Optionally, ASR could shut down the source VM before it triggers a failover.
- At this point, ASR creates an Azure VM using the processed data. This replica VM can then become the active VM once your commit, which will result in the removal of all recovery points.

Failover and failback has four main stages:

1. Failover machines to Azure or secondary site.
2. Re-protect VMs in Azure to replicate data back to the on-premises site or primary Azure region. If you failover Hyper-V VMs to a secondary on-premises site, use the **reverse replicate** option to replicate the protected VMs data back to the primary site before failover.
3. Run a planned failover to failback Hyper-V VMs from the secondary site or Azure to the primary site. For VMware VMs and Physical servers, run an unplanned failover to failback from Azure to the on-premises site. To failback Azure VMs from the secondary Azure region to the primary Azure region, run a failover job.

4. Re-protect VMs that you failed back to the primary site so that they replicate to secondary site or Azure. For Hyper-V VMs, use the reverse replicate job to replicate data to the secondary site.

See also

Visit the following websites for more information:

- **Replication architecture for Hyper-V to Azure**: `https://docs.microsoft.com/en-us/azure/site-recovery/concepts-hyper-v-to-azure-architecture`.
- **Replication architecture for VMM site to VMM secondary site**: `https://docs.microsoft.com/en-us/azure/site-recovery/concepts-hyper-v-to-secondary-architecture`.
- **Replication architecture for VMware to Azure**: `https://docs.microsoft.com/en-us/azure/site-recovery/concepts-vmware-to-azure-architecture`.
- **Replication architecture for Physical server to Azure**: `https://docs.microsoft.com/en-us/azure/site-recovery/concepts-physical-to-azure-architecture`.
- **Replication architecture for Azure to Azure**: `https://docs.microsoft.com/en-us/azure/site-recovery/concepts-azure-to-azure-architecture`.
- **Failback to an alternate location**: `https://docs.microsoft.com/en-us/azure/site-recovery/site-recovery-failback-from-azure-to-hyper-v#failback-to-an-alternate-location`.

5
Configuration Management and Automation with OMS

IT organizations are faced with many challenges today, ranging from supporting workloads in an ever-changing modern technology landscape to ensuring optimal service delivery to the business while navigating the constraints of shrinking budgets. IT operations teams are expected to do more with fewer resources and, in spite of the latest tools and platforms that such teams have at their disposal, they are faced with the age-old problems of inconsistent deployment, configuration, and update processes; these lead to unscheduled system outages, challenges of configuration drift on workloads, heterogeneous workload management, and lengthy backlogs of error-prone, repetitive to-do lists that detract from time and resources that should otherwise be expended on tasks and initiatives that would provide value and optimize the service delivery to the business. In this chapter, we will explore the automation and control capabilities in OMS and learn about how organizations can leverage automation and configuration management to manage rapid change and deliver continuous IT services across their hybrid environment. Topics include the following:

- Working with Process Automation
- Configuration management with Azure Automation
- Working with OMS Automation and Control management solutions

Working with Process Automation

Azure Automation is a cloud-based automation and configuration service that enables users and organizations to deliver continuous IT services and enable consistent management and compliance on heterogeneous workloads across hybrid environments. Azure Automation provides such capabilities as the following:

- **Inventory and change tracking**: Get an inventory of your workloads and track changes to services, software, registries, daemons, and files on heterogeneous workloads in your hybrid environment
- **Process Automation:** Lower overhead and cumulative costs and leverage efficiencies by automating frequent, long-running, error-prone tasks, and free up your resources to focus on initiatives that add value to the business
- **Configuration management**: Consistently deploy, configure, update, and monitor your workload configurations using configuration management in Azure with Azure Automation **Desired State Configuration** (**DSC**)
- **Update management**: Automatically assess and monitor update compliance and schedule update deployments to keep heterogeneous workloads across your hybrid environment up-to-date

As IT operations teams adopt DevOps tenets and navigate such concepts as infrastructure as code to operationalize crucial business services and optimize the service delivery to the business, automation and configuration management capabilities in OMS Automation will facilitate the translation and implementation of tried and true software development practices into effective infrastructure automation.

Getting ready

To get started with Azure Automation, create an Automation account. An Automation account serves as a means to logically separate your Azure Automation resources, such as runbooks, Hybrid worker groups, update management schedules, shared resources, and DSC nodes and configurations. You can create multiple Automation accounts in an Azure subscription.

Creating an Automation account

If you do not already have an Automation account, follow these steps to create one:

 You can create an Automation account in other ways, including using ARM templates, and AzureRM PowerShell.

1. Log into the Azure portal at `https://portal.azure.com`.
2. In the Azure portal, type **automation account** in the **Search resources** search field and, under the **SERVICES** option, select **Automation Accounts** as shown in the following screenshot:

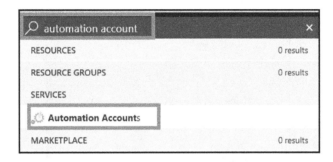

Figure 5.1

3. In **Automation Accounts**, click the **+Add** button, and then select choices for the following items:

   - Provide a name for the new Automation account.
   - Select a subscription to link to by selecting from the drop-down list if the default selected is not appropriate.
   - For the **Resource group** option, choose **Create new** resource group and enter a name in the text field or select **Use existing** to use an existing resource group that is already set up.
   - Select an available location from the **Location** field.
   - Select **Yes** under the **Create Azure Run As account** option. Note that you will need to have permissions to be able to create this **Run As** account in Azure Active Directory. You will still be able to proceed with this task if you select **No** here.

4. Click the **Create** button to create the Automation account as shown in the following screenshot:

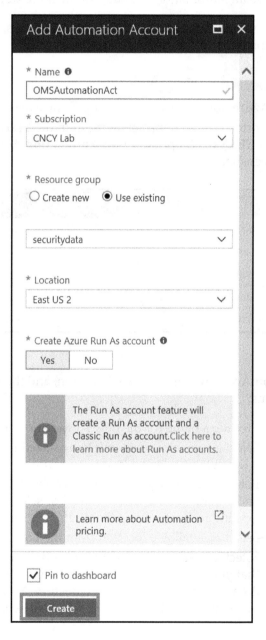

Figure 5.2

5. Once created, the Automation account is pinned to the Azure dashboard and you can click on the account to see the account overview page:

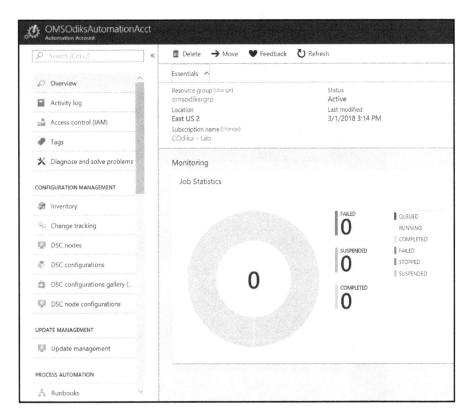

Figure 5.3

Installing the Automation solution in OMS workspace

To add the **Automation and Control** solution offering, you must create an Automation account or select an existing Automation account:

1. Navigate to the Azure portal and click the **New** button. Type **Automation & Control** into the marketplace search field and press *Enter*.

2. Select **Automation & Control** in the **Everything** blade and click on the **Create** button.

3. In create a new solution blade, click the **OMS Workspace**, select your **OMS Workspace**, and check the **Automation Hybrid Worker** and other recommended solutions you would like to install and click the **OMS Workspace Settings** tab.

4. In the resulting blade, confirm your workspace, Azure subscription, location, resource group and pricing tier information and click **Automation account**.

5. In the **Automation Accounts** blade, select an existing Automation account or click **Create an Automation account**:

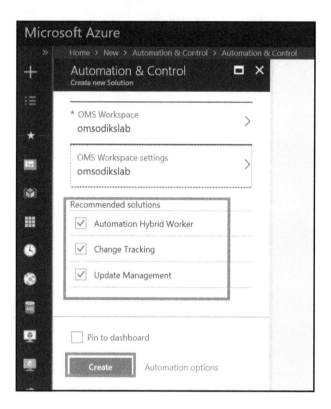

Figure 5.4

6. After the deployments are complete, click **OK** in the **OMS Workspace** blade and upon completion of deployment, click **Create** in the **Automation & Control** blade to finish adding the Automation and Control solution offering to your workspace.

The Automation account is now associated with your Log Analytics workspace, and the installed Automation and Control solutions in your Log Analytics workspace.

In the next section, we will show how you can use the Process Automation feature in Azure Automation to automate frequent, error-prone and time-consuming management tasks on your workloads in Azure and, by using a hybrid runbook worker, automate processes in your on-premises environments. When working with Process Automation, you will work with Azure Automation resources such as the following:

- **Runbooks**: A runbook in Azure Automation is a set of related tasks that work together to perform an automated process. You can create Azure Automation runbooks through the browser-based user interface in the Azure portal, or you can import and modify runbooks from the runbook gallery to suit your purposes.
- **Jobs:** Azure Automation jobs are created when you start runbooks in Azure Automation. A job is a single instance of a runbook execution. The job status indicates the status of the runbook execution.
- **Hybrid worker groups:** The Hybrid runbook worker feature in Azure Automation enables you to run Azure Automation runbooks on computers in your on-premises data centers. A hybrid worker group can be comprised of one or more agents or hybrid workers.

How to do it...

In this section, we will explore Process Automation tasks in Azure Automation and use runbooks to automate tasks on Azure VMs and, with Hybrid worker groups, automate tasks on machines in your on-premises data centers.

Creating a new runbook in Azure Portal

Take the following steps to create a new runbook in Azure Portal:

1. Navigate to the Azure portal at `http://portal.azure.com` and sign in.
2. In the Azure portal, type **Automation Accounts** and select and open your Automation account.
3. From the hub, select **Runbooks** and open the list of runbooks.

4. Click on the **Add a runbook** button and then **Create a new runbook** as shown in the following screenshot:

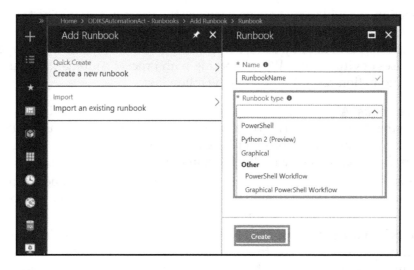

Figure 5.5

5. Enter a name in the **Name** field and select your runbook type. At this time, the following are the types of runbooks you can create:

- **PowerShell**: These are runbooks that are based on Windows PowerShell. You can create and edit this using any standard text editor in Azure or elsewhere. PowerShell runbooks allow for complex logic and they nest other runbooks.

- **Python 2 (Preview)**: Python runbooks compile under Python 2. This runbook type gives you access to the extensive standard Python library. At this time, Python 3 is not supported.

- **Graphical**: Graphical runbooks are runbooks that you create and edit with the graphical editor in the Azure Portal. These runbooks are based on Windows PowerShell and generate PowerShell code, but the code is not exposed for viewing or modification.

- **PowerShell Workflow**: PowerShell Workflow runbooks are based on Windows PowerShell Workflow and, like PowerShell runbooks, are text runbooks. You can create and modify the code in any standard text editor in either the Azure portal or offline using a tool such as PowerShell ISE.

- **Graphical PowerShell Workflow**: Graphical PowerShell Workflow runbooks are based on Windows PowerShell Workflow. Like the graphical runbooks, these can only be created and edited using the graphical editor in the Azure portal.

6. Click **Create** to create the runbook and open the editor.

Once created, you can edit the PowerShell or Python code for your runbook, or, in the case of a graphical runbook, modify the graphical workflow. Once you are done with your edits, you will need to publish the runbook before you can run it.

Publishing a runbook in Azure portal

Take the following steps to publish your runbook in the Azure portal:

1. In your Automation account in the Azure portal, click on **Runbooks** under **Process Automation**.
2. Click a runbook to open it and click on the **Edit** button.
3. Click the **Publish** button and answer **Yes** to the verification prompt:

Figure 5.6

Now that we've gone over the basics, let's add a runbook in Azure and start the runbook to perform an operation. In this exercise, we will add a runbook from the **Runbooks Gallery** in Azure. The Runbook Gallery contains various runbooks from Microsoft and from the community. You can import these runbooks and use them in your environments.

Importing and starting a runbook from the Azure Runbooks Gallery

To import and start a runbook from the Azure Runbooks Gallery, take the followings steps:

1. Navigate to the Azure portal at `http://portal.azure.com` and sign in.
2. In the Azure portal, type **Automation Accounts** and select and open your Automation account.
3. In the Automation Account blade, click **Runbooks gallery** under **PROCESS AUTOMATION**.
4. In the gallery, search for **Easy shutdown** in the gallery search field and, from the returned list of runbooks, select the **Easy Shutdown/ Start for ARM and Classic VMs** PowerShell Workflow runbook:

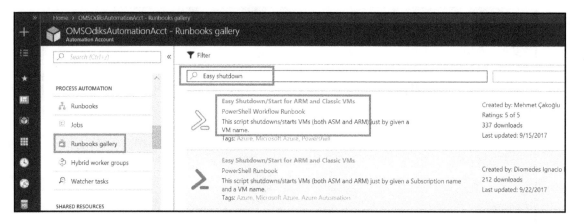

Figure 5.7

5. In the runbook source page, click on **View Source Project** to view details about the runbook in the TechNet Script Center. You can also review the code before importing the runbook:

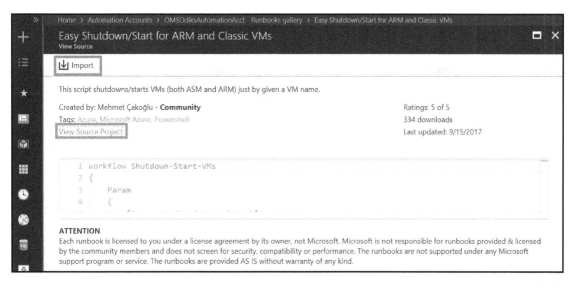

Figure 5.8

6. Once you've viewed the details about the PowerShell Workflow runbook, click the **Import** button and click **OK** to accept the default name of **Shutdown-Start-VMs** and to import the runbook.

7. In the runbook page, click on **Edit** to view the runbook code and make any changes necessary. The default runbook code is sufficient for this illustration:

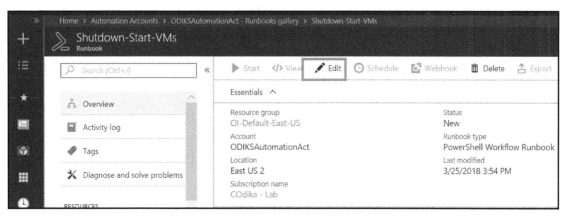

Figure 5.9

8. Once code review is complete, click **Publish** to make the runbook ready for execution and click **Yes** at the prompt:

Figure 5.10

9. Once published, close the runbook page to return to your Automation account, and click **Credentials** under **SHARED RESOURCES** to open the **Credentials** blade.

10. Click on **Add a credential** button at the top of the blade.

11. In the **New Credential** form, enter Credential01 in the **Name** field. This is the default credential asset variable in the code, but you can update the variable and use another name if you prefer.

12. Enter the name and password of an account that will be used to connect to your Azure subscription into the **User name** and **Password** fields respectively and confirm the password. Click **Create** to create the credential asset.

13. In the Automation Account, under **PROCESS AUTOMATION**, click on **Runbooks** and click on **Shutdown-Start-VMs** in the list of runbooks.

14. In the runbook page, click the **Start** button to start the runbook.

15. In the **Parameters** page, enter a name of the Azure VM you would like to shut down or start up.

16. In the **SHUTDOWN** drop-down menu, select **True** to shut down the target VM or **False** to start up the VM. Select **Azure** in the **Run on** settings to execute the runbook against Azure and click **OK** to submit the runbook:

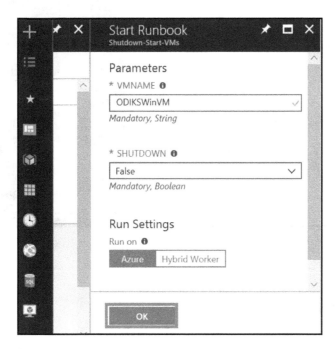

Figure 5.11

Once submitted, the runbook starts and a job is created.

17. In the runbook job page, click **Output** to see the status of the runbook job. As seen in the following screenshot, the output shows that the runbook finds the target VM and either starts or stops it depending on your parameter selection:

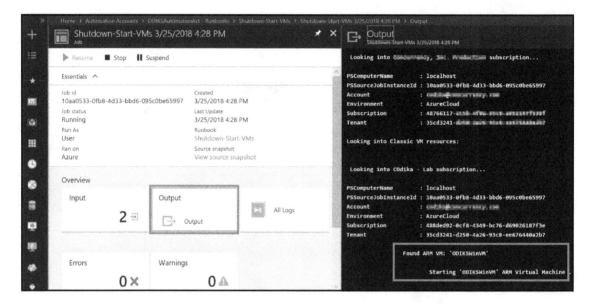

Figure 5.12

How it works...

Process Automation is a capability in Azure Automation that enables users and organizations to transform service delivery by automating long-running, error-prone and repetitive tasks in order to focus on tasks that add value to the business. Process Automation is comprised of various components, including runbooks, jobs, and Azure Automations shared resources or assets.

Runbooks

As described earlier, runbooks in Azure Automation are a set of related tasks that work together to perform an automated process. You can create Azure Automation runbooks through the browser-based user interface in the Azure portal, or you can import and modify runbooks from the Runbook Gallery to suit your purposes. At this time, there are five types of runbooks that you can create and use with Azure Automation:

- **PowerShell:** These are runbooks that are based on Windows PowerShell. You can create and edit this using any standard text editor in Azure or elsewhere. PowerShell runbooks allow for complex logic and they nest other runbooks.
- **Python 2**: Python runbooks compile under Python 2. This runbook type gives you access to the extensive standard Python library. Note that, at this time, Python 3 is not supported.
- **Graphical**: Graphical runbooks are runbooks that you create and edit with the graphical editor in the Azure Portal. These runbooks are based on Windows PowerShell and generate PowerShell code, but the code is not exposed for viewing or modification.
- **PowerShell Workflow**: PowerShell Workflow runbooks are based on Windows PowerShell Workflow and, like PowerShell runbooks, are text runbooks. You can create and modify the code in any standard text editor in either the Azure Portal or offline using a tool such as PowerShell ISE.
- **Graphical PowerShell Workflow**: Graphical PowerShell Workflow runbooks are based on Windows PowerShell Workflow. Like the graphical runbooks, these can only be created and edited using the graphical editor in the Azure Portal.

While much of this chapter shows how to work with runbook, and other Azure Automation resources from within the Azure portal, there are various other methods for starting runbooks and creating and interacting with Azure Automation shared resources and assets. Some other ways of triggering runbooks are the following:

- **Windows PowerShell**: You can create and start runbooks using Windows PowerShell cmdlets. To do this, you will need to authenticate with either an OAuth user service principal or certificate to your Azure subscription.
- **Webhooks**: You can use webhooks to start runbooks in Azure Automation, using a single HTTP POST request. You can also use webhooks to start a runbook in response to a Log Analytics alert rule. With this option, you will use a security token in the webhook URL to authenticate to your Azure subscription.
- **Schedule automation tasks**: Various automation tasks, such as the update deployment task that updates your heterogeneous workloads, will start runbooks on a predefined schedule. The update deployment feature is part of the Update management solution in Azure Automation and OMS Automation and Control.
- **Azure Automation API**: You can also start runbooks by leveraging the REST API for Azure Automation, using any code that can make HTTP requests. Authentication with this method will be either using an OAuth user or service principal or certificate to your Azure subscription.

Jobs

Azure Automation jobs are created when you start runbooks in Azure Automation. A job is a single instance of a runbook execution. The job status indicates the status of the runbook execution. You can view job statistics for all runbooks executed from your Automation account:

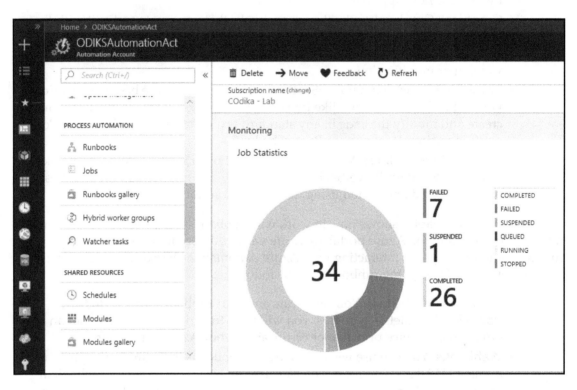

Figure 5.13

You can also view job statistics from within the runbook page as seen in the following screenshot:

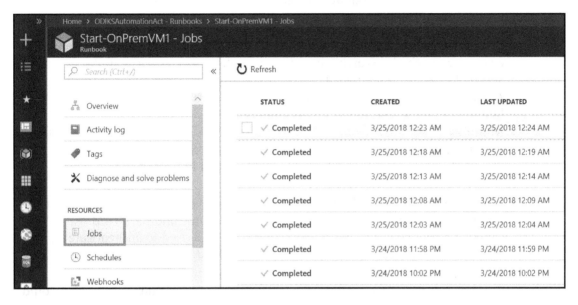

Figure 5.14

Job statuses indicate the outcome of a runbook execution. The following table lists some job statuses for Azure Automation runbooks:

Job status	Status description
Completed	This indicates that the job successfully completed.
Failed	This status indicates that the job failed to start or encountered an error. It could also indicate that certain runbook types failed to compile.
Suspended	This status indicates that the job was suspended either by the user or system. A job with this status can be resumed.
Stopped	This status indicates that the user stopped the job before completion.
Resuming	This indicates that a job that was previously suspended has resumed execution.

Table 5.1

Shared resources

Azure Automation accounts have shared resources which can be used by all runbooks in an Automation account. Also referred to as assets, shared resources include the following:

- **Schedules**: Schedules are used with runbooks and enable them to be executed at a set time. A schedule can be linked to multiple runbooks and a runbook can be subject to various schedules. For instance, the update deployment feature in Azure Automation Update management executes runbooks to patch heterogeneous workloads at various pre-defined schedules.

- **Modules**: These are a group of PowerShell cmdlets that you can execute with the various runbook types using any supported methods. Modules in Azure Automation, are like PowerShell modules that you import to enable some workload-specific functionality in PowerShell.

- **Credentials**: A credential asset is used to authenticate against services and it holds a PSCredential object comprising of a username and password. When called in a runbook, this object is then retrieved and used to authenticate against resources in order for the runbook to perform the desired task.

- **Connections:** Connection assets enable users to store all of the information required to connect to an external application or service. Such information could include user name, password, service name, URL, port, and so on. By enabling you to store all variables, parameters, and credentials needed to connect to an external service in one asset, connections eliminate the need for multiple connection variables and credentials.

- **Certificates**: Certificate assets facilitate authentication to Azure, for instance using Windows PowerShell or the Azure Automation REST API, to start a runbook or perform some other task.

- **Variables:** Variable assets hold various types of information that you can use in runbooks and with other Automation resources. You can create variables of various datatypes such as string, integer, Boolean, and so on.

With Process Automation in Azure Automation, you can execute runbooks to automate tasks in your hybrid environment. Once a runbook is started, the runbook executes against resources in Azure or, if set to run on-premises, the hybrid worker group in your automation account relays the runbook to a hybrid worker in your on-premises environment to run it against local resources. Once the runbook performs the defined tasks, job, results are returned indicating status of tasks. The following figure depicts Azure Automation workflows for various Azure Automation features, including process automation and configuration management:

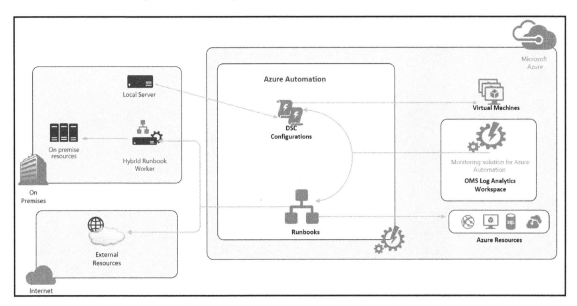

Figure 5.15

There's more...

As mentioned in the preceding sections, Azure Automation runbooks run in the Azure cloud and cannot directly access resources in other environments. To address this, Azure Automation has a **Hybrid Runbook Worker** feature that enables you to execute runbooks against resources in other environments. To use this feature, you will need to create a hybrid runbook worker group in an Azure Automation account. The hybrid worker group is comprised of one or more hybrid runbook worker. More workers in a group enable high availability for the group. When you start a runbook and run it on a hybrid worker, you will have to choose the hybrid worker group that the runbook will execute on. There is not an option to specify what worker the runbook runs on.

The group members will determine which worker services the request and runs the runbook:

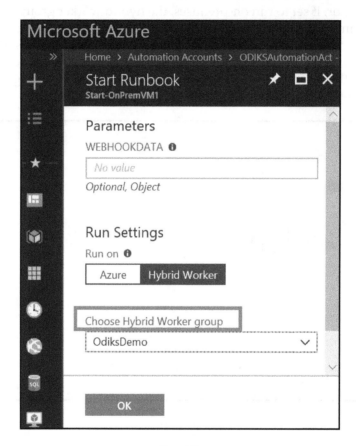

Figure 5.16

Each hybrid worker installed in your environment requires the Microsoft Monitoring Agent. The worker uses the Microsoft Monitoring Agent with which it interacts as well as the Azure Automation account to register the worker to the hybrid worker group, receive jobs from the account, and report job status to the account. You can install the Hybrid Runbook worker either automatically using a script or manually through a series of steps.

Installing and configuring a Windows Hybrid Worker

Before installing the Hybrid worker, ensure that the **Microsoft Monitoring Agent** (**MMA**) is installed on the Hybrid worker, after which you can proceed with the following steps:

1. Navigate to the PowerShell Gallery to view information about the Hybrid worker runbook at `https://www.powershellgallery.com/packages/New-OnPremiseHybridWorker/1.4/DisplayScript`.

2. Run `Get-PSRepository` to confirm that the PowerShell gallery is seen as a registered script repository on the machine:

```
PS C:\Program Files\Update Services\Tools> Get-PSRepository

Name            InstallationPolicy    SourceLocation
----            ------------------    --------------
PSGallery       Untrusted             https://www.powershellgallery.com/api/v2/
```

Figure 5.17

3. On the hybrid worker of another machine, run the following to download the hybrid worker script:

   ```
   Save-script –Name New-OnPremiseHybridWorker –Path
   <path>
   ```

4. Once saved, navigate to the hybrid worker and run Windows PowerShell as an administrator.

5. Navigate to the script path and run the script with the relevant values for the following script arguments:

   ```
   .New-OnPremiseHybridWorker.ps1 –AutomationAccountName
   <NameofAutomationAccount> –AAResourceGroupName
   <NameofResourceGroup>`
   –OMSResourceGroupName <NameofOResourceGroup> –HybridGroupName
   <NameofHRWGroup> `
   –SubscriptionId <AzureSubscriptionId> –WorkspaceName
   <NameOfLogAnalyticsWorkspace
   ```

6. Accept the prompts and enter any requested authentication credentials.
7. After installing the hybrid worker, it will now be visible in the Automation Account under **Automation Accounts** | **HYBRID WORKER GROUPS** | **Group Name:**

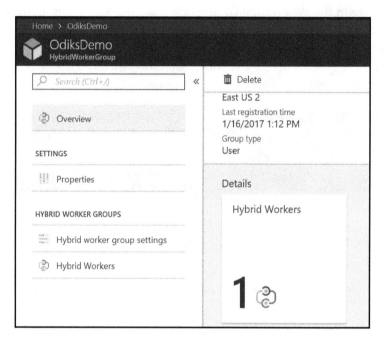

Figure 5.18

Running a runbook on hybrid worker

In this scenario, we will execute a fairly simple runbook on a hybrid worker. The runbook will look for all files in a directory specified in a runbook source parameter and copy to another hybrid worker directory specified in a runbook target parameter:

```
workflow File-Copy

{

    Param

    (

        [parameter(Mandatory=$true)]
        [String] $FileSource,
```

```
        [parameter(Mandatory=$true)]
        [String] $FileDestination
    )

    Write-Output "Runbook is executing on On-premises Hybrid worker:
$env:ComputerName"

    Write-Output "File Destination: $FileDestination"

    Write-Output "Source of File: $FileSource"

    $execute = InlineScript
    {
        Try

        {
            Copy-Item -Path "$using:FileSource" -Destination
"$using:FileDestination" -recurse
        }

        catch
        {
            $errorMessage = $error[0].Exception.Message
        }

        if($errorMessage -eq $null)
        {
            return "Files were copied successfully"
        }
        else
        {
            return " Copy Operation Failed: Encountered error(s)  while
copying files. Error message=[$errorMessage]"
        }
    }

    Write-Output $execute
    Write-Output "Runbook execution has completed"

}
```

Perform the following steps:

1. You can download this PowerShell Workflow runbook from the GitHub at
   `https://github.com/MSOMSBook/BookChapters`. The file is named
   `FileCopy.ps1`.
2. Navigate to the Azure Portal at `http://portal.azure.com` and sign in.

3. In the Azure portal, type **Automation Accounts** and select and open your Automation account.
4. In **Automation Account**, select **Runbooks**, click **Add a runbook** at the top of the page and select **Import an existing runbook**.
5. In the **Import** blade, for the **Runbook file** field, click the browse button, and select the runbook you downloaded from GitHub in step 1. This will automatically fill in the **Runbook type** and **Name** fields.
6. Click **Create** to finish importing the runbook:

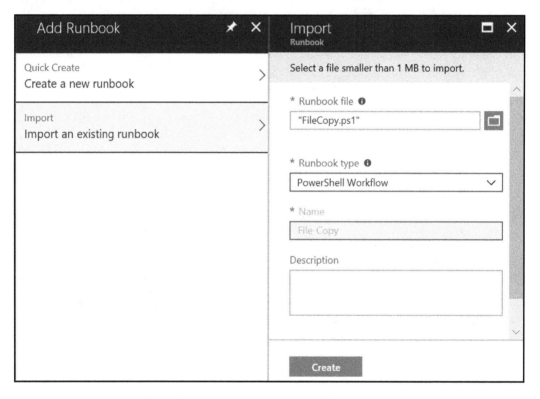

Figure 5.19

7. After importing the runbook, select the runbook, and click **Edit** at the top of the menu.
8. Once in the **Edit** menu, click **Publish** to make the runbook available for execution, and click **Yes** at the prompt.
9. Once published, click **Start** to execute the runbook.

10. In the **Parameters** blade, enter runbook parameters for the file source and file destination shown as following:

- **FILESOURCE**: Enter a directory for the location of files/ folders you would like to copy
- **FILEDESTINATIO**N: Enter a directory where you would like the copied files/folders to be copied to:

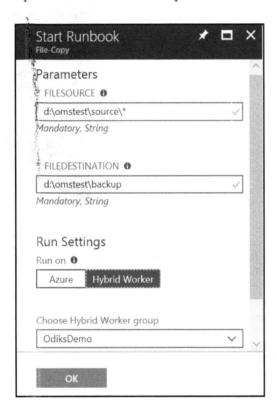

Figure 5.20

11. Select **Hybrid Worker** under **Run on** and choose a hybrid worker group from the drop-down menu. Click **OK** to finish and start the runbook.

12. Once started, a job instance blade will open in the Azure portal. Click the **Output** tile to see the result indicating that the files in the source directory were successfully copied to the target directory:

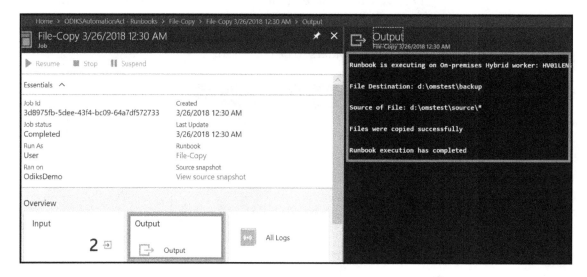

Figure 5.21

13. Navigate to the target directory on the hybrid worker and confirm that the files were copied to the target directory:

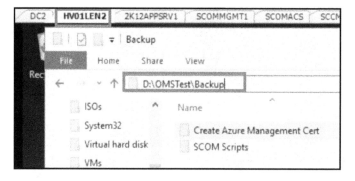

Figure 5.22

See also

- **How to deploy a Linux Hybrid Runbook Worker**: `https://docs.microsoft.com/en-us/azure/automation/automation-linux-hrw-install`.
- **Forward job status and job streams from Automation to Log Analytics**: `https://docs.microsoft.com/en-us/azure/automation/automation-manage-send-joblogs-log-analytics`.

Configuration management with Azure Automation

Configuration management in Azure Automation enables users and organizations to manage and configure their heterogeneous workloads by leveraging such capabilities as inventory collection, change tracking, and desired state configuration. Azure Automation configuration management is based on PowerShell DSC and it enables you to create, manage, compile, and test your DSC configurations, as well as manage nodes that will be subject to your configurations.

How to do it...

In this section we will review steps for creating a sample configuration for the Windows web server IIS role, and steps for compiling, applying, and testing the configuration.

Creating an Azure Automation DSC configuration

In this example, we will use a simple DSC configuration that looks for the IIS Windows feature:

1. Open a text editor, such as PowerShell ISE or Notepad ++.
2. Enter the following simple Web Server (IIS) configuration into the editor and save it as `DSCConfig.ps1`:

```
configuration DSCConfig
{
    Node WebServer
    {
        WindowsFeature IIS
        {
```

```
            Ensure = 'Present'
            Name = 'Web-Server'
            IncludeAllSubFeature = $true


        }
    }

    Node NotWebServer
    {
        WindowsFeature IIS
        {
            Ensure = 'Absent'
            Name = 'Web-Server'


        }
    }
}
```

3. Navigate to the Azure portal at `http://portal.azure.com` and sign in.
4. In the Azure portal, type **Automation Accounts** and select and open your Automation account.
5. In **Automation Account** page, select **DSC Configurations** and click **+Add a configuration.**
6. On the **Import Configuration** page, click the browse button to import the saved configuration file. This automatically populates the **Name** field as well. Click **OK** to import the configuration:

Figure 5.23

7. The imported configuration is now visible in the Automation Account at **Automation Accounts** | **CONFIGURATION MANAGEMENT** | **DSC configurations.**

8. In **DSC configurations**, click the imported DSC configuration and click **Compile** and then click **Yes** at the prompt:

Figure 5.24

This kicks off a compilation job and you can monitor the job status in the DSC configuration blade, **Automation Accounts** | **Configuration Management** | **DSC configurations** | **<DSC Configuration name>**:

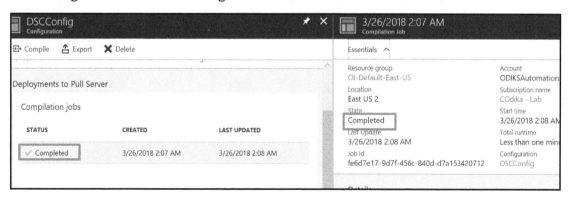

Figure 5.25

9. In the Automation account, navigate to **CONFIGURATION MANAGEMENT** | **DSC node configurations**. You can now see that the MOF files for the node configuration you created have been deployed to and are now available on the pull server:

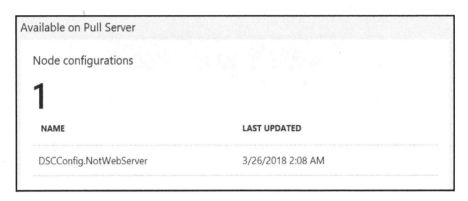

Figure 5.26

10. Click on **DSC nodes** in the Automation account and click **Add Azure VM**.

11. Select a VM from the list of VMs on the **Virtual Machines** page and click **Connect**.

12. In the **Registration** page, click on the drop-down for the **Node configuration name** and select your node configuration. Leave the other default settings or modify where necessary and click **OK**:

Figure 5.27

Nodes are then assessed for compliance with the node configuration. You can review node compliance in **Azure Automation** I **CONFIGURATION MANAGEMENT** I **DSC nodes:**

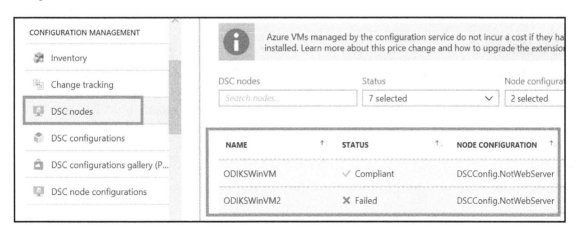

Figure 5.28

How it works...

DSC refers to a documented set of characteristics on computers in a given environment. The configurations can vary widely in complexity and, as such, have immense value for such use cases as compliance enforcement and continuous deployment. Azure Automation DSC is based on PowerShell DSC and, because it is a cloud service, enables configuration management at scale and supports the management of heterogeneous physical computers and VM nodes, enabling nodes to connect to a DSC Pull server and automatically receive configurations. Node configurations are MOF files that are deployed to the pull server where they are then accessed by the nodes.

Once the nodes receive the configurations, they compare the desired settings or behavior defined in the configurations with their local state and report compliance back to Azure Automation.

See also

For more information, visit the following links:

- **DSC Configurations**: `https://docs.microsoft.com/en-us/powershell/dsc/configurations`.
- **Forward Azure Automation DSC reporting data to Log Analytics**: `https://docs.microsoft.com/en-us/azure/automation/automation-dsc-diagnostics`.

Working with OMS Automation and Control solutions

As part of the Automation and Control service offerings, Azure Automation provides update management, assessment, and deployment for remediation and change tracking features. These features are available through the **Update management** and **Change tracking** automation solutions in Log Analytics and are also visible in the Azure Automation account:

- **Update management**: This solution identifies missing system updates and orchestrates installation of these updates across Windows and Linux servers, both in your data center and in any public cloud. The Update management solution supports both update assessments using automation and update deployments on supported operating systems.

- **Change tracking:** This solution enables you to troubleshoot operational and other issues by identifying and tracking changes in your environment. The solution tracks software and file changes on Windows and Linux computers and changes to Windows registry keys, Windows services, and Linux daemons.

How to do it...

You can use the Update management to view the update assessment for servers in your environment, as well as create deployments to install updates on servers that need to be patched.

Adding the Update management solution to OMS Log Analytics workspace

Adding the Update management solution to the OMS Log Analytics workspace requires you to have an Azure Automation account. You can either install this solution from the OMS portal, or you could deploy the solution as part of the Automation and Control offering in the Azure portal:

1. Navigate to your OMS portal at `https://www.mms.microsoft.com` in your browser and sign in.
2. While in the OMS portal, click on the **Solutions Gallery** and click the **Automation & Control** offering under solution offers.

3. Click **Configure Workspace** to configure an automation account:

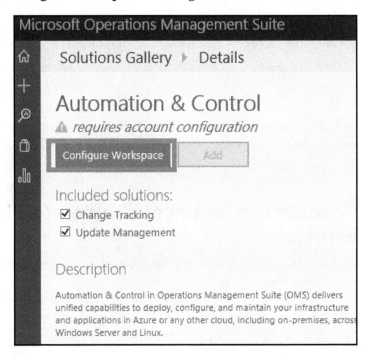

Figure 5.29

4. In the **Automation Account** blade, select **Use existing** and from the drop-down menu, select your Automation account:

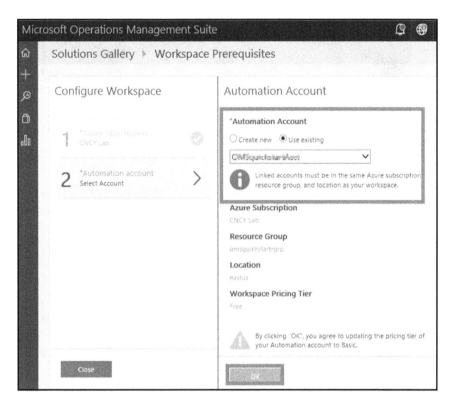

Figure 5.30

5. Click **OK** and click **Close** to finish.
6. Return to the **Solutions Gallery** and click the **Automation & Control** offering.

7. Under **Automation & Control**, confirm that the options for **Update Management** and, optionally, **Change Tracking** are checked. Click **Add** to add the solutions to your workspace:

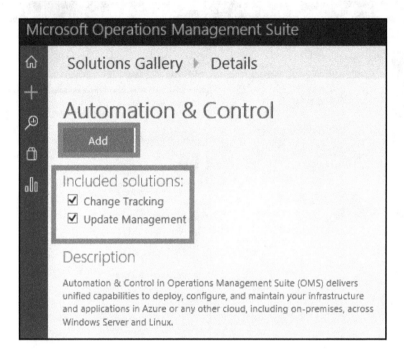

Figure 5.31

Installing updates with Update management

Update management enables you to install updates on servers that are assessed and found to be missing updates that are approved for deployment:

1. In the **Update Management** dashboard, under **Update Deployments**, click **Manage Update Deployments**.

2. In the **Update Deployments** page, click **Add** to open the **New Update Deployment** page:

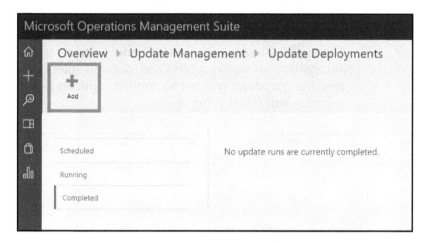

Figure 5.32

3. In the **New Update Deployment** page, enter values for the following fields:

- **Name**: A unique name for the update deployment.
- **Computers**: The names of computers or computer groups to include and target in the Update deployment. Clicking in the entry field will enumerate all eligible computers and groups in your workspace.
- **Time Zone**: The time zone to use for the start time.
- **Schedule Type**: The type of schedule. Choose between one time, weekly recurring, or monthly recurring.
- **Start Time**: The date and time to start the update deployment.

- **Duration (min)**: This is the number of minutes the update is allowed to run. All updates must be run within this time frame. Any uninstalled updates will be applied at the next scheduled time. This is the equivalent of a maintenance window. The duration must be a minimum of 30 minutes and less than six hours. The last 20 minutes of the maintenance window will be used by the automation for restart actions and, once the interval is reached, any remaining updates will not be applied. Updates that are in-progress will finish being applied.

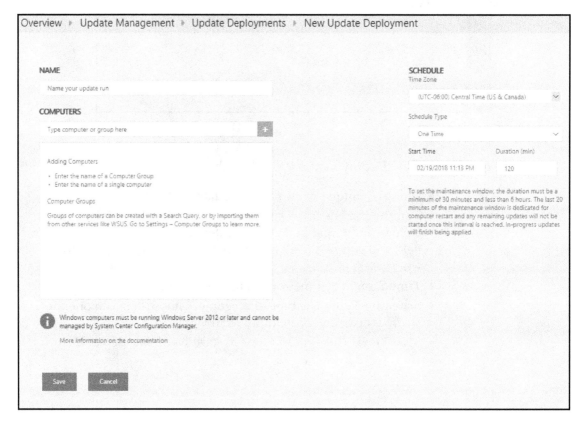

Figure 5.33

Configuring change tracking from the OMS portal

Take the following steps to configure **Change Tracking** from the OMS Portal:

1. In the **Change Tracking** dashboard, click **Configure**. This will take you to the settings page in your OMS workspace.

2. In the **Settings** page, select one or more of the settings as follows:

    - **Windows File Tracking**: In the search field, enter the path to the file you would like to track and click **+** to add it to the list of tracked files and click **Save**.

    - **Windows Registry Tracking**: In the search field, enter the registry path for the registry key you would like to track. Click **+** to add it to the list of tracked registry keys. You can also check the enabled box for the suggested registry keys to enable them. Click **Save** once done.

    - **Linux File Tracking**: In the search field, enter the path to the Linux file you would like to track and click **Save**:

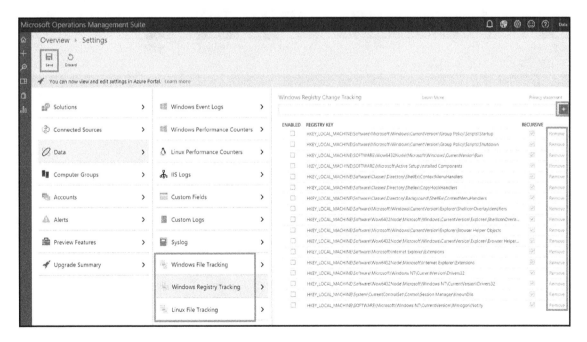

Figure 5.34

To disable change tracking for any Windows registry keys or Windows and Linux files, simply click the **Remove** button for tracked entry in the **Settings** page and click **Save** to finish.

Similarly, you can configure tracking settings from your Automation account in the Azure portal.

Configuring Change Tracking from the Azure Portal

Take the following steps to configure **Change Tracking** from the Azure Portal:

1. Log into the Azure portal at `https://portal.azure.com`.
2. In the Azure portal, type **Automation Account** in the **Search resources** search field and, under **Services**, select **Automation Account**.
3. Select your automation account from the list of accounts.
4. In your Automation account, click **Change tracking (Preview)** under **CONFIGURATION MANAGEMENT** and click **Edit Settings**:

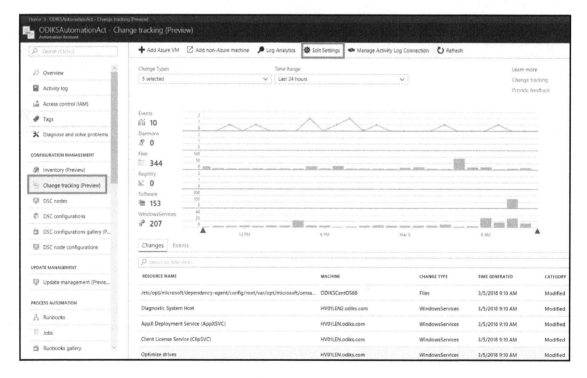

Figure 5.35

5. On the **Change tracking** page, select a tab to track a corresponding configuration:

- **Windows File Tracking**: Click **+Add** to add a new file to track. On the **Add Windows File for Change Tracking** blade, enter the information for the file to track and click **Save** once done.
- **Windows Registry Tracking**: Click the **+Add** button to add a registry key to track. On the **Add Windows Registry for Change Tracking** blade, enter the information for the key to track and click **Save** once done.
- **Linux File Tracking**: Click **+Add** to add a new file to track. On the **Add Linux File for Change Tracking** blade, enter the information for the file to track and click **Save** once done.

How it works...

The Update management solution analyses update metadata and state data collected from servers in your on-premises data centre and in the cloud, assesses the update state of the servers, and provides you with automation capabilities for patching any servers with approved updates. Update management supports the following connected sources:

- **SCOM management group**: The solution collects and analyses information about updates from agents in a SCOM management group that is connected to OMS
- **Windows updates**: The solution can collect information about system updates from Windows computers and can initiate installation of updates that are required
- **Linux agents:** The solution can collect information about system updates from Linux computers and can initiate installation of updates that are required

At various intervals, OMS agent computers run scans for update compliance. On Windows computers, the default interval is every 12 hours. The scan is also initiated on Windows computers within 15 minutes of restarting the OMS agent, prior to installation of the update and after installation of the update. Linux computers run compliance scans every three hours by default and, upon OMS Linux agent restart, the scan is run within 15 minutes. Once the scan is run, the OMS agent forwards the data to Log Analytics and the Update management solution analyses the data and summarizes update information in the solution visualizations. Update management assesses a computer's update state, based on what source the computer is configured to synchronize with.

In a scenario where a Windows computer is configured to report to WSUS, the update state assessment from Windows updates may differ from what WSUS indicates, depending on when WSUS last synchronized with Microsoft Update. This concept also applies to Linux computers if they are configured to report to a local repo or to a public repo.

After you enable this solution in your workspace, any Windows computer that is connected directly to your OMS workspace is configured automatically as a Hybrid Runbook Worker to support solution runbooks. When you create an update deployment to install software on computers in your workspace, the updates are installed by runbooks in Azure Automation. When you create the update deployment, it creates a schedule that starts a master runbook, which in turn starts the child runbook on each agent that you configured to install the required updates.

 Only required updates are applied. Optional updates are not applied by the update deployment.

The Change Tracking solution is part of the Automation and Control OMS solution offering. The solution enables you to troubleshoot operational and other issues by identifying and tracking changes in your environment. The solution tracks software and file changes on Windows and Linux computers and changes to Windows registry keys, Windows services, and Linux daemons.

The Change Tracking solution requires an Azure Automation account and can be added to your workspace either through the Automation and Control offering or directly to your Log Analytics workspace. Once added to your workspace, the solution adds the Change Tracking tile to your OMS dashboard and you can see this in your workspace overview page. The tile will display a summary of changes over the last 24 hours:

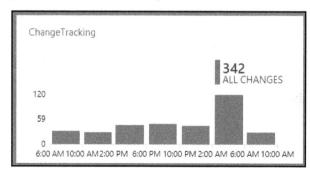

Figure 5.36

Click on the tile to open the solution dashboard. The dashboard groups solution data is based on:

- **Configuration Changes Summary**: A summary of changes across all categories for Linux daemons, Windows services, Windows and Linux software, Windows registry, and Windows and Linux files with counts over the last 24 hours.
- **Changes by Configuration Type**: This lists and counts changes by type of configuration in the last 24 hours.
- **Software Changes**: This lists and counts software changes that occurred in the last 24 hours and provides a breakdown by number and count of Windows applications and Linux packages.
- **Windows Service Changes**: This lists and counts Windows services changes that occurred in the past 24 hours.
- **Linux Daemon Changes:** This lists and counts Linux daemon changes that occurred in the past 24 hours:

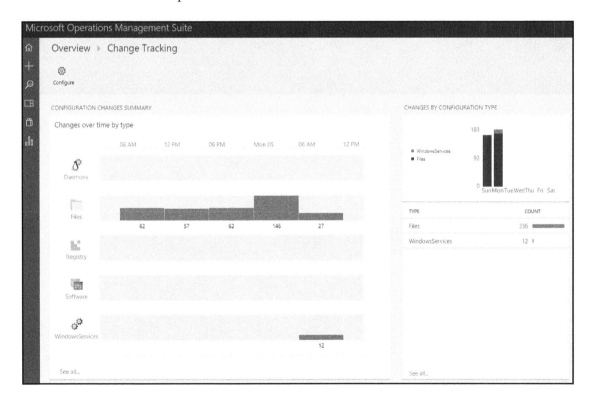

Figure 5.37

Once added to your workspace, the Change Tracking solution will start tracking software changes on your Windows and Linux computers, and changes to Windows services and Linux daemons, as well as changes to configuration files in the `/etc` directory (`/etc/*conf`) on your Linux computers. You can track additional Windows registry keys, Windows files, and Linux files and you can configure change tracking and inventory from either the OMS portal or the Azure portal.

6
Working with Security and Compliance in OMS

In this chapter, we will take a comprehensive look at the Security and Compliance solution offering in OMS, and explore the OMS Security and Audit solution, related solutions, and security-related capabilities in OMS. We will cover the following topics:

- Using the Security and Audit solution
- Understanding Security and Audit data
- Using the Antimalware Assessment solution
- Using Baseline Assessment
- Using the Update Management solution

Introduction

Growing and ever-changing security threats are some of the toughest challenges that organizations face today. As threat actors and defenders adapt to the exponential growth of business data, and advances in technology and security-related capabilities, the need for organizations to implement a coherent cybersecurity strategy is greater than ever. As IT security and operations team grapple with the challenges of managing and securing highly complex, cross-platform, and hybrid cloud systems that are increasingly subject to a rising number of sophisticated cyber attacks, organizations are coming to terms with the reality that a security strategy that revolves around traditional, perimeter-based defenses alone is no longer a sound strategy. This outdated strategy should be supplanted by cybersecurity that is cloud-enabled and based on, among other things, real-time analysis of data and patterns of user behavior.

With the growing need for organizations to comply with security audits and conform to various compliance requirements and standards, Security and Compliance in OMS enables organizations to meet their compliance requirements through the comprehensive and searchable OMS platform.

The Security and Compliance offering in OMS enables organizations to leverage Microsoft Security and third-party intelligence for threat prevention, detection, and response. As a cloud-native security solution, Security and Compliance within OMS presents a unified view of all security-related issues in OMS, providing organizations with quick and easy threat and security posture detection.

Once you enable the Security and Compliance solution offering, it gathers all the machine data from across your hybrid environment, including on-premise and in any cloud environments, such as Azure and AWS. Using security best practices recommendations and security baselines established by Microsoft's security teams, and the most advanced third-party security providers in the world, the Security and Compliance capability then analyzes the collected data and associates patterns based on gathered intelligence to provide you with a comprehensive view of your security posture in a single pane of glass. Security and compliance requires no configuration to provide relevant security insights. Once you connect agent sources to OMS, the solution offering will automatically select and collect the necessary data to unlock relevant insights into your environment.

In April 2016, a European privacy law, the **General Data Protection Regulation** (**GDPR**) was approved and is due to take effect in May 2018. GDPR is being touted as the most important change in data privacy regulation in over two decades, and it imposes new data privacy rules on companies, government agencies, and any organizations that do business in and with the **European Union** (**EU**). This is of particular significance because of the positive implications of such a regulation on data privacy, the benefits of the inevitable shift in the way organizations across the region and business partners around the world will now approach data privacy, and because non-compliant organizations could be subject to hefty fines, as is often the case with such regulations.

As the dominant leader in the enterprise computing space, Microsoft provides organizations with an array of cloud services and on-premises solutions to enable them to meet compliance requirements such as the GDPR reporting and assessment requirements. One of these capabilities is the security and compliance offering, which leverages Log Analytics and other services and capabilities in Azure to provide organizations with security and data collection and analysis options for identifying and repairing gaps in security policies.

Using the Security and Audit solution

The OMS Security and Audit solution is one of the key capabilities of the Security and Compliance offering in OMS. The Security and Audit solution provides a comprehensive view into the IT security posture of your organization by enabling you to monitor your environment for potential threats and vulnerabilities. The Security and Audit solution uses built-in search queries and intuitive visualizations to highlight security issues that should be addressed. With threat intelligence, malware detection, and other security capabilities, the solution provides you with increased visibility to prevent, detect, and respond to various security threats. In this section, we will explore the Security and Audit solution and the various solution features and capabilities.

Getting ready

To use the Security and Audit solution in OMS, enable the Security and Compliance solution offering for your OMS workspace. Additionally, you will need to connect sources such as direct agents or a **System Center Operations Manager** (**SCOM**) management group to your OMS workspace in order to collect and analyze security and audit data from the sources and display it in the solution. The Security and Audit solution also supports data sources from various security products, such as **Common Event format** (**CEF**) events and Cisco ASA events.

Additionally, you will need to add the Update Management solution from the Automation and Control solution offering in order to make use of the Update Assessment security domain. You will therefore have to create an Automation account or link an existing automation account to your OMS workspace to be able to add the Automation and Control offering, which gives you access to the Update Management solution.

 The Security and Audit solution also supports showing security insights from networking data and malicious traffic visualized on map data. To enable the collection of these respective security records, enable the WireData solution and the collection of DNS events and IIS logs.

How to do it...

Start by linking an Automation account to your OMS workspace. This can be accomplished by configuring and adding the Automation and Control solution offering, either through the Azure Portal or through your OMS workspace.

Adding the Automation account

You will only need to complete this step if you do not already have an Automation account for use with your OMS workspace.

The following steps create an automation account for use with the Automation and Control solution offering to enable use of the Update Management solution:

1. Log in to the Azure portal at `https://portal.azure.com`
2. In the Azure portal, type **Automation Account** in the Search resources search field and under Services, select **Automation Accounts**:

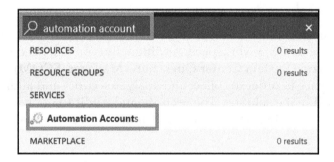

Figure 6.1

3. In Automation Accounts, click **+Add**, and then select choices for the following items:

    - Provide a name for the new Automation Account.
    - Select a **Subscription** to link to by selecting from the drop-down list if the default selected is not appropriate.
    - For **Resource group**, choose to **Create new** resource group and enter a name in the text field, or select **Use existing** to use an existing resource group already set up.
    - Select an available **Location**.
    - Select **Yes** under **Create Azure Run As account**. Note that you will need to have permissions to be able to create this run as account in Azure Active Directory. You will still be able to proceed with this task if you select **No** here.

4. Click **Create** to create the automation account:

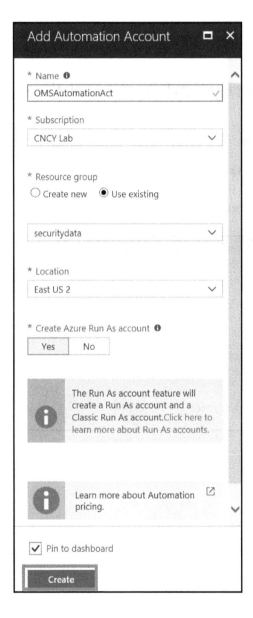

Figure 6.2

Once you create an Automation account, you are now ready to add the solution offerings in your OMS workspace.

Next, add the Security and Audit solution to your OMS workspace.

Adding the Security and Audit Solution to the OMS workspace

Perform the following steps:

1. Navigate to the **Azure Portal** (https://portal.azure.com) and sign in
2. In the Azure Portal, type log analytics in the **Search resources** search field and under **Services**, select **Log Analytics**:

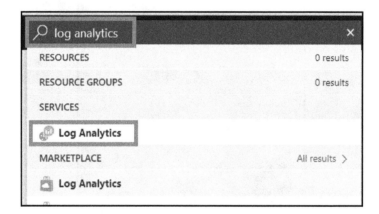

Figure 6.3

3. On the resulting page, click your Log Analytics instance, and under **Management**, click **OMS Portal** to open your OMS workspace portal:

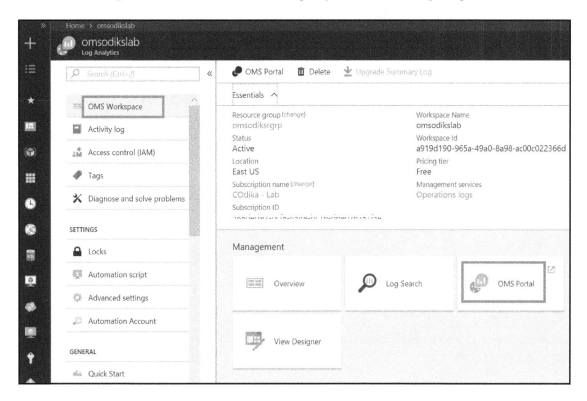

Figure 6.4

4. In the OMS Portal, click the **Solutions Gallery** link to navigate to the **Solutions Gallery**

5. In the **Solutions Gallery**, under **Solution offers**, click the **Security & Compliance** offering

6. Under **Security & Compliance**, confirm that options for **Antimalware Assessment** and **Security and Audit** are checked

7. Click **Add** to add the solutions to your OMS workspace:

Figure 6.5

Once the Security and Compliance solutions are added to your workspace, add the Update Management solution to your OMS workspace.

Adding the Update Management Solution to the OMS workspace

Perform the following steps:

1. While in the OMS portal, return to the **Solutions Gallery** and click the **Automation & Control** offering under **Solution offers**.

2. Click **Configure Workspace** to configure an automation account:

Figure 6.6

3. In the **Automation Account** blade, select **Use existing**, and from the drop-down menu, select the Automation account created in the previous section:

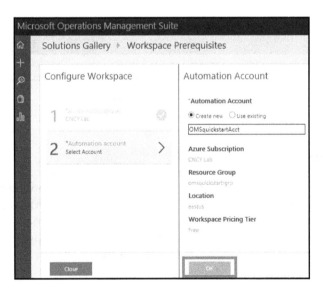

Figure 6.7

4. Click **OK**, and then click **Close** to finish.

5. Return to the **Solutions Gallery** and click **Automation & Control.**

6. Under **Automation & Control**, confirm that the options for **Update .Management**, and optionally **Change Tracking**, are checked. Click **Add** to add the solutions to your workspace:

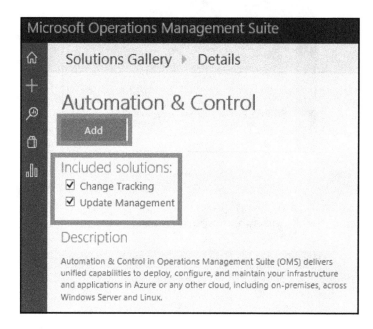

Figure 6.8

How it works...

After installing the Security and Audit solution, and depending on whether you have security data from connected sources indexed in OMS for your workspace, you will see security data in the solution tiles right away. If you install the solutions before connecting sources (agents, Cisco ASA, and so on) it may take some time for the data to get uploaded to the cloud and analyzed before it shows up in the solution tiles in your workspace.

As mentioned previously, the Security and Audit solution is designed to provide a unified view of all security related issues in your hybrid cloud environment. This unified view is possible through the native Security & Compliance solution offerings for Security & Audit, and Antimalware respectively, but also through the Update Management solution and various other solutions that enable additional security insights into other security domains, such as network security, threat intelligence, and update assessment. In essence, to enable the comprehensive collection of security records, you will need to enable the various solutions described previously, as well as the WireData 2.0 solution for networking data, IIS log collection for security insights about malicious traffic, and any other relevant security-related solutions or data sources.

The Security and Audit solution collates, logically groups, and visualizes insights from the various related solutions to provide you with a single-pane view into the security posture of your environment:

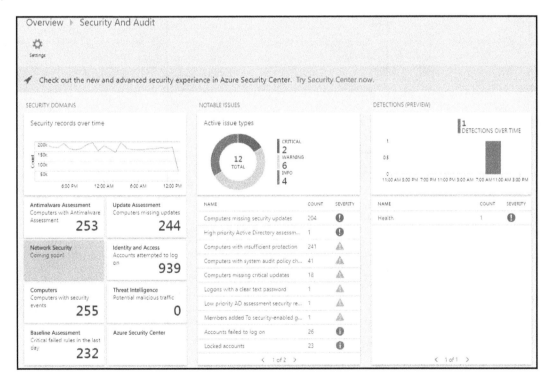

Figure 6.9

The Security and Audit dashboard groups security data into four broad categories:

- Security domains

- Notable issues
- Detections (preview)
- Threat intelligence

Security domains

This category succinctly presents security records relating to update assessment, antimalware assessment, network security, identity and access, and threat intelligence, enabling you to visualize your security posture from these perspectives. All tiles in this category are interactive and clicking on the various tiles will take you either to the search blade to see the underlying query and resulting security records, or to the underlying resources in the case of Azure Security Center:

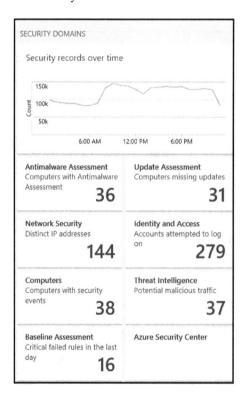

Figure 6.10

Notable issues

This category presents a quick visualization of noteworthy security issues in your environment grouped by severity. Issues are deemed notable based on security records contained in the various perspectives of the security domains. The solution analyzes all relevant security records and effectively flags issues it recommends you should look into further:

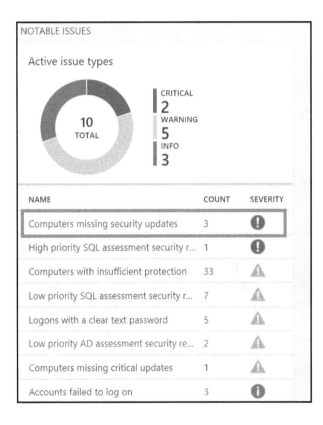

Figure 6.11

Clicking on any of the listed notable issues will take you to the search blade showing the query and security records listed as a notable issue:

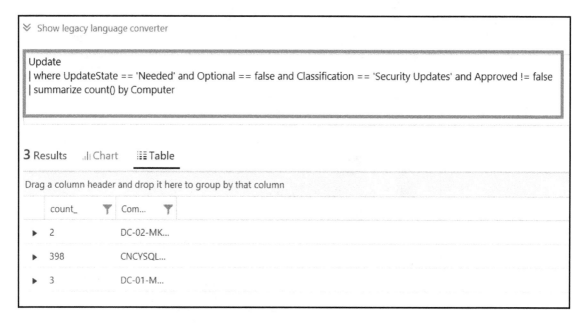

Show legacy language converter

Update
| where UpdateState == 'Needed' and Optional == false and Classification == 'Security Updates' and Approved != false
| summarize count() by Computer

3 Results   Chart   Table

Drag a column header and drop it here to group by that column

count_	Com...
2	DC-02-MK...
398	CNCYSQL...
3	DC-01-M...

Figure 6.12

The notable issues capability of the Security and Audit solution makes use of all the security records in your environment available. These records could be based on analysis of the data from the Security and Audit solution (leveraging Active Directory, Advanced Threat Analytics data, and so on), as well as from Wire Data, Update Management, Malware Assessment, and other security-related and assessment solutions, such as the SQL Health Check solution, and logs such as IIS, firewall, and security appliance logs.

Detections (preview)

This category of the Security and Audit solution enables you to quickly identify suspicious activities and potential threats to your environment, as well as the determined severity of the threat. This particular capability leverages the power of OMS in Azure, the benefits of machine learning, and big data to analyze indexed security data for your workspace, and references security intelligence to enable you to detect certain threats in your environment. While this capability can point out certain threats, in other instances it will simply alert you to unusual and suspicious activities to facilitate investigation as part of your organization's incident response process. Data for this category of the Security and Audit solution is stored in the **SecurityDetection** table in the OMS repository for your workspace. The solution tile presents a view of detections over time, as well as a listing of specific current detections in your environment:

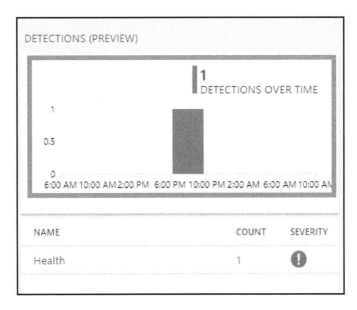

Figure 6.13

The solution tile will enumerate issues based on severity. This enables you to determine how to address the referenced issues. When you click on a listed issue, it takes you to the search blade showing the query and security record for the detection:

Figure 6.14

The security record shows you details about the detection, along with steps that you can take to remediate the issue.

> In responding to any identified threats, endeavor to leverage any incident response processes in your organization to address identified threats.

Threat intelligence

This section of the solution leverages security data from leading security and threat intelligence vendors, and data collected by the **Microsoft Threat Intelligence Center** (**MSTIC**), under the auspices of Microsoft's consortium of security teams, responsible for securing Microsoft's organizational global infrastructure, and cloud services, which is arguably the world's biggest cloud service. The insights derived from this treasure trove of data and capabilities informs an intelligent security graph that in turn informs formidable strategies for securing enterprises against cybersecurity threats. This intelligence data is then analyzed and correlated against log data for your environment to provide insights into possible attack patterns to enable you to detect and respond to impending, potential, or ongoing threats with increased visibility into the specific actions of threat actors.

This threat intelligence overview provides information about servers with malicious IP traffic, the nature of the malicious threat, and a depiction of the source of the IPs on an interactive map. The yellow pin indicators on the map show incoming traffic from malicious IPs.

While outgoing malicious traffic is likely an indication of a compromised machine, and should be investigated immediately, incoming traffic is not nearly as severe because endpoints exposed to the internet are bound to see this sort of traffic. However, it is recommended that you review this incoming traffic to ensure that no connection attempts were successful.

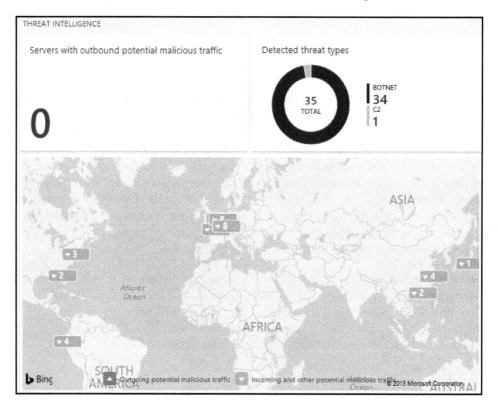

Figure 6.15

When you click on a threat intelligence tile for detected threat types, it takes you to the search blade showing the query and security record for the referenced threat types:

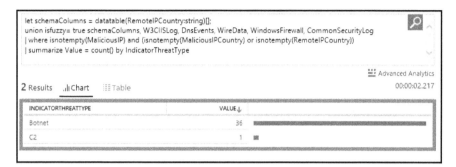

Figure 6.16

You can then delve deeper into the security records to see specific information about the types of threat.

Also, you can interact with the map by clicking on any of the referenced incoming threats identified in your environment. When you click on the yellow push up pins, you will get a popup with the option to open a detailed threat intelligence dashboard, through which you can further investigate the issue:

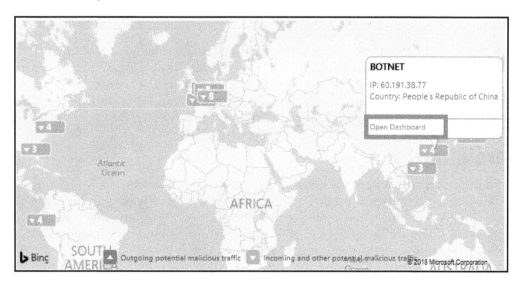

Figure 6.17

Once in the **Threat Intelligence** dashboard, you can explore the enumerated threat types, as well as details of the various threats:

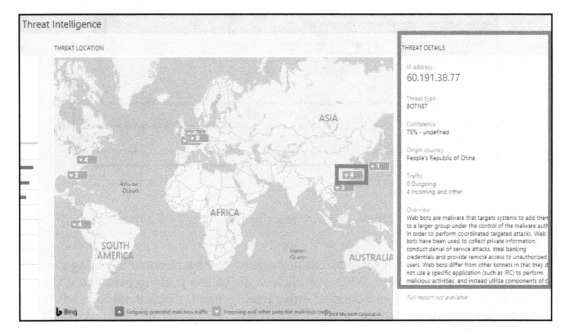

Figure 6.18

In its analysis of threat data for your environment, the threat intelligence capability makes use of data from the Wire Data solution, as well as IIS and firewall logs, and correlates information from the intelligent security graph against this data. It is therefore recommended that you have these data sources defined in your OMS workspace.

There's more...

In addition to many of the security insights provided by the Security and Audit solution and other OMS features out of the box, you can extend the security data and functionality you get with this solution by customizing any unsupported logs from other data sources to conform to the **Common Event Format** (**CEF**) standard format and making them suitable for ingestion and use with the Security and Audit solution.

Manage Security and Audit event data collection

By default, OMS security collects all events from Windows Security, Firewall event logs, and AppLocker. As a true hybrid cloud platform, OMS leverages the big data capabilities of the cloud and can ingest essentially any data you send to the service. This is subject to the pricing data tier that you opt for, with the various data rate and retention limits. While this ability to collect vast amounts of data can prove very useful in some scenarios, in other scenarios it could be cost-prohibitive.

OMS enables you to therefore filter the security events that you are most interested in, based on four broad classifications of security events:

- **All events:** This option is for users who want to collect all security-related events. This is the default setting in OMS.
- **Common**: This option gives users a set of events that enables them to conduct a full audit trail. This option will be sufficient for most users.
- **Minimal**: This option enables a small subset of relevant security events for users who want to be able to leverage the solution without the impact of event volume from all security logs. Admittedly, the determination about the relevancy of these events is somewhat subjectively based on industry standards, as well as research conducted by Microsoft with various customers around the world. Review the following event IDs and ensure that the logs collected here address the specific scenarios you are interested in monitoring for.
- **None**: This option disables security event collection from all security and App Locker logs. Users who opt for this can still derive value from various capabilities in the Security and Audit solution, but will not be able to benefit from any of the log-driven capabilities.

Setting	Windows Security Event IDs	AppLocker Event IDs
Minimal	1102, 4626, 4625, 4657, 4663, 4688, 4700, 4702, 4719, 4720, 4722, 4723, 4724, 4727, 4728, 4732, 4735, 4737,4739, 4740, 4754, 4755, 4756, 4767, 4825, 4946, 4948, 4956, 5024, 5033	8001, 8002

Common	299, 300, 324, 340, 403, 404, 410, 411, 412, 413, 431, 500, 501, 1100, 1102, 4626, 4625, 4657, 4663, 4688, 4700, 4702, 4719, 4720, 4722, 4723, 4724, 4727, 4728, 4732, 4735, 4737,4739, 4740, 4754, 4755, 4756, 4767, 4825, 4946, 4948, 4956, 5024, 5033, 1107, 1108, 4608, 4610, 4611, 4614, 4616, 4622, 4634, 4647, 4648, 4649, 4658, 4661, 4662, 4665, 4666, 4667, 4670, 4673, 4674, 4675, 4689, 4690, 4697, 4704, 4705, 4716, 4717, 4718, 4725, 4726, 4729, 4733, 4738, 4742, 4744, 4745, 4746, 4750, 4751, 4752, 4757, 4760, 4761, 4762, 4764, 4768, 4771, 4774, 4778, 4779, 4781, 4793, 4797, 4798, 4799, 4800, 4801, 4802, 4803, 4826, 4870, 4886, 4887, 4888, 4893, 4898, 4902, 4904, 4905, 4907, 4931, 4932, 4933, 4985, 5059, 5136, 5137, 5140, 5145, 5632, 6144, 6145, 6272, 6273, 6278, 8222, 26401, 30004	8001, 8002

Table 6.1

Filtering Security events in OMS

Perform the following steps:

1. Browse to your OMS portal at `https://www.mms.microsoft.com`.
2. In the OMS portal, click the **Security and Audit solution** tile.
3. Once in **Security and Audit**, click **Settings** at the top:

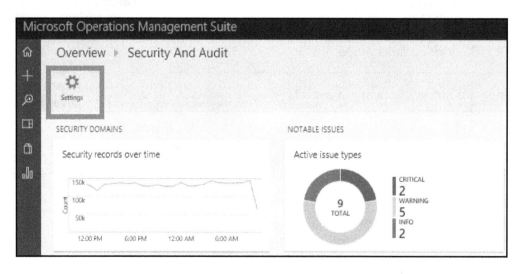

Figure 6.19

4. Once in **Settings**, choose from the four security data collection settings as shown in the following screenshot:

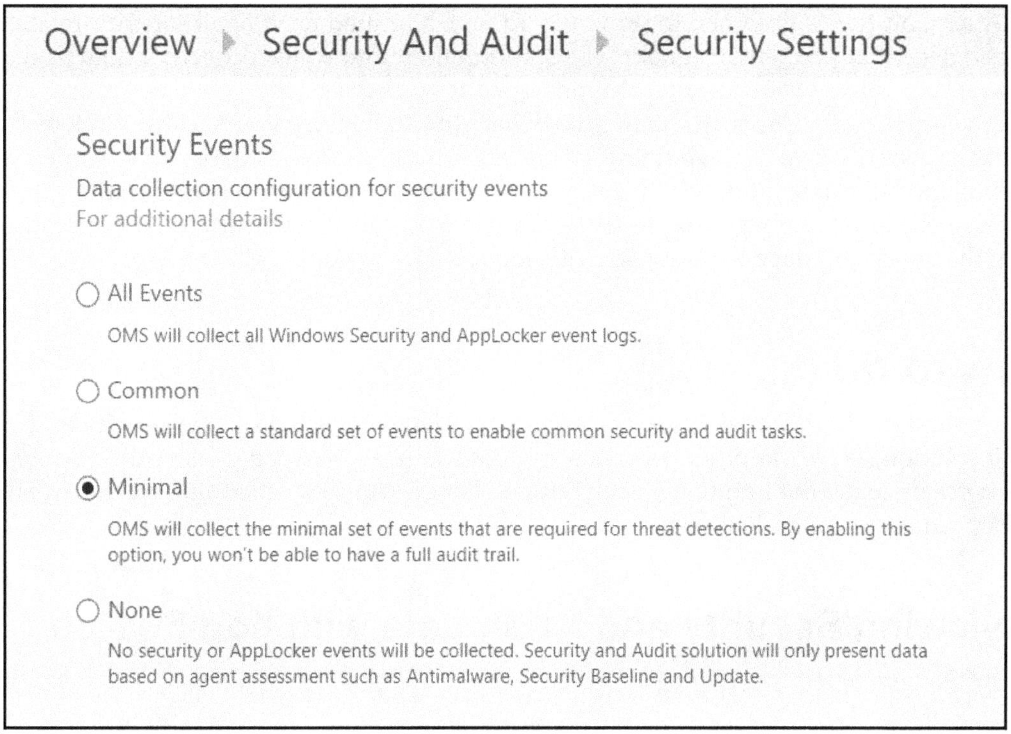

Overview ▸ Security And Audit ▸ Security Settings

Security Events
Data collection configuration for security events
For additional details

○ All Events
   OMS will collect all Windows Security and AppLocker event logs.

○ Common
   OMS will collect a standard set of events to enable common security and audit tasks.

◉ Minimal
   OMS will collect the minimal set of events that are required for threat detections. By enabling this option, you won't be able to have a full audit trail.

○ None
   No security or AppLocker events will be collected. Security and Audit solution will only present data based on agent assessment such as Antimalware, Security Baseline and Update.

Figure 6.20

Selecting an option automatically configures security event data collection based on the selected setting.

See also

Visit the following links for more information:

- *Connect security products to the OMS Security and Audit solution*: `https://docs.microsoft.com/en-us/azure/operations-management-suite/oms-security-connect-products`
- *Exploring the OMS Experience center*: `www.mrchiyo.com/exploring-the-microsoft-operations-management-suite-oms-experience-center/`

Understanding Security and Audit data

Recall that, as part of the Security and Compliance solution offering in OMS, the Security and Audit solution is designed to provide you with a unified view of all security-related issues detected in your environment. The solution therefore weaves together data from disparate but related sources and solutions in your workspace, and leverages information from the intelligent security graph to unlock insights and enable you to prevent, detect, and remediate security threats in your environment. You can explore Security and Audit data by using the built-in solution visualizations, which enable you to interact with the underlying queries and resulting security records. You can also perform query operations using the query language to query security-related data in your OMS workspace.

How to do it...

Security and Audit data makes use of various data types collected by the Security and Audit solution, as well as other solutions and data sources. You can explore the various data types by using the intuitive visualizations that are built into the solution, or by using the Log Analytics query language.

Reviewing Security and Audit data with Log Search

Perform the following steps:

1. Navigate to the **OMS Portal** (https://www.mms.microsoft.com.) and sign in.

2. Click on the Search icon to navigate to the **Log Search** page.

3. In the **Log Search** page, type the following query in the search field to return all collected data in your **Log Analytics** workspace and list the various data types indexed for your workspace:

```
search *
| summarize by Type
| sort by Type
```

How it works...

The preceding query returns a list of the various types of data in your workspace. A cursory review of the various data types could easily indicate which types of data are related to security, as shown in the following screenshot. However, the Security and Audit solution makes use of various other data types in the list, including (but not limited to) Wire Data, DnsEvents, W3CIISLog, and Update:

Figure 6.21

The Security and Audit solution works with data collected from Windows Security Event logs, firewall logs, and AppLocker logs on Windows machines. On cross-platform machines, OMS collects security data from Syslog.

Examples of syslog security log records are shown in the following screenshots:

Figure 6.22

Figure 6.23

Once all of this data is indexed in OMS, the various data types are stored as records in tables that correspond to the various data types. Refer to `Chapter 2`, *Searching and Analyzing OMS Data*, for details on how data is indexed and queried using the query language.

The following table shows a mapping of security and audit capabilities to various solutions, data sources, and tables queried:

 This table should be used as a guide to understand how the various security domains, solutions, and data sources are related. The information contained in this table is by no means comprehensive.

Security Domain	Data Sources and Types	Solutions & logs	Data record types
Antimalware Assessment	• configuration data • metadata and state data	Antimalware Assessment	ProtectionStatus
Update Assessment	update metadata and state data	Update Management	• Update • UpdateSummary
Network Security	metadata about network traffic	WireData 2.0	WireData
Identity and Access	• Windows security events from Active Directory and **Advanced Threat Analytics (ATA)** • Windows firewall logs • Windows application events	Security and Audit	• SecurityEvent • Syslog

Computers	security metadata and state data	Security and Audit	• SecurityEvent • LinuxAuditLog • ProtectionStatus • SecurityBaselineSummary • SecurityDetection • CommonSecurityLog
Threat Intelligence	• IIS logs, WireData • Windows Firewall logs • metadata about network traffic	• WireData 2.0 • IIS Logs	• W3CIISLog • WireData • WindowsFirewall • CommonSecurityLog
Baseline Assessment	• configuration data • metadata and state data	Security and Audit	• SecurityBaselineSummary • SecurityBaseline
Azure Security Center (ASC)	NA	Security and Audit	This simply links to Azure Security Center in the Azure portal.
Notable Issues	• syslog, configuration data • metadata and state data • WMI data, registry data • performance data and others.	• Security and Audit • SQL Health Check • WireData 2.0 • Antimalware Assessment • Update Management • other relevant Assessment solutions • IIS logs.	All Security and Audit, and assessment data tables including Syslog, SQLAssessmentRecommendation etc.
Detections (Preview)	• Windows security events • IIS logs • Windows Firewall logs	• Security and Audit • WireData • IIS logs	• SecurityDetection • SecurityAlert

Figure 6.24

You can review the security records in your workspace for the various security domains in this table by using the Log Analytics query language to query for records in the tables that correspond to your security domain of interest. For instance, to search for data for both Windows and cross-platform machines relating to the Identity and Access security domain, you can use a simple query such as the following to filter your workspace data, and apply further query filters to derive relevant insights:

```
search *
| where Type == "SecurityEvent" or Type =="Syslog"
```

The preceding code provides a different way to visualize security data. This can be used along with, or in lieu of, the intuitive visualizations that are provided as part of the Security and Audit solution. For instance, you could just as easily visualize Identity and Access data for your workspace by clicking the Identity and Access tile in the Security and Audit solution:

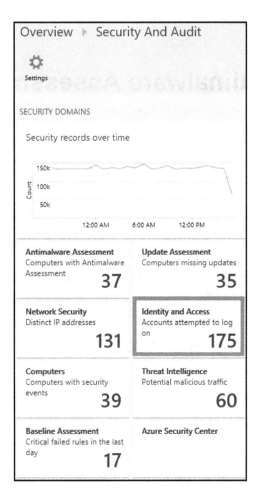

Figure 6.25

See also

For more information, visit the following website:

- *Monitoring resources in the OMS Security and Audit solution:* `https://docs.microsoft.com/en-us/azure/operations-management-suite/oms-security-monitoring-resources`

Using the Antimalware Assessment solution

The Antimalware Assessment solution in Log Analytics enables you to monitor the status of Antimalware protection in your environment. The solution detects whether supported antimalware solutions are installed on your machines, and whether the solutions are operational. You can install this solution from the Solutions Gallery in your OMS workspace or add it to your Log Analytics through the Azure marketplace in the Azure Portal.

How to do it...

If you haven't completed the *How to do it* section in the *Using the Security and Audit solution* recipe, you can follow these steps:

Adding the Security and Audit Solution to the OMS workspace

Perform the following steps:

1. Navigate to your **OMS Portal** (`https://www.mms.microsoft.com`) and sign in.
2. In the OMS portal, click the **Solutions Gallery** link to navigate to the **Solutions Gallery**
3. In the **Solutions Gallery**, under **Solution offers**, click the **Security & Compliance** offering.
4. Under **Security & Compliance**, confirm that the options for **Antimalware Assessment** and **Security and Audit** are checked.

5. Click **Add** to add the solutions to your OMS workspace:

Figure 6.26

Reviewing malware threats in your environment

Once the Antimalware Assessment solution is added to your workspace, you can review the state of antimalware protection in your environment by following these steps:

1. Click the **Antimalware Assessment** tile in your **Overview** page:

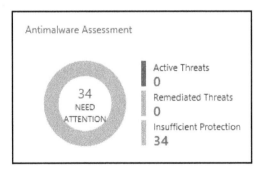

Figure 6.27

2. Once in the **Antimalware** dashboard, review the **THREAT STATUS** and **DETECTED THREATS** areas and click a server name with identified threats, if any:

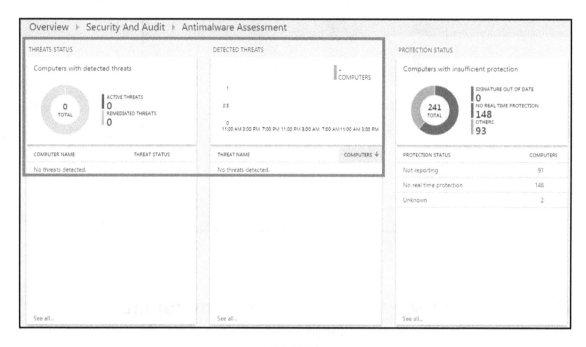

Figure 6.28

Note that, when you have adequate protection on your computers, your antimalware solution will identify and quarantine any active threats on your machines, and you can use the solution to further analyze and understand the nature of the threat.

Reviewing malware protection status.

To review the malware protection status, perform the following steps:

1. In the **Antimalware solution** dashboard, in the **PROTECTION STATUS** area, click **No real-time protection** to evaluate computers that might be vulnerable:

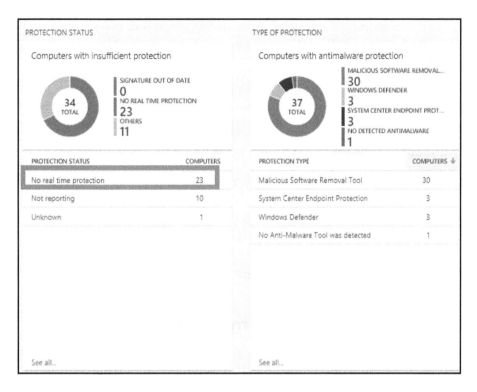

Figure 6.29

2. This takes you to a search page with a list of servers without real-time protection

Computers that have an unsupported antimalware solution or antimalware solution version will be listed as not having real-time protection.

How it works...

When you install the Antimalware Assessment solution in your workspace, the OMS agents installed on connected sources for your workspace collect data about the protection status of computers in your environment, and about detected threats.

In determining the state of antimalware protection in your environment, the Antimalware solution collects and analyzes metadata, state data, and configuration data.

This data is then relayed to the Log Analytics service, where the data gets analyzed and insights into your malware protection status are visualized in the solution dashboard.

Log Analytics supports the following products for Antimalware Assessment:

- Windows Defender on Windows 8, Windows 8.1, Windows 10, and Windows Server 2016
- System Center Endpoint Protection (v 4.5.216 and later)
- Windows Security Center (WSC) on Windows 8, Windows 8.1, Windows 10, and Windows 2016
- Servers with Windows Management Framework (WMF) 3.0, WMF 4.0

Support for third-party Antimalware products

In addition to supporting assessments for the products listed previously, at this time, the Antimalware Assessment solution in OMS also supports the following third-party antimalware solutions:

- Symantec Endpoint Protection 12.1.1100 and higher
- Trend Micro Deep Security version 9.6.

You can expect more guidance from Microsoft on added support for other third-party solutions in the near future. The OMS product team is actively working to expand this solution's support for other third-party antimalware solutions and versions.

The Antimalware Assessment solution detects whether supported anti-malware solutions are installed on your machines, and whether these solutions are operational. The solution is able to determine if antimalware solutions on your machines are:

- Enabled and running
- Using antimalware and antivirus signatures that are not older than seven days
- Running scans on machines

Using baseline assessment

Security baseline assessment is one of the assessment capabilities of OMS Security. The Security and Audit solution uses this capability to help you assess how compliant your machines are with an established configuration for highly secure server deployments.

This assessment is part of the Security and Audit solution. You will need to install the Security and Audit solution to access this capability in your OMS workspace. Note that baseline assessment supports both Windows and Linux machines.

How to do it...

Perform the following steps to use security baseline assessment:

Adding the Security and Audit Solution to the OMS workspace

Perform the following steps:

1. Navigate to your **OMS Portal** (`https://www.mms.microsoft.com`) and sign in.
2. In the OMS Portal, click the **Solutions Gallery** link to navigate to the **Solutions Gallery**
3. In the **Solutions Gallery**, under **Solution offers**, click the **Security & Compliance** offering.
4. Under **Security & Compliance**, confirm that the **Security and Audit** option is checked.

5. Click **Add** to add the solution to your OMS workspace:

Figure 6.30

Reviewing security baseline assessment in OMS

Perform the following steps:

1. Navigate to your **OMS Portal** (https://www.mms.microsoft.com) in your browser and sign in.

2. On the **Overview** page, click the **Security and Audit** tile.

3. In the **Security and Audit** dashboard, click **Baseline Assessment** under **Security Domains**. This opens the **Security Baseline Assessment** dashboard:

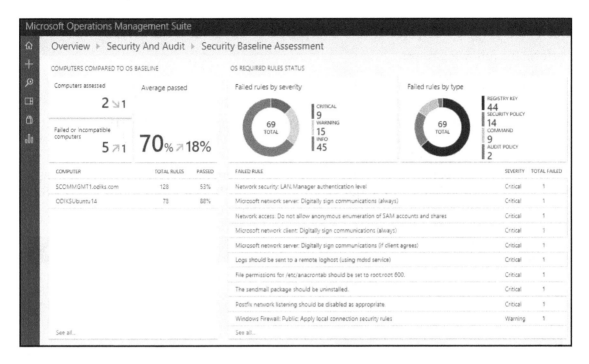

Figure 6.31

Baseline assessments are available for computers and web servers.

Reviewing computers compared to the baseline

Perform the following steps:

1. In the **Security Baseline Assessment** dashboard, you can see the computer baseline perspective on the left side of the dashboard.
2. The left pane shows the number of computers compared to the baseline, the average percentage of passed rules on the evaluated servers, and a list of servers that were assessed.
3. The right pane lists the rules that failed by severity and type. Click on the computers in the **Computer** pane, under **COMPUTERS COMPARED TO OS BASELINE**, to access the search query and records:

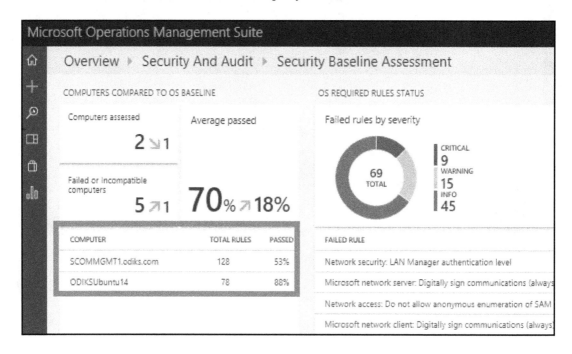

Figure 6.32

4. In the resulting search window, review the search query and records indicating rules that failed on the reference machine:

SecurityBaseline
| where BaselineType in ('WindowsOS', 'Linux') and AnalyzeResult=='Failed' and Computer=="ODIKSUbuntu14"

9 Results ≡ List ⊞ Table

2/18/2018 7:02:28.523 PM | SecurityBaseline
　... TimeGenerated   : 2/18/2018 7:02:28.523 PM
　... Computer   : ODIKSUbuntu14
　... BaselineType   : Linux
　... OSName   : Linux
　... CceId   : CCE-14027-7
　... RuleSeverity   : Warning
　... BaselineRuleType : Command
　... Description   : Disable support for RDS.
　... AnalyzeResult   : Failed
　[+] show more

2/18/2018 7:02:28.523 PM | SecurityBaseline
　... TimeGenerated   : 2/18/2018 7:02:28.523 PM
　... Computer   : ODIKSUbuntu14
　... BaselineType   : Linux
　... OSName   : Linux
　... CceId   : CCE-17248-6
　... RuleSeverity   : Critical
　... BaselineRuleType : Command
　... Description   : Logs should be sent to a remote loghost (using mdsd service)
　... AnalyzeResult   : Failed

Figure 6.33

5. Use the following query to aggregate all of the data for rules that the evaluated computers failed, and return the number of various rule types your machines are assessed against:

```
SecurityBaseline
| where BaselineType in ('WindowsOS', 'Linux') and
AnalyzeResult=='Failed'
| summarize AgregatedValue = count() by BaselineRuleType
```

6. Click on the relevant rule type to further investigate the assessment result:

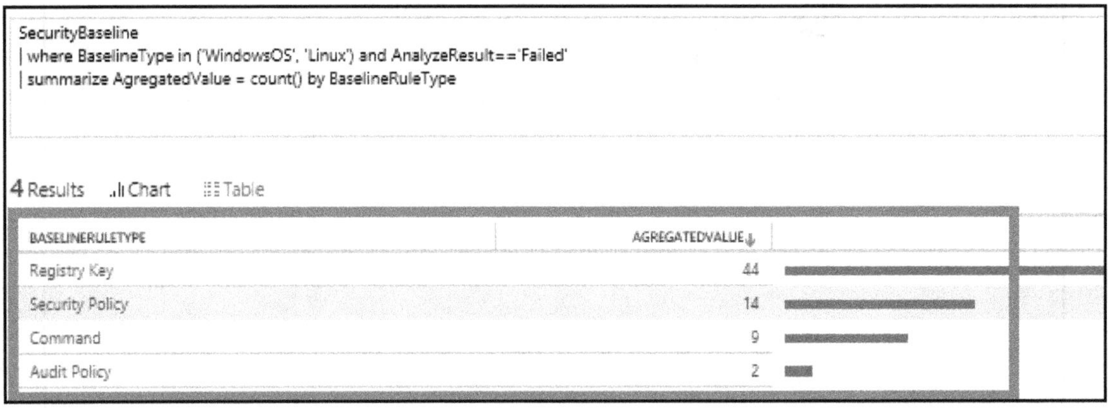

SecurityBaseline
| where BaselineType in ('WindowsOS', 'Linux') and AnalyzeResult=='Failed'
| summarize AgregatedValue = count() by BaselineRuleType

4 Results   .ıl Chart   ☷ Table

BASELINERULETYPE	AGREGATEDVALUE↓	
Registry Key	44	
Security Policy	14	
Command	9	
Audit Policy	2	

Figure 6.34

Reviewing Web Servers computers compared to the baseline

Perform the following steps to review web server computers:

1. In the **Security Baseline Assessment** dashboard, you will see the web baseline perspective next to the OS baseline perspective.
2. The left pane shows the number of web servers compared to the baseline, the average percentage of passed rules on the evaluated servers, and a list of web servers that were assessed.

3. The right pane lists the rules that failed by severity and type. Click on **See all…** under **Failed Rule**:

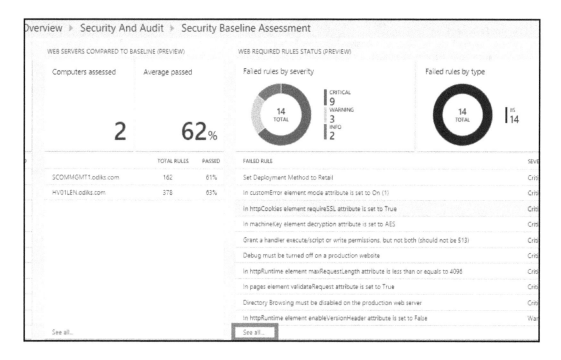

Figure 6.35

4. In the resulting search window, review the search query and click on **Table** to review failed rules:

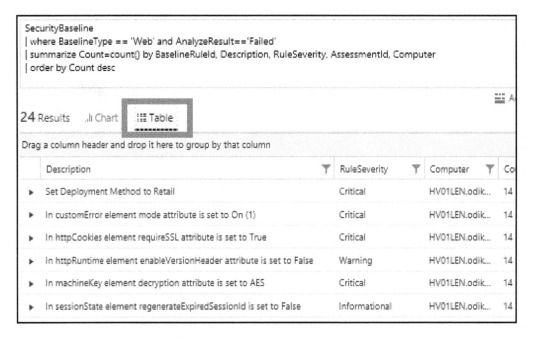

```
SecurityBaseline
| where BaselineType == 'Web' and AnalyzeResult=='Failed'
| summarize Count=count() by BaselineRuleId, Description, RuleSeverity, AssessmentId, Computer
| order by Count desc
```

24 Results   .ıl Chart   ⦂⦂⦂ Table

Drag a column header and drop it here to group by that column

Description	RuleSeverity	Computer	Co
▸ Set Deployment Method to Retail	Critical	HV01LEN.odik...	14
▸ In customError element mode attribute is set to On (1)	Critical	HV01LEN.odik...	14
▸ In httpCookies element requireSSL attribute is set to True	Critical	HV01LEN.odik...	14
▸ In httpRuntime element enableVersionHeader attribute is set to False	Warning	HV01LEN.odik...	14
▸ In machineKey element decryption attribute is set to AES	Critical	HV01LEN.odik...	14
▸ In sessionState element regenerateExpiredSessionId is set to False	Informational	HV01LEN.odik...	14

Figure 6.36

How it works...

As organizations navigate the evolving and ever-changing technology landscape, they must also navigate and prepare for escalating and more targeted cybersecurity threats. These are threats faced by every organization; however, the nature of threats that are specific to some organizations differs from those for other organizations. For example, a manufacturing firm may focus on protecting its programmable logic controllers and factory line assets, while a financial services firm may focus on protecting confidential client transaction records and other data. Given these differences in focus, organizations across verticals share the common and fundamental need to secure their applications and devices. A set of rules was therefore created to provide an established set of configurations for highly secure computer deployments. This set of rules is called a **security baseline**.

The baseline assessment is based on a machine configuration (Windows and Linux) that represents highly secure server deployments. The configurations are really a set of rules that include configurations for registry keys, security policy settings, and audit policy settings provided with Microsoft's recommendations for the various settings. The configuration settings are based on feedback from Microsoft security teams, product groups, government organizations, and global partners and customers. The upshot is that the security baselines represent an industry standard configuration that is broadly known and rigorously tested to prevent or mitigate various cybersecurity threats.

The baseline assessment runs:

- **Registry key** rules that check that registry keys are correctly set
- **Audit policy** rules that review your audit policy against best practices
- **Security policy** rules that review users' permissions on machines
- **Commands** that review configurations on machines

Data for the Security Baseline Assessment is stored in the **SecurityBaseline** and **SecurityBaselineSummary** tables in OMS for your workspace. You can use the query language to view and filter the assessment results for your environment. For instance, use the following query to see what types of baseline rules your machines are being evaluated against:

```
SecurityBaselineSummary
| summarize by BaselineType
```

You can further filter the query to gain more insights. Microsoft makes available the Common Configuration Identifiers and Baseline Rules used by OMS Security. You can download and review them from the following link.

See also

Visit the following links for more information:

- *Azure Security Center Common Configuration Identifiers and Baseline Rules*: https://gallery.technet.microsoft.com/Azure-Security-Center-a789e335?redir=0

Using the Update Management solution

The Update Management solution in OMS is part of the Automation & Control offering. Update Management identifies missing system updates and orchestrates the installation of these updates across Windows and Linux servers, both in your data center and in any public cloud. The Update Management solution supports both update assessments and, using automation, update deployments on supported operating systems.

Getting ready

To use the Update Management solution, ensure you do the following:

- Create and configure an Azure Automation account.
- Ensure that machines are running supported operating systems. See the *Supported operating systems* subsection.
- Target machines with Windows agents should either have access to Microsoft update or be configured to communicate with **Windows Server Update Services (WSUS)**. Target machines cannot be managed by System Center Configuration Manager.
- OMS Linux agents should have access to an update repository.
- OMS Linux agents should not be multi-homed to report to multiple OMS workspaces. This is not a supported configuration.

Supported operating systems

At this time, the Update solution supports update assessments against Windows Server 2008 and higher, and update deployments against Windows Server 2008 R2 SP1 and higher.

For update deployment support on Windows Server 2008 R2 SP1 machines, computers must have .NET Framework 4.5 and WMF 5.0 or later.

The solution also supports the following versions of Linux:

- CentOS 6 (x86/ x64) and 7 (x64)
- Red Hat Enterprise 6 (x86/x64) and 7 (x64)
- SUSE Linux Enterprise Server 11 (x86/x64) and 12 (x64)
- Ubuntu 12.04 LTS and newer (x86/x64)

How to do it...

You can use Update Management to view the update assessment for servers in your environment, and create deployments to install updates on servers that need to be patched.

Adding the Update Management Solution to OMS workspace

This requires you to have an Azure Automation account. You can either install this solution from the OMS portal, or you could deploy the solution as part of the Automation & Control offering in the Azure portal:

1. Navigate to the **OMS Portal** (`https://www.mms.microsoft.com`) in your browser and sign in.
2. While in the OMS Portal, click on the **Solutions Gallery** and click the **Automation & Control** offering under **Solution offers**.
3. Click **Configure Workspace** to configure an automation account:

Figure 6.37

4. In the **Automation Account** blade, select **Use existing**, and from the drop-down menu, select your **Automation Account**:

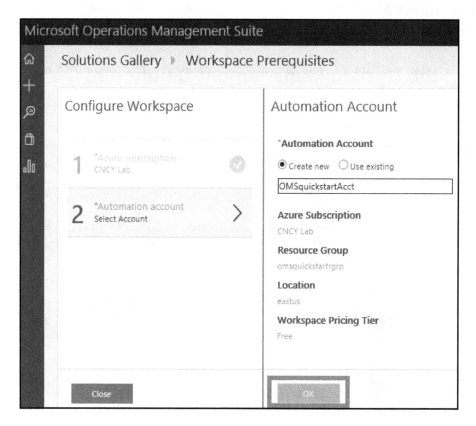

Figure 6.38

5. Click **OK**, and click **Close** to finish.
6. Return to the **Solutions Gallery** and click the **Automation & Control** offering.

7. Under **Automation & Control**, confirm that the options for **Update Management**, and optionally **Change Tracking**, are checked. Click **Add** to add the solutions to your workspace:

Figure 6.39

Using the Update Management solution.

Perform the following steps to use the Update Management solution:

1. In the OMS portal, click on the **System Update Management** solution tile to open the **Update Management** dashboard:

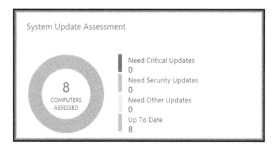

Figure 6.40

2. The dashboard displays information about assessed computers and missing updates, categorized by operating system type and update classification. Click on the **Windows Computers** tile to review any missing updates:

Figure 6.41

3. On the resulting search page, click a search record to review the missing update information:

Figure 6.42

4. Return to the **Update Management** dashboard, and click on the **Linux Computers** tile to review any missing updates:

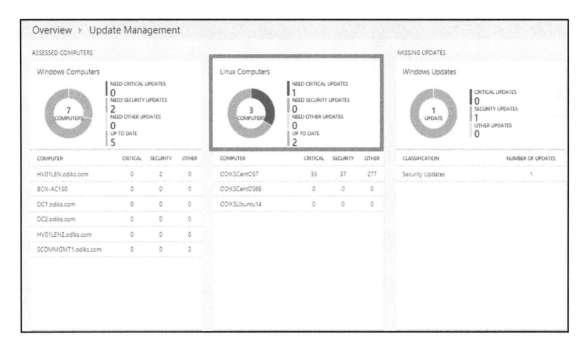

Figure 6.43

5. On the resulting search page, click on the **Table** button to tabulate the search records:

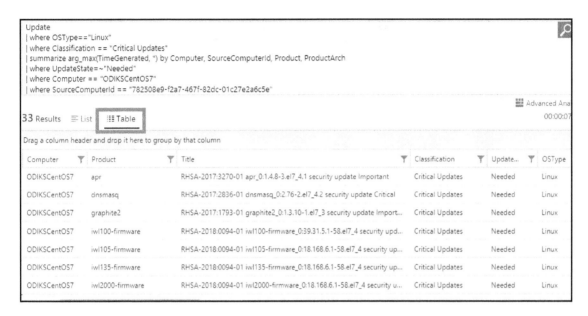

Figure 6.44

Installing updates with Update Management

Update Management enables you to install updates on servers that are assessed and found to be missing updates that are approved for deployment:

1. In the **Update Management** dashboard, under **Update Deployments**, click **Manage Update Deployments**.

2. In the **Update Deployments** page, click **Add** to open the **New Update Deployment** page:

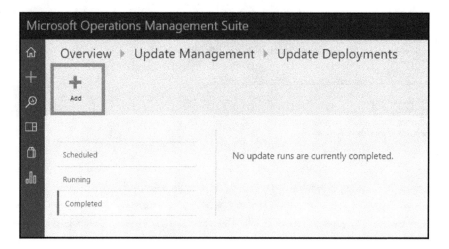

Figure 6.45

3. On the **New Update Deployment** page, enter values for the following fields:

- **Name**: A unique name for the update deployment.
- **Computers**: Names of computers or computer groups to include and target in the Update deployment. Clicking in the entry field will enumerate all eligible computers and groups in your workspace.
- **Time Zone**: Time zone to use for the start time.
- **Schedule Type**: Type of schedule. Choose between one-time, weekly recurring, or monthly recurring.
- **Start Time**: Date and time to start the update deployment.

- **Duration**: This is the number of minutes the update is allowed to run. All updates must be run within this time frame. Any uninstalled updates will be applied at the next scheduled time. This is the equivalent of a maintenance window. The duration must be a minimum of 30 minutes and less than 6 hours. The last 20 minutes of the maintenance window will be used by the automation for restart actions; once the interval is reached, any remaining updates will not be applied. Updates that are in progress will finish being applied:

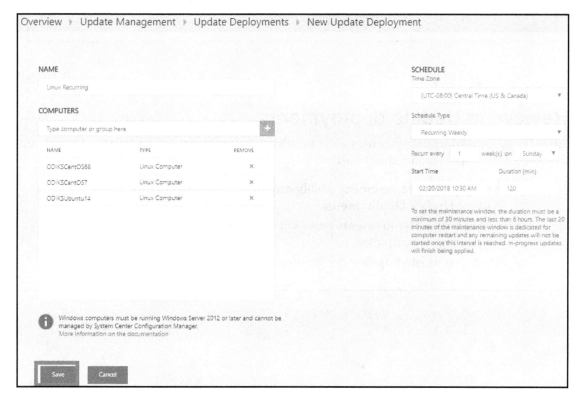

Figure 6.46

4. Click **Save** to schedule and save your deployment.

5. Once saved, the scheduled deployment now shows up in the **Update Deployments** page as a scheduled deployment:

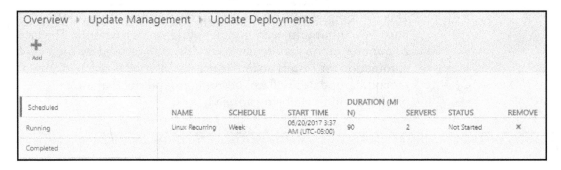

Figure 6.47

Reviewing Update deployments

After the scheduled update executes and completes, you can review the completed updates in the **Update Deployments** dashboard.

1. In the **Update Management** dashboard, under **Update Deployments**, click **Manage Update Deployments**.
2. In the **Update Deployments** page, click **Completed** to view scheduled update runs that have completed.
3. Select a completed update deployment to view the detail screen:

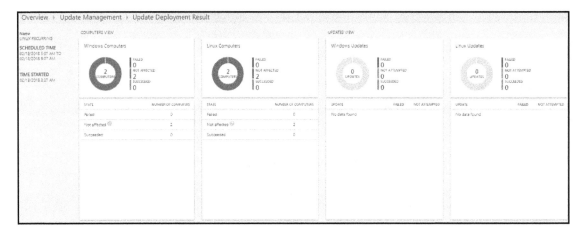

Figure 6.48

4. You can click the various tiles to see more information about the applied updates for affected computers.

How it works...

The Update Management solution analyzes update metadata and state data collected from servers in your on-premises data centre and in the cloud, assesses the update state of the servers, and provides you with automation capabilities for patching any servers with approved updates. Update management supports the following connected sources:

- **System Center Operations Manager (SCOM) Management group**: The solution collects and analyzes information about updates from agents in an SCOM management group that is connected to OMS.
- **Windows updates**: The solution can collect information about system updates from Windows computers and can initiate the installation of updates that are required.
- **Linux agents:** The solution can collect information about system updates from Linux computers and can initiate the installation of updates that are required.

At various intervals, OMS agent computers run scans for update compliance. On Windows computers, the default interval is every 12 hours. The scan is also initiated on Windows computers within 15 minutes of restarting the OMS agent, prior to the installation of the update and after installation of the update. Linux computers run compliance scans every 3 hours by default; on OMS Linux agent restart, the scan is run within 15 minutes. Once the scan is run, the OMS agent forwards the data to Log Analytics, and the Update Management solution analyzes the data and summarizes update information in the solution visualizations. Update management assesses a computer's update state, based on which source the computer is configured to synchronize with.

In a scenario where a Windows computer is configured to report to WSUS, the update state assessment from Windows updates may differ from what WSUS indicates, depending on when WSUS last synchronized with Microsoft Update. This concept also applies to Linux computers if they are configured to report to a local repo or to a public repo.

After you enable this solution in your workspace, any Windows computer that is connected directly to your OMS workspace is configured automatically as a Hybrid Runbook Worker to support solution runbooks. When you create an update deployment to install software on computers in your workspace, the updates are installed by runbooks in Azure Automation. When you create the update deployment, it creates a schedule that starts a master runbook, which in turn starts the child runbook on each agent that you configured, to install the required updates.

 Only required updates are applied. Optional updates are not applied by the Update deployment.

See also

Visit the following websites for more information:

- **Manage updates for multiple VMs:** https://docs.microsoft.com/en-us/azure/automation/manage-update-multi
- **Integrate ConfigMgr with OMS Update Management:** https://docs.microsoft.com/en-us/azure/automation/oms-solution-updatemgmt-sccmintegration

7
Using Wire Data 2.0 and Service Map

This chapter will take a look at the Wire Data 2.0 and Service Map solutions, which are part of the Insights and Analytics solution offerings in OMS Log Analytics. Both solutions use data from the Microsoft Dependency Agent to provide you with, among other capabilities, insights into your network traffic and application discovery and mapping, respectively.

In this chapter we will include the following recipes:

- Using Wire Data 2.0
- Using Service Map

Introduction

Network services are key to the availability and performance of business critical applications, and a change in network usage can impact the performance and reliability of networks and the applications that depend on them. It is therefore important to have a solution that provides you with insights into the network traffic in your infrastructure and that enables you to understand how application components relate to one another and any existing network dependencies..

Using Wire Data 2.0

The Wire Data 2.0 solution is a network traffic monitoring solution that consolidates network and performance data from your Windows and supported Linux computers and provides you with visibility of connections into and out of your network. The Wire Data 2.0 solution builds on and extends the capabilities of the legacy Wire Data solution, and introduces support for Windows Server 2008 R2 and later Windows Server versions, as well as support for some Linux operating system distributions. This solution requires the Microsoft Dependency Agent for network data collection on Windows and Linux computers.

How to do it...

To use the Wire Data 2.0 solution, enable the Insights and Analytics offering in the Azure Portal or add the solution directly from the Solution Gallery in the OMS portal or the Azure marketplace. Although the Dependency Agent is responsible for monitoring and collecting the relevant Wire data, it relies on the OMS agent for its connections to Log Analytics, and, as such, you must install the OMS agents on any Windows or Linux computers that you wish to collect wire data from. Note that the Dependency Agent must be installed on 64-bit machines because the solution does not support 32-bit operating system architectures. Also, ensure that you install the Dependency Agent on a supported operating system. The following operating systems are currently supported:

- Windows Server 2008 R2 (requires SP1) and higher
- Windows Desktop 7 and higher
- Red Hat Enterprise Linux (RHEL) Server 5, 6, 7 (x64)
- Oracle Linux (RHEL kernel) 5, 6 (x64)
- SUSE Linux Enterprise Server 10 SP4, 11 (x64)

Once you meet the aforementioned requirements, install the Dependency Agent on all computers on which you would like to collect wire data. On Windows computers, you will need to run the agent file `InstallDependencyAgent-Windows.exe`. You can download the file from `https://docs.microsoft.com/en-us/azure/operations-management-suite/operations-management-suite-service-map-configure`. You can run this via the command line or, to deploy it to many servers, use a script with PowerShell or use **Desired State Configuration** (**DSC**) to enforce it as a configuration requirement. If you are managing Azure VMs with Azure Log Analytics, you can also deploy the Dependency Agent using the Azure VM extension.

On supported Linux computers, you will need to download and run the Dependency Agent installation file `InstallDependencyAgent-linux64.bin` and download this from `https://aka.ms/dependencyagentlinux` with relevant permissions.

> You may need to add execute permissions to the Dependency Agent installation file before installation. You can use the `chmod +x InstallDependencyAgent-Linux64.bin` command to accomplish this.

How it works...

The solution consolidates network and performance data from your Windows and Linux machines and enables you to correlate this data against other data in your workspace to glean insights about network connections into and out of your network. Wire Data simply collects data from managed computers at the application layer including data about ports and protocols used from the application-level's perspective. It neither performs packet-level analysis nor monitors for segmentation, acknowledgment, reliability, or any of the other functions at the TCP/UDP transport layer. The Wire Data 2.0 solution does not have full network data packet capture capabilities, and it is not intended for in-depth troubleshooting of network traffic at the packet level like you would do with a featured network packet analyzer like Wireshark.

One of the many benefits of using this solution for network traffic monitoring is that Wire Data uses a rather simple implementation to get you network traffic information. By simply deploying the agent on endpoints in your infrastructure, you can gain valuable insights that will enable you to detect, diagnose, and address network problems without the need to perform any monitoring configurations on your network appliances. This solution will also prove useful for monitoring network traffic in scenarios where you don't own the infrastructure network fabric, such as in managed or hosted on-premises data centers, or public cloud platforms, such as AWS or Microsoft Azure. Some applications of the Wire Data solution include the following:

- Detecting, analyzing, and fixing network issues
- Understanding application mix and changes
- Application usage accounting
- Data correlation with other log data
- Trending and capacity planning

The solution supports both directly attached agents and agents in a connected SCOM management group. In both cases, agents send wire data directly to Log Analytics endpoints without storing the data in the SCOM databases. This is because the collection mechanism is in real time and rather high volume in nature.

Once added to your workspace, the solution adds the Wire Data 2.0 tile to your OMS dashboard. The tile displays a count of agents capturing wire data, discovered local subnets, and application-level protocols discovered in the past 24 hours:

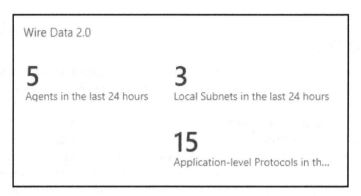

Figure 7.1

Click on the tile to open the solution dashboard. The dashboard groups solution data into the following blades for network traffic information:

- **Agents capturing network traffic**: This blade shows a count of agents collecting wire data, and lists up to 10 computers collecting wire data and the amount of data in bytes for each agent.
- **Local Subnets**: This blade shows the count of local subnets discovered by agents and list-discovered subnets and the number of bytes sent over each subnet.
- **Application-level Protocols**: This blade shows the number of agent-discovered application protocols that are in use in your network, as well as the number of bytes of data sent using the protocol:

Figure 7.2

The Wire Data 2.0 solution creates data records of the *WireData* type from the input data. The Wire Data 2.0 solution is also instrumental in providing various insights, such as network security insights through the Security and Audit solution, which correlates network traffic data collected by the Wire Data 2.0 solution with other log data to provide insight about your security posture from a network security's perspective. For instance, the following query correlates data from various sources, including wire data, and provides you with threat intelligence data based on potentially malicious incoming traffic on your network:

```
let schemaColumns = datatable(RemoteIPCountry:string)[];
union isfuzzy= true schemaColumns, W3CIISLog, DnsEvents, WireData,
WindowsFirewall, CommonSecurityLog
| where isnotempty(MaliciousIP) and (isnotempty(MaliciousIPCountry) or
isnotempty(RemoteIPCountry))
| extend Country = iff(isnotempty(MaliciousIPCountry), MaliciousIPCountry,
iff(isnotempty(RemoteIPCountry), RemoteIPCountry, ''))
| where Country == "Italy"
```

The query correlates various data types and sources and returns information about potentially malicious traffic seen originating from Italy. The query result is as seen here:

Figure 7.3

The Wire Data 2.0 solution is available to the Free and OMS (per node) pricing tiers.

Using Service Map

Service Map is part of the Insights and Analytics offering in OMS Log Analytics. The Service Map solution was made possible by, among other things, Microsoft's strategic acquisition of BlueStripe Software. BlueStripe's *FactFinder* tool was an established leader in dynamic application dependency mapping, and Microsoft has since integrated this tool as a cloud-based offering in Log Analytics to complement the vast array of other hybrid cloud management capabilities and services that exist in OMS. Service Map was initially known as **Application Dependency Monitor** (**ADM**) and has since evolved into a full-fledged service application dependency mapping solution with numerous practical applications and use cases.

Service Map discovers application components and TCP-connected processes on Windows and Linux computers automatically, maps the connections that the processes make, and builds a detailed topology view of the connections down to the IP and ports on servers across your infrastructure. Service Map also provides relevant data from other solutions, including performance data, alert data, log data, change tracking data, updates, security, and service desk data. This disparate data from the disparate sources is woven together to provide you with a rich tapestry of insights into your systems and the applications that run on them. Service Map requires the Microsoft Dependency Agent for data collection.

How to do it...

To use Service Map, enable the Insights and Analytics offering in the Azure Portal, or add the solution directly from the Solution Gallery in the OMS Portal or the Azure marketplace. While the Dependency Agent is responsible for monitoring and collecting the relevant Wire data, it relies on the OMS agent for its connections to Log Analytics, and as such you must install the OMS agents on any Windows or Linux computers that you wish to collect wire data from. Note that the Dependency Agent must be installed on 64-bit machines because the solution does not support 32-bit operating system architectures. Also, ensure that you install the Dependency Agent on a supported operating system. The following operating systems are currently supported:

- Windows Server 2008 R2 (requires SP1) and higher
- Windows Desktop 7 and higher
- Red Hat Enterprise Linux (RHEL) Server 5, 6, 7 (x64)
- Oracle Linux (RHEL kernel) 5, 6 (x64)
- SUSE Linux Enterprise Server 10 SP4, 11 (x64)

Once you meet the previous requirements, install the Dependency Agent on all computers on which you would like to collect wire data. On Windows computers, you will need to run the agent file `InstallDependencyAgent-Windows.exe` and download from `https://aka.ms/dependencyagentwindows`. You can run this via the command line or to deploy it to many servers, use a script with PowerShell or use DSC to enforce as a configuration requirement. If you are managing Azure VMs with Azure Log Analytics, you can also deploy the Dependency Agent using the Azure VM extension.

On supported Linux computers, you will need to download and run the Dependency Agent installation file `InstallDependencyAgent-linux64.bin` and download from `https://aka.ms/dependencyagentlinux` with relevant permissions.

Tip: You may need to add execute permissions to the Dependency Agent installation file before installation. You can use the `chmod +x InstallDependencyAgent-Linux64.bin` command to accomplish this.

Once you connect supported sources to OMS Log Analytics and install the Dependency Agent, no further configuration is required for Service Map to collect data.

How it works...

Service Map gets its data from the Dependency Agent. Once the agent is installed on supported Windows and Linux computers, the agents gather and send monitoring data to Log Analytics endpoints. Once the data is in Log Analytics, Service Map analyzes the monitoring data and maps the connections between servers, ports, and processes across any TCP-connected architecture, regardless of whether your workloads are in the your on-premises data center or in a public cloud, such as AWS or Microsoft Azure. This incredible capability has several attendant practical use cases:

- **Application Discovery**: Service Map automatically creates an intuitive topology view that maps all TCP-connected servers, services, ports, and processes, showing you live connections and historical perspectives of your application to enable you to quickly identify changes to your application or any issues that might affect application availability and/or performance.

- **Migration Planning**: The dependency mapping feature in Service Map will give you the confidence you need to migrate your applications to the cloud or other on-premises sites. Once you discover the application components and all the services and components that your application relies on, you can rest assured that, once you implement your migration plan, Service Map will enable you to confirm that all application components are connected and quickly identify any operational issues that could affect application availability and performance.

- **Disaster Recovery and Business Continuity (DR/BCP) Planning**: This use case is closely related to the previously mentioned migration benefits. With dependency mapping in Service Map, you can visualize all of the components of your application and the relationship between components. This will enable you to verify your recovery plan to ensure that application components are recovered in the correct order to ensure application availability.

- **Incident Management**: Service Map integrates various workflows that facilitate incident and problem management and enable you to quickly identify and isolate problems when they arise and arms you with actionable insights for root-cause analysis.

- **Patch Management**: The dependency mapping capability in Service Map gives you a clear picture of what systems are connected to your applications and systems and how they could be affected during the update and patching process. Service Map also integrates with System Update Assessment workflows to show you the update state of your systems.

Service Map supports both directly attached agents and agents in a connected SCOM management group. In both cases, the Dependency Agent collects the mapping and other relevant data used by Service Map and uses the OMS Agent to send the data directly to Log Analytics. Once this data is in Log Analytics, Service Map analyzes the data to provide you with the dependency mapping and insights about TCP connections to and from your systems and applications. Service Map also integrates with other solutions to show you relevant data around performance, security, updates, logs, change tracking, alerts, and other data that pertains to your systems and applications.

Once added to your workspace, the solution adds the Service Map tile to your OMS Log Analytics dashboard. The tile shows a count of machines with the Microsoft Dependency Agent installed and reporting in the past 30 minutes, a count of all machines that have ever sent relevant data and a breakdown of machines for Windows and Linux:

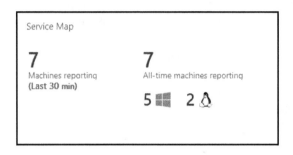

Figure 7.4

Click on the tile to open the Service Map console. In the left pane of your screen, there is a list of all computers that have the Dependency Agent installed. Click on a computer to see the connections for that computer. In the console, you will see the selected computer and a list of processes running on the computer, as well as a map of external and other connections to the computer:

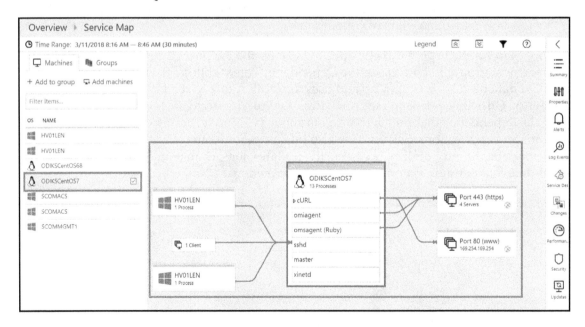

Figure 7.5

You will also see various options in the console that provide you with incredibly detailed insight about connection information about all machines that are direct TCP clients or servers of the machine, as well as IP address and port information for all connections made to any processes on the machine:

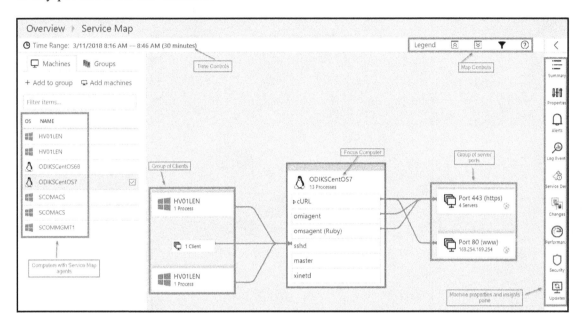

Figure 7.6

Once your selected machine is displayed in the console with attendant connections, you can click on **Time Range** to select a different time frame for which to view your machine connections. This is useful to determine what changes occurred on a machine over a period of time and to correlate with **Change Tracking** data, for instance. By default, Service Map shows the past 30 minutes of dependency information for the selected machine:

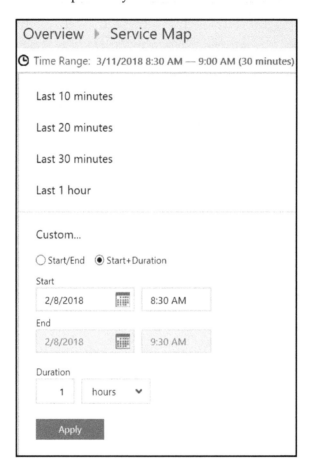

Figure 7.7

At this time, you can select a time range of up to 1 hour. You can view up to 30 days of historical Service Map data for your machines in paid workspaces and 7 days of historical data in free workspaces. Once you select your time range of interest, select the focus machine to view processes, and this expands the **Properties** pane, which provides an overview of the machine's properties:

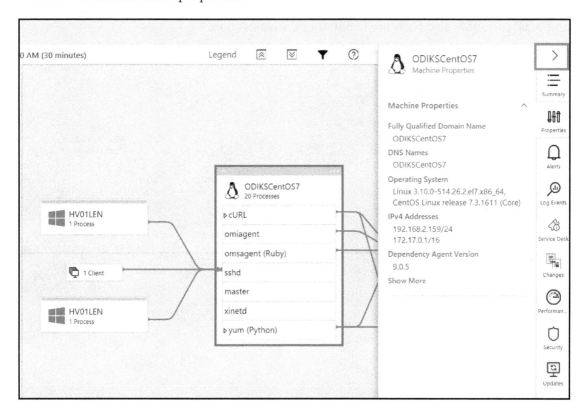

Figure 7.8

You can toggle the pane button to open or hide the detailed right pane view. In the map for your selected machine, you will see connected clients grouped to the left of the focus machine. The connected clients comprises both monitored computers and a client group of unmonitored IP addresses connecting to the focus machine. For client connections, you will see very detailed information about the names and properties of monitored clients, as well as what services on the monitored client is initiating a connection to your focus computer and what processes and ports are facilitating the connection:

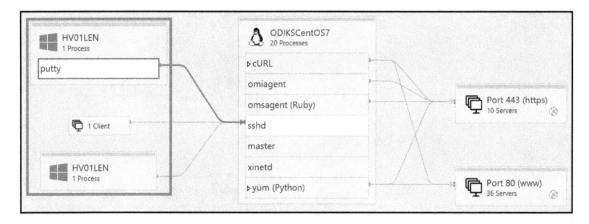

Figure 7.9

As seen in the previous figure, the client `HV01LEN` is connected to the CentOS server via **Putty** utility, and the connection is over **SSH**:

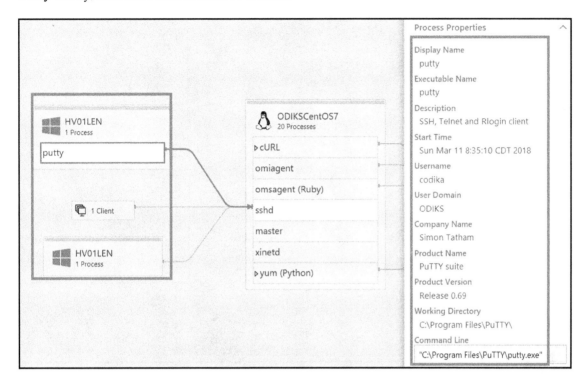

Figure 7.10

Clicking on the client also shows the IP and port information of the servers in the client group:

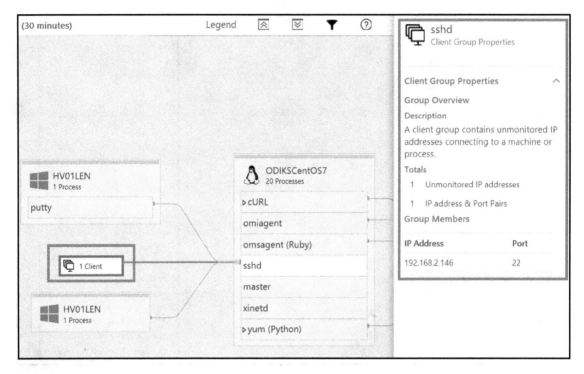

Figure 7.11

Similarly, for the focus machine, you will see a grouping of connections made by the machine to the right of the focus machine. The connected servers comprises both monitored computers and Server Port Groups, which represent ports on servers that do not have the Microsoft Dependency Agent installed:

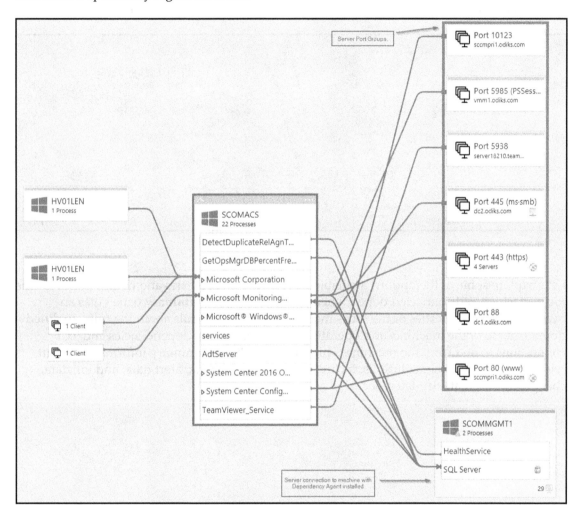

Figure 7.12

Server port groups show a grouping of connections to endpoints over specific ports, and the connections over a specific port are intuitively grouped together, and for each connection over a given port, the name or IP address of the endpoint is listed in the port group. As seen here, all connections made over HTTPS are grouped together, and the IP addresses of the endpoints are listed:

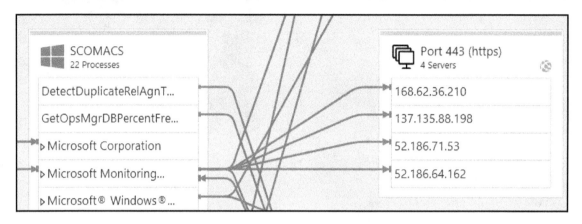

Figure 7.13

Let's explore some of the options available to you on the properties and details panes for the focus machine and connected dependencies. The **Computer Summary** pane gives an overview of the properties of the focus machine, including details about the fully qualified domain name of the machine, and operating system, counts of dependencies and TCP connections to and from the machine. This pane also shows summary information about relevant data from other solutions, including performance data, alert data, and log data, change tracking data, updates, security, and service desk data:

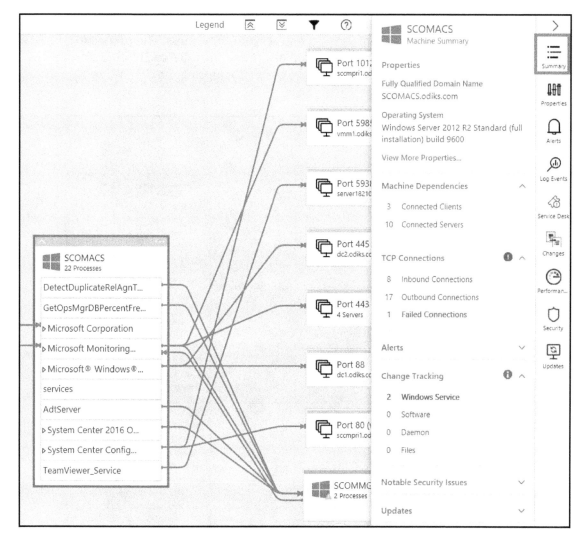

Figure 7.14

Furthermore, while in the **Summary** pane, you can click on any of the connected monitored or unmonitored clients, servers, or port groups to view the summary information for them.

The **Machine Properties** pane gives you additional context about the properties of selected machines, clients, client groups, and servers and server port groups. The property information displayed depends on the selected object and includes such information as the fully qualified domain names of objects, DNS names, OS information, IP addresses, and other machine properties:

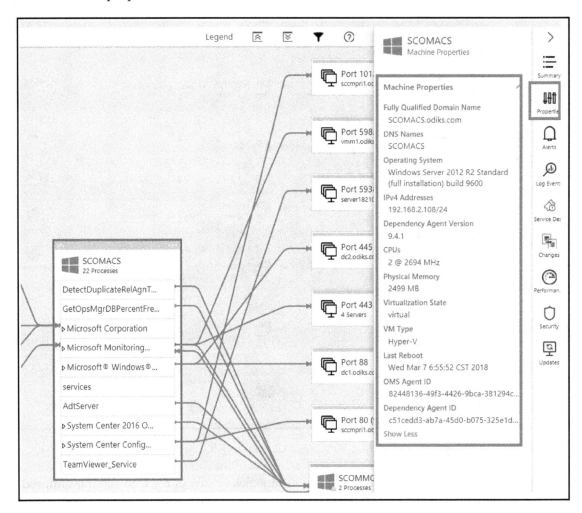

Figure 7.15

As mentioned earlier, Service Map also automatically integrates with other solutions to provide you with contextual information that relates to your systems and applications. The **Alerts** pane shows any alerts that have been generated for the selected machine or connected systems that are being monitored. The alerts displayed are alerts generated by a Log Analytics *metric measurement* alert rule. A sample query that you can use to create such a rule is:

```
Perf
| where CounterName == "% Processor Time" and ObjectName == "Processor" and
InstanceName == "_Total"
| summarize AggregatedValue = avg(CounterValue) by Computer,
bin(TimeGenerated, 5m)
```

Importantly, the query aggregates query result records and groups output by the computer for a specified interval. Any alerts fired by the query rule are shown in Service Map if they relate to the selected object in the Service Map console:

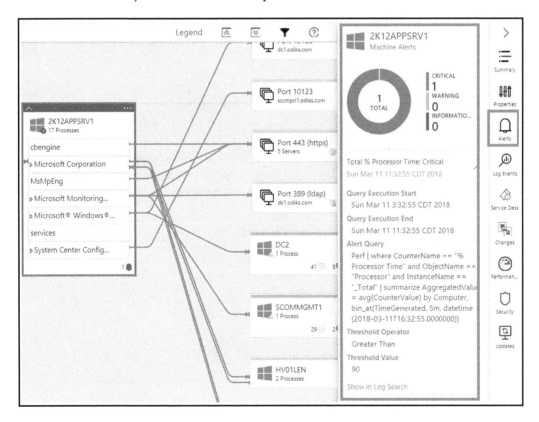

Figure 7.16

Service Map automatically integrates with OMS Log Search, and, for the selected server in the Service Map console, you can click on the **Log Events** pane to see a count of all available logs for the specified time range:

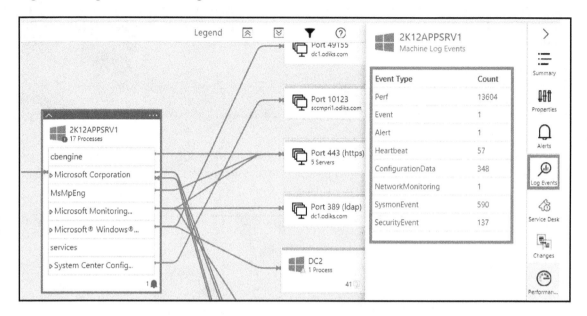

Figure 7.17

Service Map automatically integrates with the **IT Service Management Connector** (**ITSMC**), and when you configure both solutions in your workspace, you can click on the **Service Desk** pane to view related service management events for the selected server or connected system in the Service Map console:

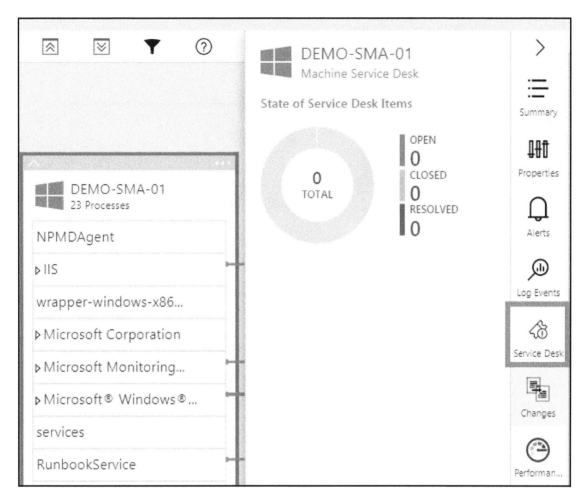

Figure 7.18

When the data for the selected object is visible in the **Service Desk** pane, you can view details about the work item in your connected ITSM solution and about the Log Search in Log Analytics.

Service Map automatically integrates with the **Change Tracking** solution to show you data relating to any service or software changes on the selected system in the Service Map console. Click on the **Changes** pane to see a list of changes, listed in order of occurrence with the most recent listed first:

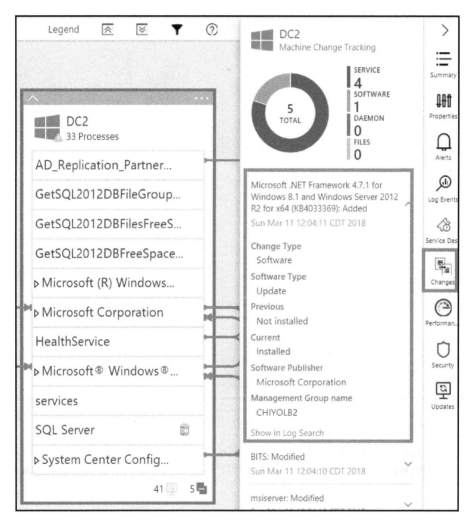

Figure 7.19

You can also click on the details option and Log Search link to see a summary about the change and detailed Log Search record, respectively:

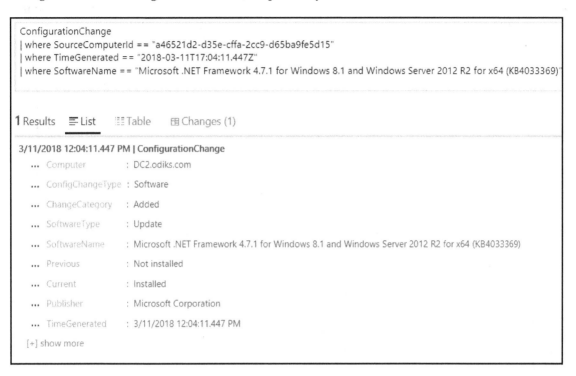

Figure 7.20

Service Map also displays performance metrics for the selected system in the Service Map console when you have performance data collection enabled and configured for your Windows and or Linux computers in your OMS workspace. Click on the **Performance** pane to view information about top processes by **Network Bytes Sent and Received** and information about such metrics as **Memory Utilization**, **CPU Utilization**, and **Network Bytes/second Sent and Received**:

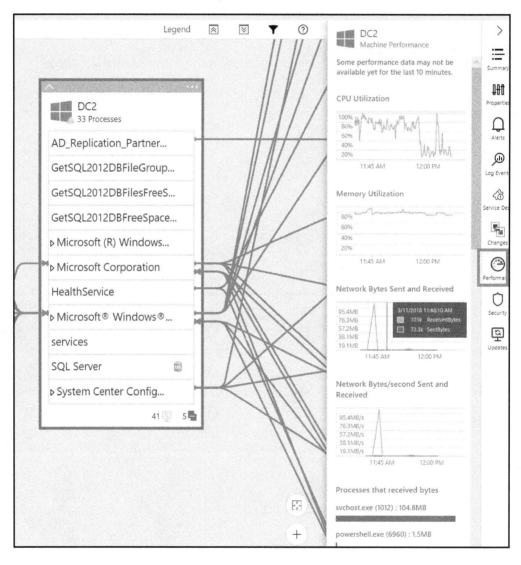

Figure 7.21

Service Map automatically integrates with the Security and Audit solution when you install and configure both solutions in your workspace. Click on the **Security** pane to see a list of notable and outstanding security issues for the selected computer, for the selected time range. You can also click on the link for the notable issue to see the Log Search record for the issue:

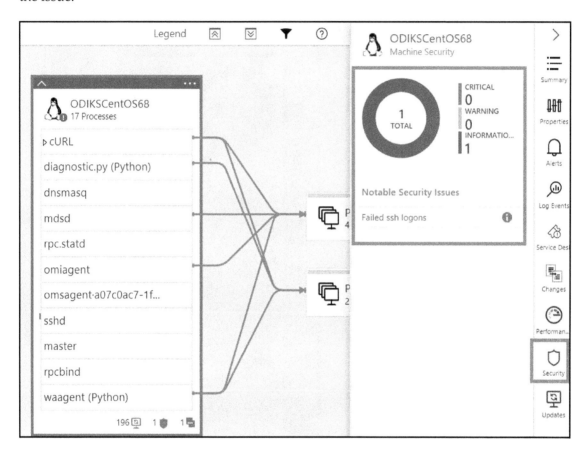

Figure 7.22

Service Map also integrates automatically with update management when you install and configure both solutions in your Log Analytics workspace:

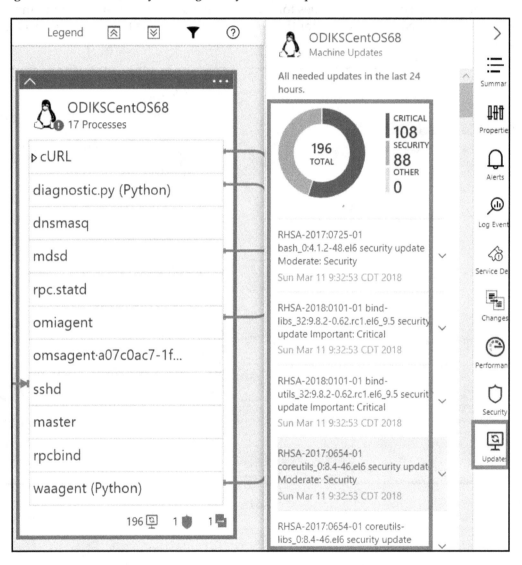

Figure 7.23

Click on the **Updates** pane to see a summary of missing updates for the selected time range, as seen earlier. Service Map creates computer and process inventory data that is stored in the OMS repository for your workspace. At this time, you can query this data with Log Search and reference the `ServiceMapComputer_CL` and/or `ServiceMapProcess_CL` data tables for the computer and process inventory data, respectively. You can use some of the sample queries below to search Service Map inventory data.

List all computers with the Service Map agent installed:

```
ServiceMapComputer_CL
| summarize arg_max(TimeGenerated, *) by Computer
```

List all processes for a specific computer:

```
ServiceMapProcess_CL
| where Computer == "ODIKSCentOS68"
| summarize arg_max(TimeGenerated, *) by ProductName_s
```

List all computers running SQL:

```
ServiceMapComputer_CL
| where ResourceName_s in ((search in (ServiceMapProcess_CL) "*sql*"
| distinct MachineResourceName_s))
| distinct ComputerName_s
```

At this time, Service Map is available to the **Free** and **OMS (per node)** pricing tiers. Service Map data for the free tier is stored for 7 days and for 30 days in paid workspaces.

There's more...

Service Map is able to discover particular application roles on your managed systems. As seen here, Service Map can determine when a machine has processes that hold application server, web server, or database roles, and can map connections to and from your systems from the perspective of these applications:

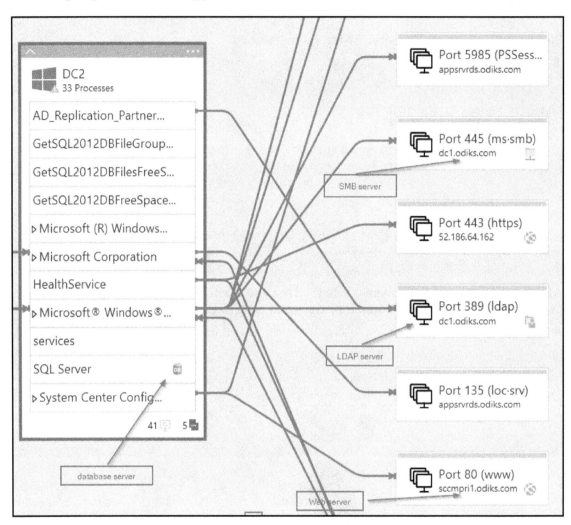

Figure 7.24

Service Map can also indicate when a failed connection to a dependent or connected system has occurred. Failed connections are depicted for computers and processes with a dashed red line indicating issues with a system reaching a particular port or process. The ability to map these dependencies and visualize connections in this way makes Service Map a truly formidable tool for many of the use cases listed earlier in this chapter. For instance in the following screenshot, the server **SCOMACS** has a dependency on the **SQL Server** database engine on the server **SCOMMGMT1**, which holds application databases, and to which it is connected:

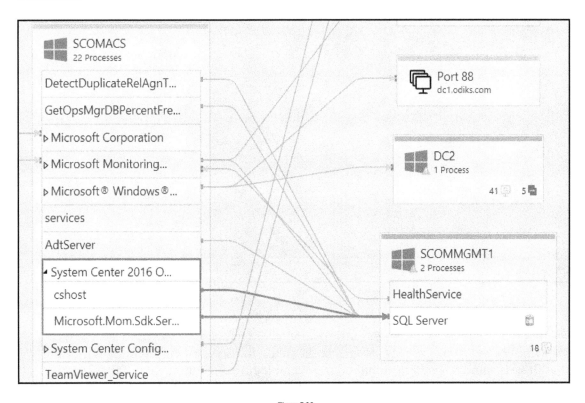

Figure 7.25

Once the connection is severed, as seen in the following image, Service Map displays a failed connection to the remote SQL instance on which the application depends:

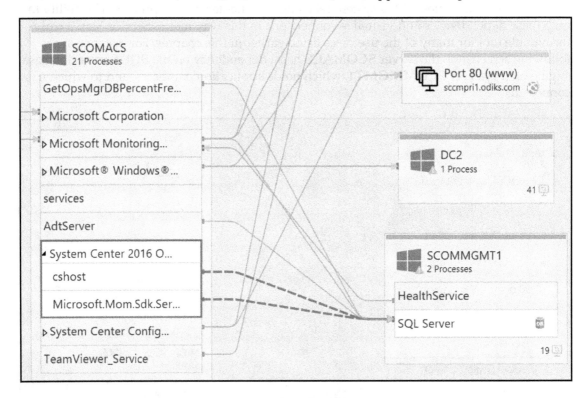

Figure 7.26

Furthermore, Service Map conveys information about a focus or connected system using *status badges* and *border coloring,* as seen in the following screenshot. The badges indicate that there is some relevant information from an integrated solution about the selected object. At this time, status badges are available for alerts, service desk events, change tracking events, update information, and security events:

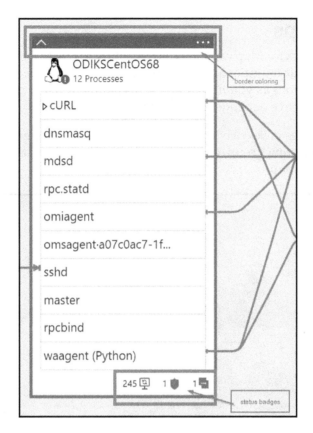

Figure 7.27

Clicking on a status badge will open the related solution pane and display the data for that solution. Border coloring refers to the colors assigned to the borders of the machine nodes to reflect severity of issues that relate to the selected computer. Red indicates a critical issue, yellow indicates a warning issue, and blue indicates an informational issue. A gray border indicates that a node has no issues. The color of a machine's border will reflect the most severe state of any of the status badges for a machine.

Machine Groups

Another very useful Service Map capability is the ability to create logical groups of servers so as to see maps of your multitier applications, application clusters, and so on, and truly visualize your applications as you think of them, as interconnected, multitier applications with components that have dependencies on other systems.

You can group machines in Service Map together and create a new group of machines or add machines to an existing group. Once created, select the group name to view the map for the selected machine group:

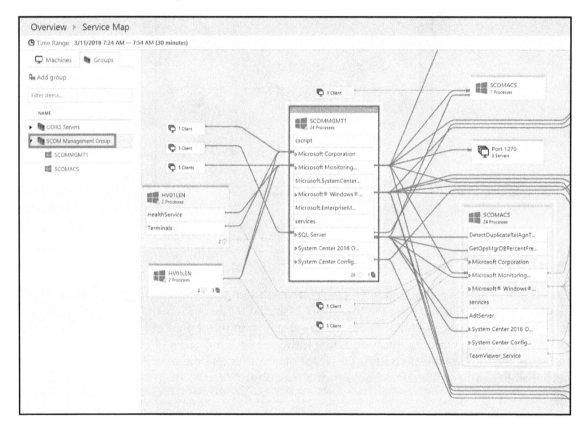

Figure 7.28

The machines that belong to the group are shown with a white outline in the map, and you can choose to isolate or filter specific processes for the machine group using the map controls. Click on Filter and select **Group-connected processes** to see only processes and connections that relate to the machine group, rather than all processes, which is the default:

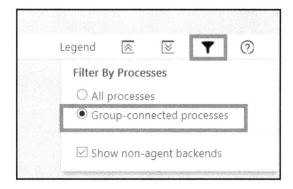

Figure 7.29

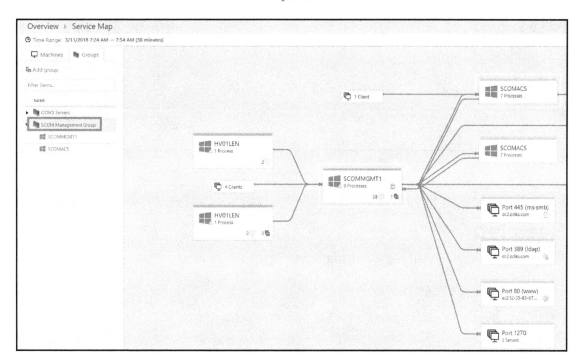

Figure 7.30

You can also toggle the options to expand or collapse all the systems and connections in the map. For example, expanding all the connections in the previously mentioned map gives me a more detailed view of connections as seen here:

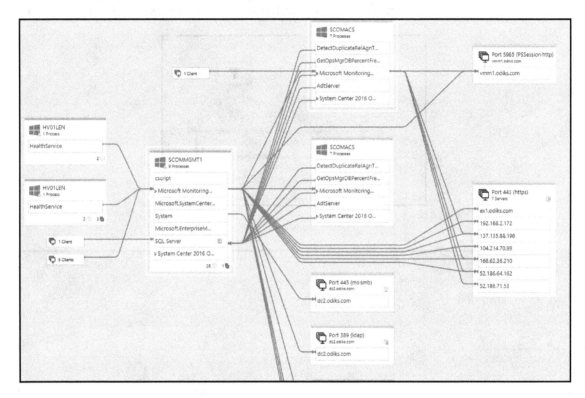

Figure 7.31

See also

For more information visit the following link:

- **Integrate Service Map with SCOM**:
  https://docs.microsoft.com/en-us/azure/operations-management-suite/
  operations-management-suite-service-map-scom

Exploring Other Management Solutions

8

In this chapter, we will explore management solutions that you can use to address various management scenarios within your infrastructure. The following topics will be covered:

- Installing other management solutions
- Reviewing other management solutions
- Log Analytics Assessment solutions

Introduction

As a hybrid management platform, OMS Log Analytics enables IT operations teams to collect and analyze data for various management scenarios using management solutions.

Installing other management solutions

Management solutions contain the logic, data acquisition, and visualization rules that provide assessments, metrics, and insights about specific workloads and areas of your infrastructure.

Getting ready

In order to fully use the visualization and automation resources contained in various management solutions, you will need a Log Analytics workspace and an Azure Automation account configured with your workspace.

Create an Automation account

If you do not already have an Automation account, follow these steps to create one:

1. Log in to the Azure portal at `https://portal.azure.com`.
2. In the Azure portal, type **Automation Account** in the `Search resources` search field and under `Services`, select **Automation Account**:

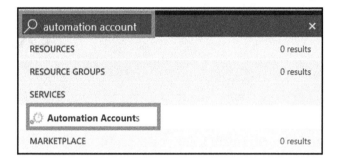

Figure 8.1

3. In Automation Accounts, click on **+Add** and then select choices for the following items:

   - Provide a name for the new Automation Account.
   - Select a **Subscription** to link by selecting from the drop-down list if the default selected is not appropriate.
   - For **Resource Group**, choose **Create new** resource group and enter a name in the text field, or select **Use existing** to use an existing resource group already set up.
   - Select an available **Location**.
   - Select **Yes** under **Create Azure Run As account**. Note that you will need to have permissions to be able to create this Run As account in Azure Active Directory. You will still be able to proceed with this task if you select **No** here.

4. Click on **Create** to create the automation account:

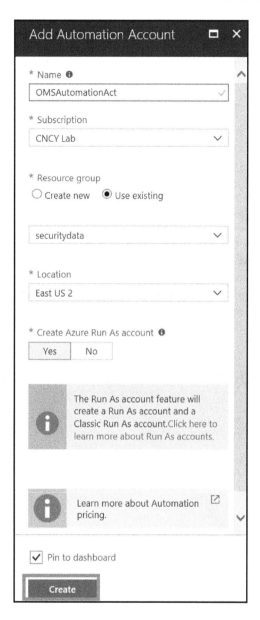

Figure 8.2

Once created, the automation account can then be associated with your Log Analytics workspace.

How to do it...

You can add management solutions to your OMS workspace through the following various methods:

- From the Azure Marketplace
- From the OMS Portal
- Using Azure Quickstart templates
- Azure Resource Manager templates

Once added to your OMS workspace, you can configure and manage the solution from the Azure Portal or from the OMS portal.

 When you install a management solution through the Azure Marketplace, a link is created between your Log Analytics workspace and an Automation account you select. When you add a solution with automation features outside of the Azure marketplace, you will have to link the Automation account to your Log Analytics workspace before you add the solution.

Installing a management solution from the Azure Portal marketplace

Perform the following steps:

1. Navigate to the **Azure Portal** (`https://portal.azure.com`) in your browser and sign in.
2. Select **+ Create a resource**, click on **Monitoring + Management,** and click on **See all**:

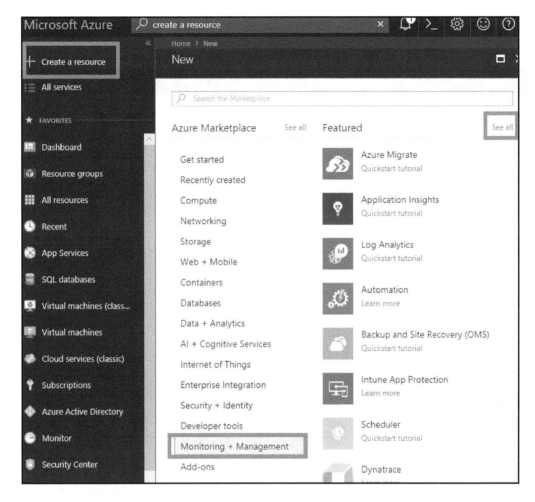

Figure 8.3

3. On the **Monitoring + Management** screen, to the right of **Monitoring + Management**, click on **More**.

4. In the **Management Solutions** blade, select a management solution to add to your workspace:

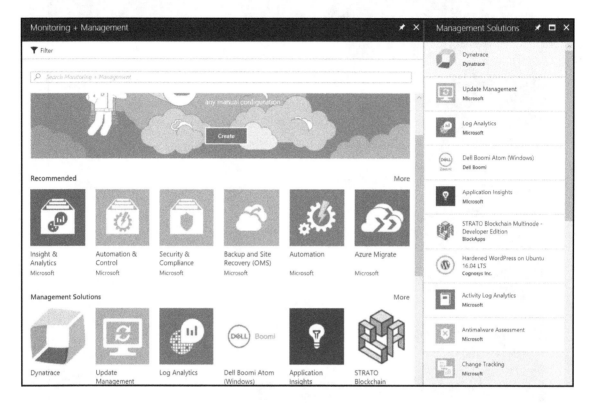

Figure 8.4

5. In the management solution blade, read the information about the management solution and click on **Create.**

6. In the blade for the selected management solution, select a workspace to associate with the management solution.

7. Review the **OMS Workspace** settings and verify or configure settings for Azure **Subscription**, **Resource group**, **Location**, and **Automation account.**

8. Click on **Create** to finish installing the solution to your OMS workspace:

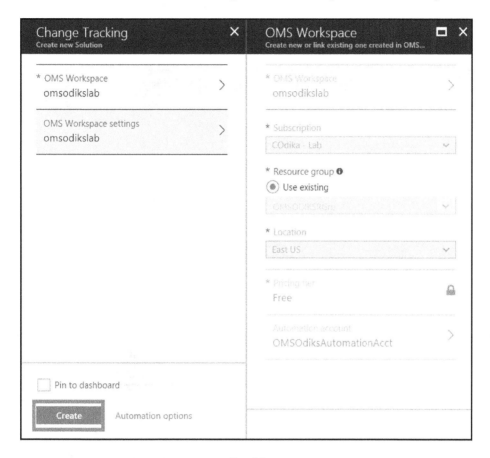

Figure 8.5

9. Once installed into your workspace, a new tile for the management solution will be visible in your workspace. Navigate to **Log Analytics**, select your workspace name, and click on **Overview** to see the tile for the installed management solution:

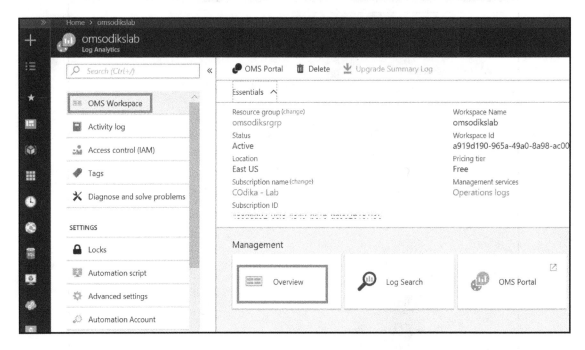

Figure 8.6

Installing a management solution from the OMS Portal

Another method of finding and adding management solutions is through the OMS portal. To install management solutions from the OMS Portal:

1. Navigate to the OMS portal and sign in. Refer to `https://www.mms.microsoft.com`.

2. On the **Overview** page, click on the **Solutions Gallery** tile to view offerings and management solutions:

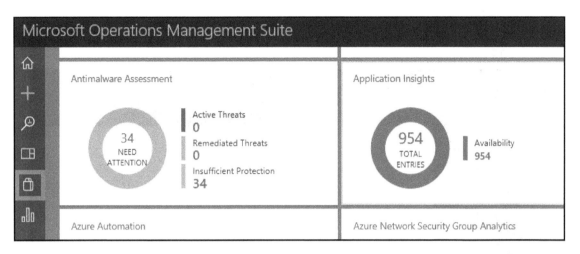

Figure 8.7

3. On the **Solutions Gallery** page, select a solution offering or management solution to add to your workspace.

4. On the **Management solution** page, click on **Add** to install the management solution in your workspace.

5. Once added, a new tile for the solution will be visible in the **Overview** page in your OMS workspace. Click on the tile to use the solution. You might have to allow some time for data processing to finish before the solution visualizations display data.

Installing a management solution from the Azure Quickstart templates

Another method of installing solutions is using Azure Quickstart templates. These templates are used by members of the Azure community to make solutions available to the public. You can download and install a quickstart template to enable a management solution capability in your workspace. To install a management solution through a template:

1. Open your browser and navigate to the **Azure Quickstart Template** page at
   `https://azure.microsoft.com/en-us/resources/templates/`

2. In the search field, search for a solution that you would like to install

3. Select the solution from the results and view details and capabilities

4. Click on the **Deploy to Azure** button

5. In the resultant **Azure Portal** page, provide required information for the template and click on **Purchase** to install the solution:

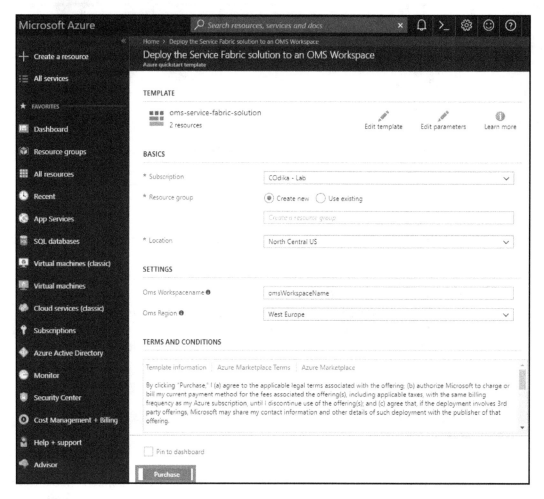

Figure 8.8

In addition to the methods described previously, you can also install solutions from the community or custom solutions that you create as a Resource Manager template. Once installed in your workspace, you can view the management solutions installed in a Log Analytics workspace through the Azure Portal and through the OMS portal.

Listing management solutions in Log Analytics workspace

Perform the following steps:

1. Navigate to the **Azure Portal** (`https://portal.azure.com`) in your browser and sign in
2. In the Azure portal, type **Log Analytics** in the `Search resources` search field and under `Services`, select **Log Analytics**
3. Select your workspace from the list and in the workspace blade, click on **Solutions**:

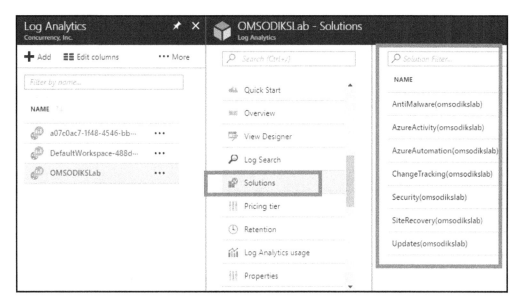

Figure 8.9

Viewing and removing solutions in OMS portal

You can also view solutions for your Log Analytics workspace in the OMS portal. Perform the following steps:

1. Navigate to the OMS portal and sign in. Refer to `https://www.mms.microsoft.com`

2. On the **Overview** page, click on the **Settings** link and select **Solutions** to display the solutions installed in the workspace:

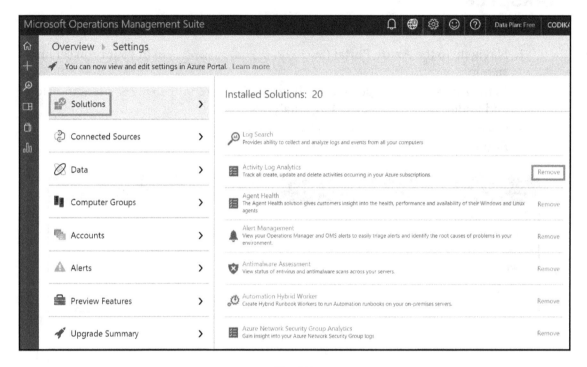

Figure 8.10

3. To remove any installed solutions, click on the **Remove** link for the solution

Once solutions are installed in your workspace, you can click on tiles for the various solutions to explore data for the management solutions.

Reviewing other Management solutions

In this section, we will review various management solutions, starting with the Agent Health solution, which helps you understand the behavior of agents connected to your workspace, and then we will move on to various other solutions that provide information around various problem areas.

How to do it...

Let's start by assessing the health of machines that are connected to your Log Analytics workspace.

Agent Health

The Agent Health solution is part of the Insights and Analytics/Log Analytics solution offering. The solution provides you with insight into the health, availability, and performance of agents connected to your Log Analytics workspace. This solution supports both Windows and Linux agents, as well as directly-attached agents and agents reporting through a SCOM management group connected to your OMS workspace. Once this solution is installed in your workspace, it installs the following solutions on your directly-attached Windows computers and in any integrated SCOM management group:

- Microsoft System Center Advisor HealthAssessment Server Channel Intelligence Pack (Microsoft.IntelligencePacks.HealthAssessmentViaServer)
- Microsoft System Center Advisor HealthAssessment Direct Channel Intelligence Pack (Microsoft.IntelligencePacks.HealthAssessmentDirect)

This solution does not require any further configuration for data collection. The solution collects heartbeat events from directly-attached Windows agents and processes heartbeat data relayed to Log Analytics from agents reporting to a SCOM management group(s). This solution collects heartbeat events every 60 seconds.

Once added to your workspace, the solution adds the Agent Health tile to your OMS dashboard, and you can see this in your workspace overview page. The tile will display the total count of agents with solution data records and the count of unresponsive agents in the past 24 hours:

Figure 8.11

Click on the tile to open the solution dashboard. The dashboard groups solution data into columns based on the following:

- **Agent count over time:** This shows a trend of a count of both Linux and Windows agents for the past seven days
- **The count of unresponsive agents:** This lists agents that have not sent a heartbeat in the past day
- **Distribution by OS type**: This gives a count of how many Windows and Linux agents you have in your environment
- **Distribution by Agent Version:** This lists and counts the various agent versions installed in your environment
- **Distribution by Agent Category**: This lists and counts the various categories of agents sending heartbeat events. Categories include those for direct agents, SCOM agents, and SCOM management servers
- **Distribution by Management Group:** This lists the SCOM management groups identified in your environment
- **Agent Geo-Location:** This lists and counts the countries where your agents are located
- **The Count of Installed Gateways**: This lists the servers that have the OMS Gateway installed:

Figure 8.12

The Agent Health solution creates data records of type `Heartbeat` from heartbeat event data. If you have an agent reporting to both an integrated SCOM management group and to your OMS workspace, the agent will send two heartbeats as reflected in the `SCAgentChannel` property of the heartbeat records for the agent, which indicates whether the agent is directly attached or reporting to a SCOM management group. Use the following query to enumerate a distribution of heartbeat data records by agent channel:

```
Heartbeat
| summarize AggregatedValue = dcount(Computer) by SCAgentChannel
| order by AggregatedValue desc
```

The following query lists a count of agents that have not sent heartbeats in the past 24 hours:

```
Heartbeat
| summarize LastCall = max(TimeGenerated) by Computer
| where LastCall < ago(24h)
```

The Agent Health solution is available to all OMS pricing tiers, including the **Free**, **Standalone (Per GB)**, and **OMS (per Node)** tiers. The solution is also available to legacy Standard and Premium (OMS) tiers.

Alert Management

The Alert Management solution is part of the Insights and Analytics/Log Analytics solution offering. The solution helps you analyze all the alerts collected for your Log Analytics workspace. The solution supports the following alerts:

- Alerts created by Log Analytics through alert rules
- Alerts imported from connected SCOM management groups
- Alerts imported from Zabbix and Nagios

Once alert data is stored in the OMS repository, the solution will work with any records of type `Alert`. Review `Chapter 3`, *Managing Alerts in OMS*, for details on creating alert rules for Log Analytics alerts, integrating SCOM with OMS, and configuring Nagios and Zabbix servers to send alerts to Log Analytics.

Once installed in your workspace, and if you have a SCOM management group integrated with your OMS workspace, the following management pack will be installed in your SCOM management group.

- **Microsoft System Center Advisor Alert Management (Microsoft.IntelligencePacks.AlertManagement):** This solution does not require additional configuration for the management pack to start collecting alerts from the connected SCOM management group. In addition, the Alert Management solution does not collect alert data directly from Windows or Linux agents. However, Log Analytics alerts and alert data records can be created from performance and event data collected from Windows and Linux agents. Once alert records are stored in the OMS repository, they are immediately made available to the solution. Once configured, it will send alerts to Log Analytics, Zabbix, and Nagios servers, which send alerts every minute, and alert data from connected SCOM management groups is sent to Log Analytics every 3 minutes.

Once added to your workspace, the solution adds the **Alert Management** tile to your OMS dashboard, and you can see this in your workspace overview page. The tile displays a count and graphical view of the number of currently active critical and warning alerts generated in the past 24 hours:

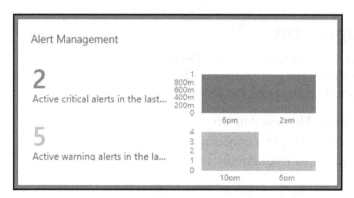

Figure 8.13

Click on the tile to open the solution dashboard. The dashboard, groups solution data into columns based on the following:

- **Critical Alerts**: This shows lists and counts all alerts with a critical severity, grouped by alert name.
- **Warning Alerts**: This lists and counts all alerts with a warning severity, grouped by alert name.

- **Active SCOM Alerts**: This lists and counts all alerts collected from SCOM with a resolution state other than closed, and alerts are grouped by SCOM alert source.
- **All Alerts**: This is a comprehensive list and count of all alerts with any severity. SCOM alerts with a resolution state of *closed* are excluded. Alerts are grouped by alert name:

Figure 8.14

The solution does not directly collect alerts created by Log Analytics or Nagios and Zabbix. The solution analyzes and works with any records of type `Alert` in the OMS repository.

Use the Alert record `SourceSystem` property to determine what system generated an alert. Alert records created by alert rules in Log Analytics have a `SourceSystem` property value of `OMS`. This can be used to distinguish them from alert records from other sources such as SCOM and from alerts such as Nagios and Zabbix. Alert records created from SCOM alerts have a `SourceSystem` property value of `OpsManager`. Nagios alerts and Zabbix alerts created alert records of type Alert with `SourceSystem` property values of `Nagios` and `Zabbix`, respectively.

You can use the following query to find a distribution of alert records by source system property in your workspace:

```
Alert
| summarize count () by SourceSystem
```

The query aggregates the content of the Alert table and returns the count of alert records by the `SourceSystem` field property.

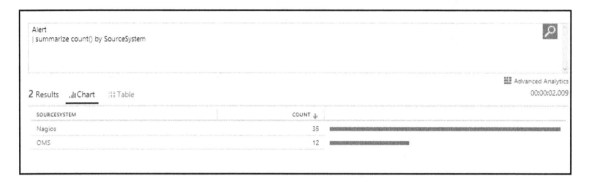

Figure 8.15

You can also use the `SourceSystem` field to specify alerts generated from a certain connected source. For instance, the following query finds alert records for alerts generated in SCOM:

```
Alert
| where SourceSystem == "OpsManager"
```

Alert records generated by the SCOM alerts in Log Analytics for instance will have a type of `Alert` and a `SourceSystem` of `OpsManager`. The properties for these records will differ slightly from those of alert records created by alert rules in Log Analytics.

The **Alert Management** solution is available to all OMS pricing tiers, including the **Free**, **Standalone (Per GB)**, and **OMS (per Node)** tiers. The solution is also available to legacy Standard and Premium (OMS) tiers.

Hyper-V Capacity and Performance

The **Capacity and Performance** solution (currently in Preview) is part of the Insights and Analytics/Log Analytics solution offering. The solution provides you with relevant capacity metrics and insights into your Hyper-V environment, and it collects metrics for memory, CPU, and storage for your hosts and the virtual machines running on them. This solution currently supports only the Windows platform, and as such only the Hyper-V hypervisor. The **Capacity and Performance** solution collects capacity and performance data from directly attached Windows agents and from agents in a connected SCOM management group. Once the solution is installed into your OMS workspace, the following solution will be installed in a connected SCOM management group:

- **Microsoft.IntelligencePacks.CapacityPerformance:**

  The solution does not require any further configuration for the management pack in SCOM to start collecting data. The solution makes use of capacity and planning-related performance data once the data is in the OMS repository for your workspace.

  Once added to your workspace, the solution adds the **Capacity and Performance** tile to your OMS dashboard, and you can see this in your workspace overview page. The tile displays a count of the number of currently active Hyper-V hosts and the number of active virtual machines that are monitored on the hosts.

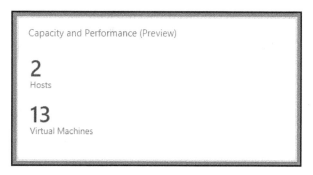

Figure 8.16

Click on the tile to open the solution dashboard. The dashboard groups solution data into columns based on the following:

- **Hosts**:
    - **Host CPU Utilization**: This shows a trend of CPU utilization of host computers in graphical form. It also lists hosts and average percentage CPU utilization for a selected time frame.
    - **Host Memory Utilization**: This shows a graphical trend of memory utilization on host computers and lists hosts with average percentage of memory utilization for a selected time frame.
- **Virtual Machines**:
    - **VM CPU Utilization**: This shows a graphical trend of CPU utilization on virtual machines. It also lists and shows the average percentage of memory utilization for a selected time frame.
    - **VM Memory Utilization**: This shows a graphical trend of memory utilization on VMs, and it also lists and shows the average percentage of memory utilization for a selected period of time.

- **VM Total Disk IOPS**: This shows a graphical trend of the total disk IOPS for VMs, and it lists VMs and shows the total disk IOPS for each for a selected time frame.
- **VM Total Disk Throughput**: This shows a graphical trend of the total disk throughput for VMs, and it lists and shows the total disk throughput for each VM for a selected time frame.

- **Clustered Shared Volumes**:
  - **Total Throughput**: This shows the sum of reads and writes on clustered shared volumes.
  - **Total IOPS:** This shows the sum of IOPS on clustered shared volumes.
  - **Total Latency**: This shows the total latency on clustered shared volumes.

- **Host Density:** This shows the number of hosts and VMs that are available to the solution:

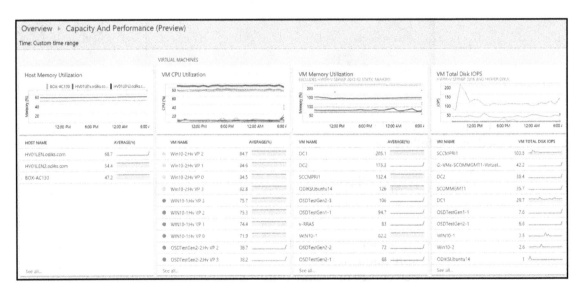

Figure 8.17

This solution collects and works with capacity and performance data from various sources including performance counters collected for relevant Hosts and VMs. All data used by the solution is in the Perf table in the OMS repository for your Log Analytics workspace. The solution works with data of type **Perf** as seen here. Use the following query to enumerate all host memory configurations:

```
Perf | where ObjectName == "Capacity and Performance"
| where CounterName == "Host Assigned Memory MB"
| summarize MB = avg(CounterValue) by InstanceName
```

The Capacity and Planning solution is available to all OMS pricing tiers, including the **Free**, **Standalone (Per GB)**, and **OMS (per Node)** tiers. The solution is also available to legacy Standard and Premium (OMS) tiers.

Change Tracking

The **Change Tracking** solution is part of the **Automation and Control OMS** solution offering. The solution enables you to troubleshoot operational and other issues by identifying and tracking changes in your environment. The solution tracks software, and file changes on Windows and Linux computers, changes to Windows registry keys, Windows services, and Linux daemons.

The **Change Tracking** solution requires an Azure Automation account, and it can be added to your workspace either through the Automation or Control offering or directly to your **Log Analytics** workspace. Once added to your workspace, the solution adds the Change Tracking tile to your OMS dashboard, and you can see this in your workspace overview page. The tile will display a summary of changes over the past 24 hours:

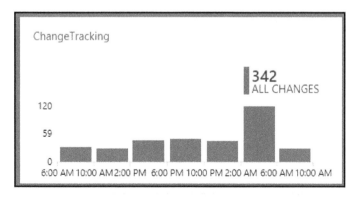

Figure 8.18

Click on the tile to open the solution dashboard. The dashboard groups solution data based on:

- **Configuration Changes Summary:** A summary of changes across all categories for Linux daemons, Windows services, Windows and Linux software, Windows registry, and Windows and Linux files with counts over the past 24 hours
- **Changes by Configuration Type:** This lists and counts changes by type of configuration in the past 24 hours
- **Software Changes:** This lists and counts software changes that occurred in the past 24 hours and provides a breakdown by number and count of Windows applications and Linux packages
- **Windows Service Changes:** This lists and counts Windows services changes that occurred in the past 24 hours
- **Linux Daemon Changes:** This lists and counts Linux daemon changes that occurred in the past 24 hours:

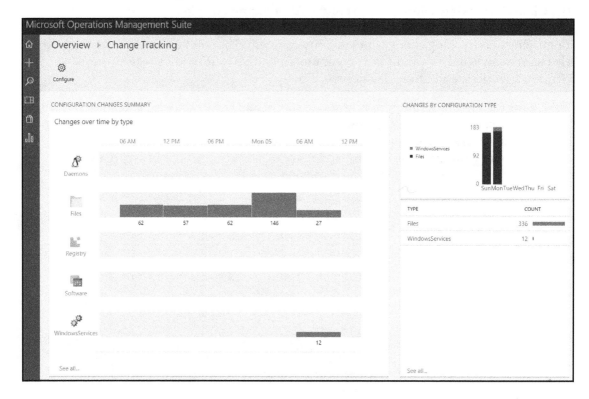

Figure 8.19

Once added to your workspace, the **Change Tracking** solution will start tracking software changes on your Windows and Linux computers and changes to Windows services and Linux daemons, as well as changes to configuration files in the /etc directory (/etc/*conf) on your Linux computers. You can track additional Windows registry keys, Windows files, and Linux files, and you can configure **Change Tracking** and inventory from either the OMS Portal or the Azure Portal.

When you configure change tracking for a Windows registry key or a Windows or Linux file, it is the entry that is enabled for both change tracking and inventory.

Configuring Change Tracking from the OMS Portal

Perform the following steps to configure Change Tracking from OMS Portal:

1. In the **Change Tracking** dashboard, click on **Configure**. This will take you to the **Settings** page in your OMS workspace.
2. In the **Settings** page, select one or more of the settings here:

    - **Windows File Tracking**: In the Search field, enter the path to the file you would like to track and click on **+** to add it to the list of tracked files, and click on **Save.**
    - **Windows Registry Tracking**: In the search field, enter the registry path for the registry key you would like to track. Click on **+** to add it to the list of tracked registry keys. You can also check the enabled box for the suggested registry keys to enable them. Click on **Save** once done:

- **Linux File Tracking**: In the search field, enter the path to the Linux file you would like to track and click on **Save**:

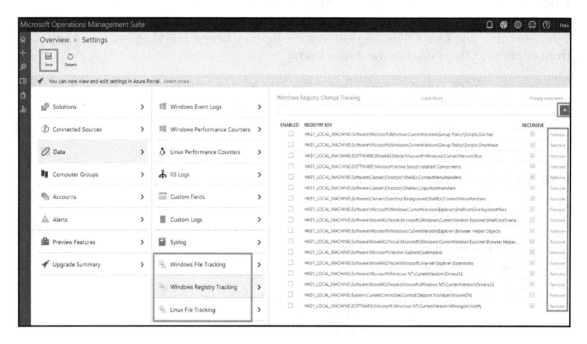

Figure 8.20

To disable change tracking for any Windows registry keys, or Windows and Linux files, simply click on the **Remove** button for tracked entry in the **Settings** page, and click on **Save** to finish.

Similarly, you can configure tracking settings from your Automation account in the Azure Portal.

Configuring Change Tracking from the Azure Portal

Perform the following steps:

1. Log in to the Azure portal at `https://portal.azure.com`
2. In the Azure portal, type **Automation Account** in the **Search Resources** search field and under **Services**, select **Automation Account**
3. Select your automation account from the list of accounts.

4. In your Automation Account, click on **Change Tracking** under **Configuration Management** and click on **Edit Settings**:

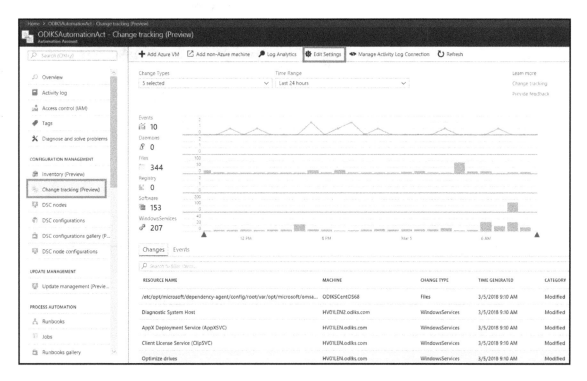

Figure 8.21

5. On the **Change Tracking** page, select a tab to track a corresponding configuration:

- **Windows File Tracking:** Click on **+Add** to add a new file to track. On the **Add Windows File for Change Tracking** blade, enter the information for the file to track and click on **Save** once done.
- **Windows Registry Tracking**: Click on the **+Add** button to add a registry key to track. On the **Add Windows Registry for Change Tracking** blade, enter the information for the key to track and click on **Save** once done.

- **Linux File Tracking**: Click on **+Add** to add a new file to track. On the **Add Linux File for Change Tracking** blade, enter the information for the file to track and click on **Save** once done:

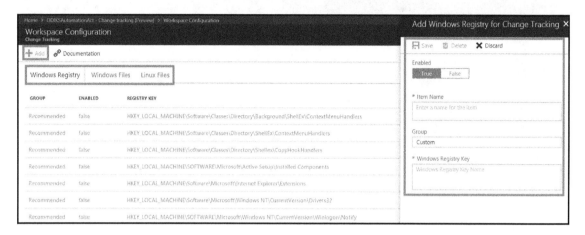

Figure 8.22

At this time, the **Change Tracking** solution does not currently support:

- Tracking file content
- Tracking network filesystems
- Tracking of Windows file directories
- Tracking path variables
- Using wild cards with Windows file tracking

The **Change Tracking** solution collects records of type `ConfigurationData` for inventory and type `ConfigurationChange` for change tracking. Some sample queries for this solution are as follows:

Query	Description
`ConfigurationChange`	All configuration changes
`ConfigurationData`	Inventory data
`ConfigurationChange` `| where ConfigChangeType == "Software"`	All software changes

ConfigurationChange | where ConfigChangeType == "Software" and SoftwareType == "Package"	All changes to Linux packages
ConfigurationData | where SoftwareType == "Package"	All Linux package inventory records

Table 8.1

The **Change Tracking** solution is available to the **Free** and **OMS (per node)** pricing data tiers.

AD Replication Status

The AD Replication Status solution is part of the Insights and Analytics solution offering. The solution analyzes the replication status for domain controllers in an Active Directory environment. This is important to ensure that domain controllers are replicating with each other. This solution supports the collection of AD replication data from both directly-attached agents and agents reporting through a SCOM management group.

In order to collect replication data, you must install agents on domain controllers that are part of the domain you would like to monitor AD replication for. Alternatively, you can configure member servers with the OMS agent to send AD replication data to Log Analytics. Once installed in your workspace, no further configuration of the solution is required for data collection. The solution collects AD replication data every five days.

Configuring a member server to send AD replication data to Log Analytics

If you don't have agents on your domain controllers, you can still collect AD replication data from member servers in your environment. To do this:

1. Verify that the member servers are part of the domain you would like to collect replication data for.
2. Install the OMS agent on the member servers directly or manage it using a connected SCOM management group.

3. Configure the following registry key on the member servers:

- **Key**:
  `HKEY_LOCAL_MACHINESYSTEMCurrentControlSetServicesHealthServiceP`
  `arametersManagementGroups<ManagementGroupName>SolutionsADReplic`
  `ation`
- **Value**: `IsTarget`
- **Value Data**: `true`

Once added to your workspace, the solution adds the AD Replication Status tile to your OMS dashboard, and you can see this in your workspace overview page. The tile displays the number of replication errors detected in your environment:

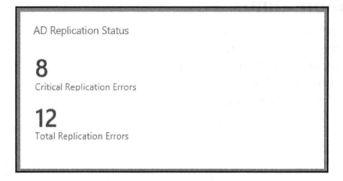

Figure 8.23

Click on the tile to open the solution dashboard. The dashboard groups solution data into columns based on the following:

- **Destination Server State:** This shows the status of the destination servers and lists destination servers with errors and number of errors
- **Source Server State**: This shows the status of source servers and lists source servers with errors and number of errors
- **Replication Error Types**: This provides information about the types of replication errors detected and the number of instances of each error
- **Tombstone Lifetime**: This provides information about replication issues that could be affected by the tombstone settings in your environment and that need to be addressed:

Figure 8.24

The AD Replication Status solution creates data records of type **ADReplicationResult**. Use the following query to show a distribution of replication information for your environment:

```
ADReplicationResult
| summarize arg_max(TimeGenerated, *) by SourceServer, DestinationServer,
PartitionName, TenantId
| where LastSyncResult != 0
| summarize AggregatedValue = count() by DestinationServer
```

The AD Replication Status solution is available to all OMS pricing tiers, including the **Free**, **Standalone (Per GB)**, and **OMS (per node)** tiers. The solution is also available to the legacy Standard and Premium (OMS) tiers.

Office 365 Analytics

The Office 365 Analytics solution is part of the Insights and Analytics solution offering. This solution is currently in Preview, which means that it is still under development, and, as such, capabilities are still being added or enhanced, and could change before final release. The Office 365 solution enables you to monitor user activities in your Office 365 accounts. You can use this solution to track administrative activities, analyze usage patterns for SharePoint, Exchange, and Azure Active Directory, and perform various other operational tasks.

Meet the following requirements before installing the Office 365 Analytics solution:

- You will need to have an Office 365 subscription.
- You have to be a global admin of the Office 365 account.

Once installed in your workspace, you will need to connect the solution to your Office 365 subscription:

1. Browse your OMS portal at `https://www.mms.microsoft.com`.
2. In the OMS portal, add the solution to your workspace from the OMS `Solutions Gallery`.
3. Go to `Settings`, click on **Connected Sources** and then on **Office 365**.
4. Click on **Connect Office 365** and sign in to Office 365 with an account that is a **Global Administrator** for your subscription:

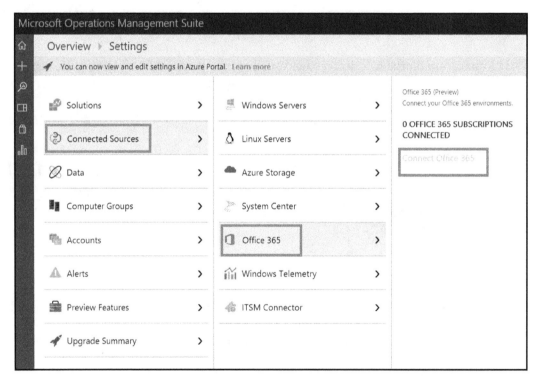

Figure 8.25

5. Once the solution is connected to your Office 365 subscription, you will see the connection information and status listed as Active. Furthermore, the solution tile in your OMS overview page will display statistics for Office 365 services:

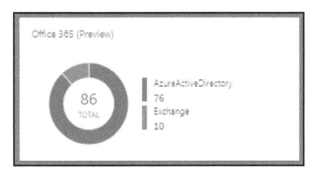

Figure 8.26

6. Click on the tile to open the solution dashboard. The dashboard groups solution data into the following columns:

- **Operations**: This provides information about active users across all of the Office 365 subscriptions that are monitored and provides counts of events for each user
- **Exchange**: This lists and counts Exchange-related operational activities, such as *Set-Mailbox* and *Remove-DistributionGroupMember*
- **SharePoint:** This lists and counts the top activities that users perform on documents in SharePoint

- **Azure Active Directory**: This lists and counts the top Azure-related user activities, such as *UserLoggedIn*, and *UserLoginFailed*:

Figure 8.27

7. The Office 365 solution creates data records of type OfficeActivity. You can use the OfficeWorkload record property to determine what Office 365 service the data record is for:

Query	Description
OfficeActivity | summarize AggregatedValue = count() by Operation	Count of all operations in your Office 365 subscription.
OfficeActivity |where OfficeWorkload == "SharePoint" and Operation == "FileAccessed" | summarize AggregatedValue = count() by UserType	File access operations listed by UserType property.

`search in (OfficeActivity) OfficeWorkload == "AzureActiveDirectory"    and "*@*"`	Search for a keyword.

Table 8.2

The Office 365 Analytics solution is available to all OMS pricing tiers, including the **Free**, **Standalone (Per GB)**, and **OMS (per Node)** tiers. The solution is also available to the legacy Standard, and Premium (OMS) tiers.

There's more...

Several more solutions are available through the Azure Marketplace and the Solution Gallery in the OMS Portal. Some examples include Such solutions as the VMware monitoring solution, which provides you with insights into the logs on your ESXi hosts, and the Application Insights Connector solution which provides you with enables you to insights into usage patterns and performance issues for applications that are monitored with the Application Insights service in Azure. See the links given in the *See also* section for more information on these solutions.

See also

Visit the following links for more information:

- VMware monitoring solution: `https://docs.microsoft.com/en-us/azure/log-analytics/log-analytics-vmware`
- Application Insights Connector solution: `https://docs.microsoft.com/en-us/azure/log-analytics/log-analytics-app-insights-connector`

Log Analytics assessment solutions

In this section, we will review assessment solutions in Log Analytics. Assessment solutions assess the risk and health of various workloads within your infrastructure and provides you with a prioritized list of recommendations across various focus areas, to enable you to quickly review and understand the assessments and the impact of the identified risks to the business. These assessments are based on Microsoft best-practices recommendations relating to risk and health factors for the various assessed workloads. Microsoft provides these assessments and configuration management capabilities to various products within its ecosystem using baseline tools and baseline-related services. With the assessment solutions in OMS, Microsoft uses an assessment-as-a-services model, which provides you with the latest and most up-to-date guidance on known risk and health factors that could affect the assessed workloads within your environment. Some of the assessment solutions that we will review are solutions for SQL Server and Active Directory.

How to do it...

As mentioned in the preceding section, you can add assessment management solutions to your Log Analytics workspace through various methods:

- From the Azure Marketplace
- From the OMS Portal
- Using Azure Quickstart templates
- Azure Resource Manager templates

Once added to your OMS workspace, you can configure and manage the solution from the Azure Portal or from the OMS portal. Refer to the *How to do it* section of the *Reviewing Management Solutions* recipe given earlier for detailed steps for the various methods for installing management solutions in OMS.

How it works...

We will review some of the assessment management solutions that are available to you in OMS. These management solutions assess risk and health factors for SQL Server and Active Directory, which support various key business services for organizations and businesses around the world.

The assessment solutions group risk and health evaluations into the following six focus areas:

- **Security and Compliance:** This focus area shows recommendations for potential security breaches and gaps, and regulatory and compliance requirements for security for the assessed workload
- **Availability and Business Continuity**: This focus area shows recommendations for service availability and highlights any risk factors that could lead to disruption of the service from a business continuity standpoint
- **Performance and Scalability**: This focus areas shows recommendations that help you ensure that you can scale the assessed workload to ensure that the service can meet increased performance and business requirements
- **Upgrade, Migration, and Deployment**: This focus area shows recommendations to enable you to upgrade, migrate, and deploy the assessed workload into your infrastructure
- **Operations and Monitoring:** This area focuses on assessments to enable you to improve and optimize your IT operational strategy as it relates to the assessed workload
- **Change and Configuration Management**: This focus area shows recommendations to ensure availability of the application through change control, and to ensure that you conform to change control best practices for tracking any changes made to the assessed workload

The assessment solutions assign a weighting value to every recommendation. The weighting value indicates the relative importance assigned to the recommendation. Weighting are aggregated values based on various key factors including the following:

- **Impact:** The impact of an issue to the availability and/or performance of a business service. This factor score is directly related to the recommendation score. A higher assessed impact results in a higher score for the recommendation.
- **Probability**: This is the likelihood that an identified issue will adversely affect a business service. This factor score is also directly related to the recommendation score. A higher assessed probability will result in a higher score for the recommendation.
- **Effort:** The amount of work involved in implementing the recommendation. This factor score is inversely related to the recommendation score. A higher assessed effort will result in a lower score for the recommendation.

Active Directory Health Check

The **Active Directory** (AD) Assessment solution is part of the Insights and Analytics solution offering. The solution provides assessments around the risk and health of your Active Directory infrastructure. The solution requires that a supported agent be installed on the domain controllers that are part of the domain you would like to evaluate. The solution supports domain controllers running Windows Server 2008 and higher, and requires a supported version of .NET Framework 4.5.2 or higher on any computers that have the Microsoft Monitoring Agent installed. The solution does not support **Azure AD** (**AAD**). The solution also supports both directly-attached agents and agents that are part of a connected SCOM management group.

After connecting domain controllers and installing the solution, no further configuration is required for the solution to start collecting configuration data. After you install the solution in your OMS workspace, a file named AdvisorAssessment.exe is added to servers with agents. The agents then read relevant configuration data and send it to the Log Analytics service endpoints. Any domain controllers that are managed in SCOM will also collect the required configuration data and relay it to the agent management server, which also sends it directly to Log Analytics. Depending on the size of your Active Directory environment, data collection will take 1 or more hours. Thereafter, the solution collects data every seven days.

Once added to your workspace, the solution adds the Active Directory Health Check tile to your OMS dashboard. The tile displays summary information for focus areas:

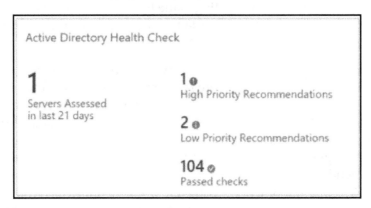

Figure 8.28

Click on the tile to open the solution dashboard. The dashboard groups solutions data into six focus areas as described earlier:

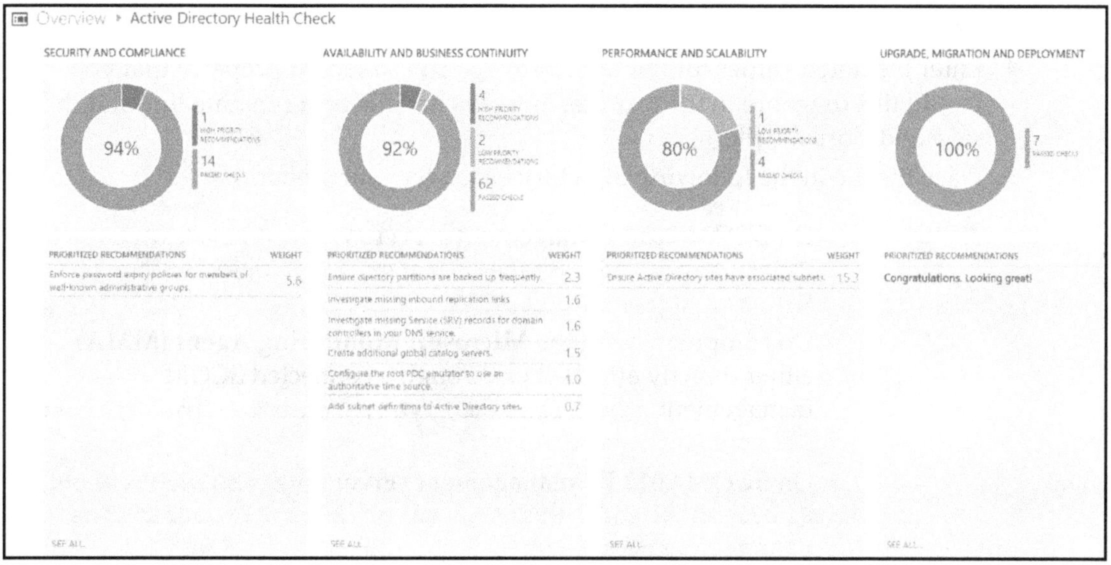

Figure 8.29

You can click on a focus area to view recommendations and take corrective actions to address the identified issues. The AD Assessment solution creates data records of type `ADAssessmentRecommendation`. You can use this data type with log search queries to review AD Assessment data.

Ignoring AD Assessment recommendations

In the event that you find an assessment recommendation to not be applicable to or relevant to your environment, you can ignore the recommendation. To ignore a recommendation, follow these steps:

1. In `Log Search` in the Azure Portal or your OMS Portal, enter the following query to list all failed recommendations:

```
ADAssessmentRecommendation | where RecommendationResult == "Failed"
| sort by Computer asc | project Computer, RecommendationId,
Recommendation
```

2. Review the returned records and choose the recommendations you would like to ignore. For each recommendation, take note of the values for the `RecommendationId` record property.

3. Create a text file and name it `IgnoreRecommendations.txt`.

4. Enter the noted values for the `RecommendationId` record property that you would like to ignore in the text file. Enter each value on a separate line and then save and close the file.

5. Place the file in the following directory based on your scenario:

   - On **SCOM 2016 management server**: `SystemDrive:\Program Files\Microsoft System Center 2016\Operations Manager\Server`
   - On computers with the **Microsoft Monitoring Agent (MMA)** either directly attached or through a connected SCOM management group: `SystemDrive\:Program Files\Microsoft Monitoring Agent\Agent`
   - On **SCOM 2012 R2 management server**: `SystemDrive\:Program Files\Microsoft System Center 2012 R2\Operations Manager\Server`

   You will have to allow the next scheduled health check to occur. The default collection frequency is seven days.

6. After the next collection schedule, run the following query to confirm that your configuration to ignore certain recommendations was successful:

   ```
   ADAssessmentRecommendation | where RecommendationResult ==
   "Ignored" | sort by Computer asc | project Computer,
   RecommendationId, Recommendation
   ```

To later enable ignored recommendations, remove the `RecommendationId` values of interest from the `IgnoreRecommendations.txt` file, and save the file. Allow a collection schedule to occur before confirming updates.

The AD Assessment solution is available to all OMS pricing tiers, including the **Free**, **Standalone (Per GB)**, and **OMS (per Node)** tiers. The solution is also available to legacy Standard and Premium (OMS) tiers.

SQL Server Health Check

The SQL Assessment solution is part of the Insights and Analytics solution offering. The solution provides assessments around the risk and health of your SQL Server environment. At this time, the solution supports SQL Server versions 2012 through 2016, and requires a supported version of .NET Framework 4 on any computers that have the **Microsoft Monitoring Agent** (**MMA**) installed. The solution also supports both directly-attached agents and agents that are part of a connected SCOM management group.

After you install the solution in your OMS workspace, a file called `AdvisorAssessment.exe` is added to servers with agents. The agents then read relevant data and send it to the Log Analytics service endpoints. Any SQL Servers that are managed in SCOM will also collect the required configuration data and relay it to the agent management server, which also sends it directly to Log Analytics. This solution has a collection frequency of seven days.

Once added to your workspace, the solution adds the SQL Health Check tile to your OMS dashboard:

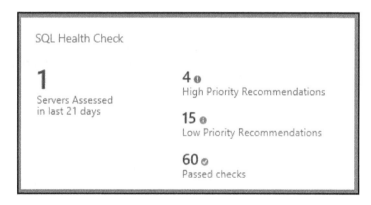

Figure 8.30

Click on the tile to open the solution dashboard. The dashboard shows solutions data in six focus areas, which are described earlier:

Figure 8.31

You can click on a focus area to view recommendations and take corrective actions to address the identified issues. The SQL Assessment solution creates data records of type `SQLAssessmenrRecommendation`. You can use this data type with log search queries to review SQL Assessment data.

Ignoring SQL Assessment recommendations

In the event that you find an assessment recommendation to not be applicable to or relevant to your environment, you can ignore the recommendation. To ignore a recommendation, follow these steps:

1. In `Log Search` in the Azure Portal or your OMS Portal, enter the following query to list all failed recommendations:

```
SQLAssessmentRecommendation | where RecommendationResult ==
"Failed" | sort by Computer asc | project Computer,
RecommendationId, Recommendation
```

2. Review the returned records and choose the recommendations you would like to ignore. For each recommendation, take note of the values for the `RecommendationId` record property.

3. Create a text file and name it `IgnoreRecommendations.txt`.

4. Enter the noted values for the `RecommendationId` record property that you would like to ignore in the text file. Enter each value on a separate line and save and close the file.

5. Place the file in the following directory based on your scenario:
    - On **SCOM 2016 management server**: `SystemDrive\:Program Files\Microsoft System Center 2016\Operations Manager\Server`
    - On computers with the **Microsoft Monitoring Agent (MMA)** either directly attached or through a connected SCOM management group: `SystemDrive\:Program Files\Microsoft Monitoring Agent\Agent`
    - On **SCOM 2012 R2 management server:** `SystemDrive\:Program Files\Microsoft System Center 2012 R2\Operations Manager\Server`

You will have to allow the next scheduled health check to occur. The default collection frequency is seven days.

5. After the next collection schedule, run the following query to confirm that your configuration to ignore certain recommendations was successful:

```
SQLAssessmentRecommendation | where RecommendationResult ==
"Ignored" | sort by Computer asc | project Computer,
RecommendationId, Recommendation
```

To later enable ignored recommendations, remove the `RecommendationId` values of interest from the `IgnoreRecommendations.txt` file, and save the file. Allow a collection schedule to occur before confirming updates.

The SQL Assessment solution is available to all OMS pricing tiers, including the **Free**, **Standalone (Per GB)**, and **OMS (per Node)** tiers. The solution is also available to legacy Standard and Premium (OMS) tiers.

See also

Visit the following link for more information:

- **SCOM Assessment Solution**: `https://docs.microsoft.com/en-us/azure/log-analytics/log-analytics-scom-assessment`

Cross Platform Management with OMS

9

Many organizations have complex, heterogeneous IT environments comprising Windows and Linux systems and workloads deployed across on-premises and cloud environments. Managing heterogeneous workloads can oftentimes prove challenging, especially when your monitoring and management solutions are tailored to only a subset of platforms, necessitating the use of multiple management and monitoring tools, which detract from ease of management. As a true hybrid management platform that supports both Windows and cross-platform systems wherever they may reside, Microsoft OMS was built from the ground up with cross-platform support in mind, and is replete with an ever-growing list of capabilities and features for monitoring and managing cross-platform workloads. This chapter will provide an overview of cross-platform management and monitoring capabilities using OMS.

The following are the recipes that we will cover in this chapter:

- Connecting Linux to OMS
- Linux data collection and metrics
- Collecting Zabbix and Nagios alerts
- Working with syslog data
- Monitoring containers with OMS Log Analytics

Introduction

When some years ago Microsoft announced the general availability of **Operations Management Suite** (**OMS**) during her flagship conference, Microsoft Ignite, it was a clear signal of a fundamental change in Microsoft's approach to and support for Linux and open source support workloads. Admittedly, organizations with investments in Microsoft's System Center have been able to monitor and manage various flavors of Linux systems using underlying tools, such as **System Center Operations Manager** (**SCOM**) and **System Center Configuration Manager** (**SCCM**). With OMS, Microsoft makes available a hybrid management platform that offers heterogeneous support and enables the seamless management of cross-platform systems, in addition to Windows systems, while complementing capabilities of the System Center tools that you have investments in. OMS simplifies the management of your cross-platform workloads, enabling you to monitor and manage cross-platform systems in your on-premises data centers, and any public cloud, and hosted at service providers. Some of the cross-platform management functions that you can perform in OMS include the following:

- **Monitoring Linux computers**: This collects data directly from your Linux computers and supported cross-platform systems wherever they may reside
- **Insights and analytics on syslog data**: This deploys the OMS agent for Linux on your supported Linux and cross-platform distributions and collect syslog data for analysis and monitoring
- **Performance data collection and metrics from Linux systems**: This collects performance counters for your Linux distributions and various applications such as MySQL and Apache HTTP server
- **Collecting alerts from cross-platform monitoring tools**: This collects alerts from open-source monitoring tools such as Zabbix and Nagios, and gleans actionable insights through analysis in Azure Log Analytics
- **Automating processes and tasks on Linux systems**: This automates operational tasks, such as jobs and updates, on your Linux systems, and simplifies configuration management for Linux workloads
- **Monitoring containers**: This monitors your containers for availability, performance, and troubleshoot issues on your containers from a single pane with the container solution in Log Analytics

Connect Linux to OMS

Azure Log Analytics supports the monitoring and management of various Linux distributions in your local datacenter and cloud environments. To connect Linux systems to Log Analytics, deploy the OMS Agent for Linux and configure it to report to your Log Analytics workspace.

Getting ready

The OMS agent for Linux supports the use of the OMS Gateway and agent communication through a proxy server. To connect Linux systems to your Log Analytics workspace, ensure that the following firewall and port requirements are met in order for the OMS agent for Linux to communicate with Log Analytics service endpoints:

Service URI	Ports	Direction
`*.oms.opinsights.azure.com`	443 (HTTPS)	Bi-directional
`*.azure-automation.net`	443 (HTTPS)	Bi-directional
`*.ods.opinsights.azure.com`	443 (HTTPS)	Bi-directional
`*.blob.core.windows.net`	443 (HTTPS)	Bi-directional

Table 9.1

Additionally, ensure that your Linux distributions are officially supported by the Linux agent. The following distributions are supported at this time:

Distribution	Versions
Amazon Linux	• 2012.09—2015.09 (x64)
CentOS Linux	• 5 (x86/x64) • 6 (x86/x64) • 7 (x86/x64)
Oracle Linux	• 5 (x86/x64) • 6 (x86/x64) • 7 (x86/x64)
Red Hat Enterprise Linux Server (RHEL)	• 5 (x86/x64) • 6 (x86/x64) • 7 (x86/x64)

Ubuntu Server	• 12.04 LTS (x86/x64) • 14.04 LTS (x86/x64) • 16.04 LTS (x86/x64)
Debian GNU/Linux	• 6 (x86/x64) • 7 (x86/x64) • 8 (x86/x64)
SUSE Linux Enterprise Server	• 11 (x86/x64) • 12 (x86/x64)

Table 9.2

To use the Linux agent with a proxy server, confirm the following syntax:

```
-p [protocol://][user:password@]proxyhost[:port]
```

You can specify the proxy server during agent installation, or by configuring the `/etc/opt/Microsoft/omsagent/proxy.conf` configuration file after agent installation. You can create or edit this configuration file, but the Linux agent must be able to read the file. The Linux agent supports both anonymous and basic authentication, and supports connecting to Log Analytics using the HTTPS protocol.

If using a proxy server, the OMS agent for Linux requires a username/password even if your proxy server does not require these. A sample proxy configuration is `https://omsuser:userpassword@proxyserver.company.com:20056`.

How to do it...

Once you have met the prerequisites for connecting Linux systems to Log Analytics, obtain your workspace ID and key, as you will need these for manually installing the Linux agent. To obtain the workspace ID and key, perform the following steps:

1. Log into the Azure portal at `https://portal.azure.com`
2. In the Azure portal, type `Log Analytics` in the search resources search field and under **Services**, select **Log Analytics**
3. Select your workspace from the list and in the workspace blade, click on **Advanced settings**

4. In the **Advanced settings** window, select **Connected Sources**, and then select **Linux Servers**

5. Copy the values for the **WORKSPACE ID** and **PRIMARY KEY**:

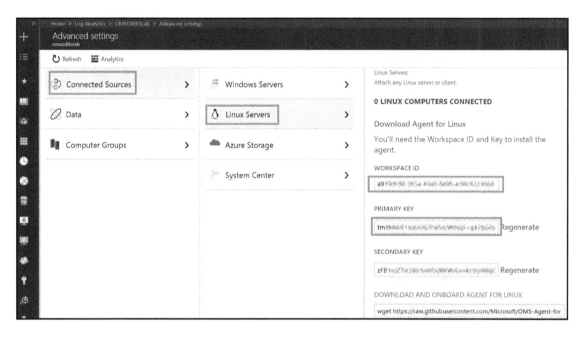

Figure 9.1

Installing and configuring the Linux agent

With you workspace credentials, you can install the Linux agent by calling a wrapper-script hosted on GitHub. Perform the following steps:

1. Run the following command to download the OMS agent for Linux, validate the checksum and install and onboard the agent to your Log Analytics workspace:

```
wget
https://raw.githubusercontent.com/Microsoft/OMS-Agent-for-Linux
/master/installer/scripts/onboard_agent.sh && sh
onboard_agent.sh -w <YOUR WORKSPACE ID> -s <YOUR WORKSPACE
PRIMARY KEY>
```

If you must use the Linux agent with a proxy, you can make use of the additional -p switch for specifying the proxy, and use the following command during installation:

```
wget
https://raw.githubusercontent.com/Microsoft/OMS-Agent-for-Linux
/master/installer/scripts/onboard_agent.sh && sh
onboard_agent.sh -p
[protocol://][user:password@]proxyhost[:port] -w <YOUR
WORKSPACE ID> -s <YOUR WORKSPACE PRIMARY KEY>
```

2. Restart the agent by running the following command:

```
sudo /opt/microsoft/omsagent/bin/service_control restart
```

Uninstalling the Linux agent

To uninstall the OMS agent for Linux, you can make use of the --purge argument, which removes the agent and its configuration:

```
wget
https://raw.githubusercontent.com/Microsoft/OMS-Agent-for-Linux/master/
installer/scripts/onboard_agent.sh && sh onboard_agent.sh --purge
```

Onboarding with the Azure VM extension

If you have Linux workloads in Azure, you can onboard to Log Analytics using the Linux Azure virtual machine extension. Azure extensions for virtual machines are small applications that provide automation tasks and post-deployment configuration on Azure VMs. The Linux Azure VM extension can install the Linux agent for OMS and onboard the machine to your Log Analytics workspace.

Using the extension with your Azure VMs, ensures that they have the latest agent capabilities, features, and fixes, as the agent is upgraded automatically.

To configure the extension, perform the following steps:

1. Log into the Azure portal at `https://portal.azure.com`.
2. In the Azure portal, type `Log Analytics` in the **Search resources** search field and under **Services**, select **Log Analytics**.
3. Select your workspace from the list and, in the workspace blade, under **Workspace Data Sources**, click on **Virtual machines**.
4. In the list of **Virtual machines**, select a virtual machine to install the agent on. The selected machine will show a status of **Not connected**.
5. In the details for the selected virtual machine, click on **Connect**. The agent is automatically installed and the machine is connected to your Log Analytics workspace:

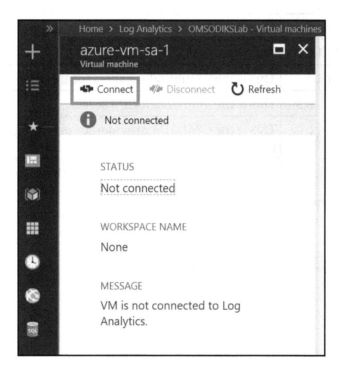

Figure 9.2

How it works...

The OMS agent for Linux is a lightweight agent with monitoring and data collection capabilities based on a CIM server listener and an open source data aggregator, Fluentd, respectively. The CIM server comprises the underlying providers for operating system, Apache, MySQL, container and other cross-platform monitoring, and the Fluentd-based data collection supports the collection of syslog, Docker data, and alert collection from Zabbix and Nagios. Through these features the Linux agent enables rich, real-time analytics for operational data.

The OMS agent for Linux is provided in a self-extracting shell script bundle that you can install. The bundle comprises multiple packages that enable the various components and features of the agent, as shown in the following table:

Agent package	Version	Description
Omsagent	1.1.0	This is the OMS Linux agent
Omsconfig	1.1.1	This is the configuration agent for the OMS agent
Omi	1.0.8.3	This is the lightweight CIM server
Scx	1.6.2	This is the OMI CIM provider for operating system performance metrics
Apache-cimprov	1.0.0	This is the Apache HTTP server performance monitoring provider for OMI
MySQL-cimprov	1.0.0	This is the MySQL server performance monitoring provider for OMI
Docker-cimprov	1.0.0	This is the Docker provider for OMI

Table 9.3

After installing the OMS Linux agent, the installer applies the following configuration changes on the Linux system:

- It creates a nonprivileged user account, which is used as the run-as account for the omsagent daemon. This account is named `omsagent`.
- The installer checks to determine whether `sudo include` directives are supported on the system, and, if so, creates a sudoers `include` file at `/etc/sudoers.d/omsagent`, to authorize the omsagent to restart the omsagent and syslog daemons. The entries will be written to `/etc/sudoers` if the `sudo include` directives are unsupported on the system.
- It modifies syslog configuration to send a subset of events to the Linux agent.

See also

OMS agent for Linux is available at `https://github.com/Microsoft/OMS-Agent-for-Linux`.

Linux data collection and metrics

Log Analytics can collect Linux operating system performance counters as well as counters for Linux applications such as MySQL and Apache HTTP server.

How to do it...

To configure performance counter data collection on connected Linux systems in your Log Analytics workspace:

1. Log into the Azure portal at `https://portal.azure.com`.
2. In the Azure portal, type `Log Analytics` in the **Search resources** search field and under **Services**, select **Log Analytics**.

3. Select your workspace from the list and, in the workspace blade, under **Settings**, click on **Advanced settings**.

4. In the **Advanced settings** window, click on **Data** and then on **Linux Performance Counters**.

5. Check the option to **Apply below configuration to my machines** and click on **Add the selected performance counters**. The listed options enable you to quickly create common counters.

6. Click on **Save** at the top of the page to save the configuration:

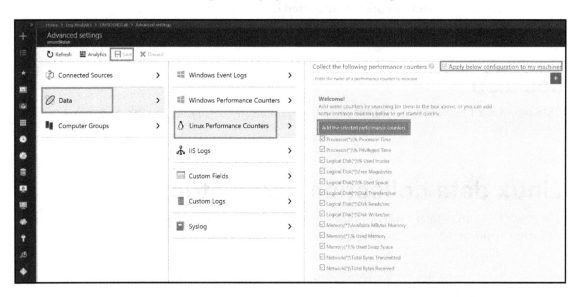

Figure 9.3

The selected counters are added and data collection is configured for a 10-second interval. You can add additional counters by searching for them, and adding them in your workspace. Once added, you can review the selected Linux performance counters in your workspace:

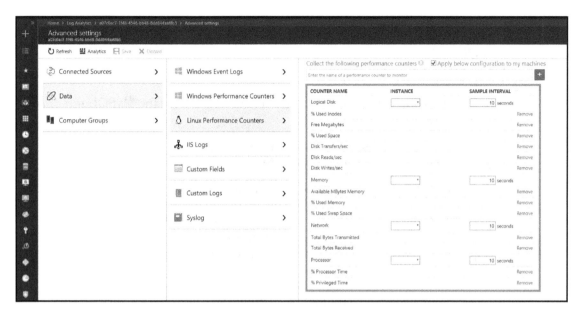

Figure 9.4

Collecting the data for Linux applications

As mentioned here, in addition to Linux system performance counters, you can collect performance counters for various Linux applications.

Collect MySQL server performance counters

When you install the OMS agent for Linux, the agent looks for an instance of MySQL server or MariaDB server, and, if detected, the `mysql-cimprov` package with the performance monitoring provider for MySQL server will be automatically installed. The provider connects to the detected MySQL server and exposes performance data for MySQL/MariaDB. The MySQL OMI provider makes use of a preconfigured MySQL user to access the MySQL server. The user will need access to the following queries:

```
SHOW GLOBAL STATUS;
SHOW GLOBAL VARIABLES;
```

The MySQL user will also require SELECT access to the following tables:

- MySQL
- Information_schema

1. Run the following commands to define a user account for the MySQL server on localhost and restart Omi:

```
sudo su omsagent -c '/opt/microsoft/mysql-
cimprov/bin/mycimprovauth default 127.0.0.1 <username>
<password>'
sudo /opt/omi/bin/service_control restart
```

It is recommended to run the `mycimprovauth` command as omsagent. As an alternative to defining the default user account on localhost, you can specify the required MySQL credentials in a file, by creating the file: `/var/opt/Microsoft/mysql-cimprov/auth/omsagent/mysql-auth`.

2. Run the following `grant` commands to grant the user the necessary privileges:

```
GRANT SELECT ON information_schema.* TO 'username'@'localhost';
GRANT SELECT ON mysql.* TO 'username'@'localhost';
```

3. In your Log Analytics workspace, configure the MySQL performance counters to collect. Log into the Azure portal at `https://portal.azure.com`.

4. In the Azure portal, type `Log Analytics` in the **Search resources** search field and, under **Services**, select **Log Analytics**.

5. Select your workspace from the list and, in the workspace blade, under **Settings**, click on **Advanced settings**.

6. In the **Advanced settings** window, click on **Data** and then on **Linux Performance Counters**.

7. In the search box, type **MySQL** and, from the returned values, select the counter names that reflect the performance counters you would like to collect, and click on the plus sign to add the counter for collection.

8. Click on **Save** at the top of the page to save the configuration:

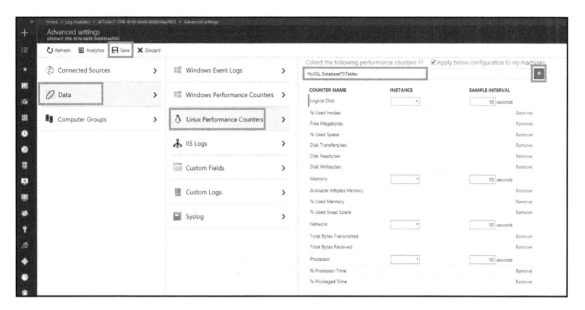

Figure 9.5

The following table lists some MySQL performance counters that you can collect in Log Analytics:

Object Name	Counter name	Performance counter
MySQL database	Disk Space in Bytes	MySQL Database(*)Disk Space in Bytes
MySQL database	Tables	MySQL Database(*)Tables
MySQL server	Aborted Connection Pct	MySQL Server(*)Aborted Connection Pct
MySQL server	Connection Use Pct	MySQL Server(*)Connection Use Pct
MySQL server	Disk Space Use in Bytes	MySQL Server(*)Disk Space Use in Bytes
MySQL server	Full Table Scan Pct	MySQL Server(*)Full Table Scan Pct
MySQL server	InnoDB Buffer Pool Hit Pct	MySQL Server(*)InnoDB Buffer Pool Hit Pct
MySQL server	InnoDB Buffer Pool Use Pct	MySQL Server(*)InnoDB Buffer Pool Use Pct
MySQL server	Key Cache Hit Pct	MySQL Server(*)Key Cache Hit Pct

MySQL server	Key Cache Write Pct	MySQL Server(*)Key Cache Write Pct
MySQL server	Key Cache Use Pct	MySQL Server(*)Key Cache Use Pct
MySQL server	Query Cache Hit Pct	MySQL Server(*)Query Cache Hit Pct
MySQL server	Query Cache Prunes Pct	MySQL Server(*)Query Cache Prunes Pct
MySQL server	Query Cache Use Pct	MySQL Server(*)Query Cache Use Pct
MySQL server	Table Cache Use Pct	MySQL Server(*)Table Cache Use Pct
MySQL server	Table Cache Hit Pct	MySQL Server(*)Table Cache Hit Pct
MySQL server	Table Lock Contention Pct	MySQL Server(*)Table Lock Contention Pct

Table 9.4

Collecting the Apache HTTP server performance counters

When you install the OMS agent for Linux, the agent looks for an instance of Apache HTTP server, and, if detected, the `apache-cimprov` package with the performance monitoring provider for Apache HTTP server will be automatically installed. The provider uses the Apache module to access performance data from the Apache HTTP server. This module must be loaded into the Apache HTTP server. Perform the following steps:

1. Use the following command to load the module into the Apache HTTP server:

   ```
   sudo /opt/microsoft/apache-cimprov/bin/apache_config.sh -c
   ```

   You can subsequently unload the module using the following command:

   ```
   sudo /opt/microsoft/apache-cimprov/bin/apache_config.sh -u
   ```

2. In your Log Analytics workspace, configure the Apache HTTP server performance counters to collect. Log into the Azure portal at `https://portal.azure.com`.

3. In the Azure portal, type `Log Analytics` in the **Search resources** search field and, under **Services**, select **Log Analytics**.

4. Select your workspace from the list and, in the workspace blade, under **Settings**, click on **Advanced settings**.

5. In the **Advanced settings** window, click on **Data**, and click on **Linux Performance Counters**.

6. In the search box, type **Apache** and, from the returned values, select the counter names that reflect the performance counters you would like to collect, and click on the **plus** sign to add the counter for collection.

7. Click on **Save** at the top of the page to save the configuration:

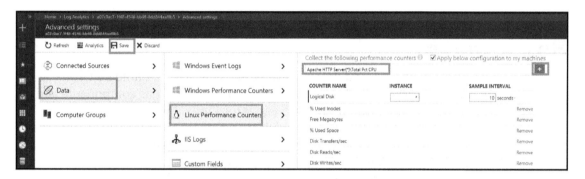

Figure 9.6

The following table lists some Apache HTTP server performance counters that you can collect in Log Analytics:

Object Name	Counter name	Performance counter
Apache HTTP server	Busy Workers	Apache HTTP Server(*)Busy Workers
Apache HTTP server	Idle Workers	Apache HTTP Server(*)Idle Workers
Apache HTTP server	Pct Busy Workers	Apache HTTP Server(*)Pct Busy Workers
Apache HTTP server	Total Pct CPU	Apache HTTP Server(*)Total Pct CPU
Apache HTTP server	Errors per Minute—client	Apache Virtual Host(*)Errors per Minute – Client

Apache HTTP server	Errors per Minute—server	Apache Virtual Host(*)Errors per Minute - Server
Apache HTTP server	KB per Request	Apache Virtual Host(*)KB per Request
Apache HTTP server	Requests KB per Second	Apache Virtual Host(*)Requests KB per Second
Apache HTTP server	Requests per Second	Apache Virtual Host(*)Requests per Second

Table 9.5

How it works...

The OMS agent for Linux is provided in a self-extracting shell script bundle that you can install. The bundle comprises multiple packages that enable the various components and features of the agent. When you install the OMS agent for Linux, the agent looks for an instance of Apache HTTP server, and, if detected, the apache-cimprov package with the performance monitoring provider for Apache HTTP server will be automatically installed. Similarly, the agent looks for an instance of MySQL server or MariaDB server, and, if detected, the mysql-cimprov package with the performance monitoring provider for MySQL server will be automatically installed. The provider connects to the detected MySQL server and exposes performance data for MySQL/MariaDB. Once the performance data is exposed and available to the Linux agent, the agent collects the performance data and sends it to the Log Analytics service where you can then consume the data.

Once you start collecting MySQL server and Apache HTTP server performance counters, you can use the following queries to find data records for these Linux applications:

```
Perf
| where ObjectName == "Apache HTTP Server"
```

And, for the MySQL server, use the following code:

```
Perf
| where ObjectName == " MySQL Server "
```

Collect Zabbix and Nagios alerts

In addition to performance counters on Linux systems and applications, you can also collect alerts from open source monitoring tools such as Nagios and Zabbix. Nagios, which is also known as Nagios Core, is an open-source computer software application that monitors systems, networks, and infrastructure. It offers monitoring and alerting for various infrastructure components, including applications, servers and routers. Zabbix is an enterprise open source monitoring software for applications and networks. Similar to Nagios, OMS supports the collection of Zabbix alerts.

How to do it...

Perform the following steps to collect alert data from Nagios and Zabbix.

Configuring the alert collection in Nagios

Perform the following steps to configure the alert collection in Nagios:

1. Navigate to the Nagios web interface and verify the location of the Nagios log file. This location could vary based on installation and configuration.

2. On the home page, click on **Alerts** under the **Reports** tab, and take note of the log file path:

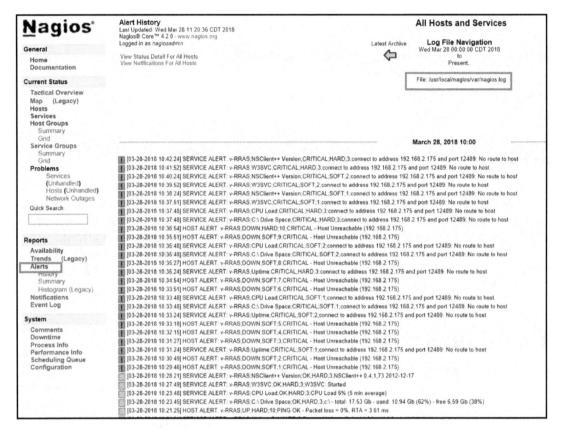

Figure 9.7

TIP

The log file path could vary based on Nagios configuration. As you can see in the preceding screenshot, the log is located at `/usr/local/nagios/var/nagios.log`. It could also be located in a path `/var/log/nagios/nagios.log`.

3. Grant the `omsagent` read access to the Nagios log file that is identified. If the `nagios.log` file is owned by the **nagios** group, you can add the **omsagent** user to the **nagios** group, using the following command:

```
sudo usermod -a -G nagios omsagent
```

4. Navigate to the configuration file located at `/etc/opt/microsoft/omsagent/conf/omsagent.conf` and ensure that the following entries are present and are not commented out:

```
<source>
  type tail
  #Update path to point to your nagios.log
  path /usr/local/nagios/var/nagios.log
  format none
  tag oms.nagios
</source>
<filter oms.nagios>
  type filter_nagios_log
</filter>
```

5. Restart the omsagent and syslog daemons using the following commands:

```
sudo sh /opt/microsoft/omsagent/bin/service_control restart
sudo service rsyslog restart
```

Once you start collecting Nagios alerts in OMS, you can use the following query to find alert records for alerts generated in Nagios.

```
Alert
| where SourceSystem == "Nagios"
```

Alert records collected by Nagios will have a **type** of **alert** and a source system of Nagios.

Configuring the Zabbix alert collection

Perform the following steps to configure the Zabbix alert collection:

1. Navigate to the configuration file located at `/etc/opt/microsoft/omsagent/conf/omsagent.conf` and ensure that the following entries are present and are not commented out:

```
<source>
  type zabbix_alerts
  run_interval 1m
  tag oms.zabbix
  zabbix_url http://localhost/zabbix/api_jsonrpc.php
  zabbix_username Admin
  zabbix_password zabbix
</source>
```

2. Restart the omsagent and syslog daemons using the following commands:

```
sudo sh /opt/microsoft/omsagent/bin/service_control restart
sudo service rsyslog restart
```

As you can see here, you need to specify a username and password in clear text. This is not an ideal configuration for obvious security reasons, so create a user account and assign only the permissions required for monitoring. Consult the Zabbix documentation on permissions in the following *See also* section.

Once you start collecting Zabbix alerts in OMS, you can use the following query to find alert records for alerts generated in Zabbix:

```
Alert
| where SourceSystem == "Zabbix"
```

Alert records collected by Nagios will have a **type** of **alert** and a source system of Zabbix.

See also

Zabbix permissions documentation is available at `https://www.zabbix.com/documentation/2.0/manual/config/users_and_usergroups/permissions`.

Work with syslog data

Log Analytics supports the collection of syslog data. This is the OMS agent for Linux that collects and sends syslog messages to the Log Analytics service.

How to do it...

Once you have met the prerequisites for connecting Linux systems to Log Analytics, and after you install the OMS agent for Linux and onboard your systems to your Log Analytics workspace, you are ready to start collecting syslog data.

To configure syslog data collection from connected Linux systems in your Log Analytics workspace, perform the following steps:

1. Log into the Azure portal at `https://portal.azure.com`.

2. In the Azure portal, type `Log Analytics` in the **Search resources** search field and, under **Services**, select **Log Analytics**.

3. Select your workspace from the list and, in the workspace blade, under **Settings**, click on **Advanced settings**.

4. In the **Advanced settings** window, click on **Data** and then on **Syslog**.

5. Check the option to **Apply below configuration to my machines**.

 When you select the option to **Apply below configuration to my machines**, all configuration changes are deployed to all Linux agents by default. Uncheck this option if you would like to manually configure syslog on each machine.

6. In the entry field, enter the name of a syslog facility to monitor, and click on the plus sign to add it to your configuration:

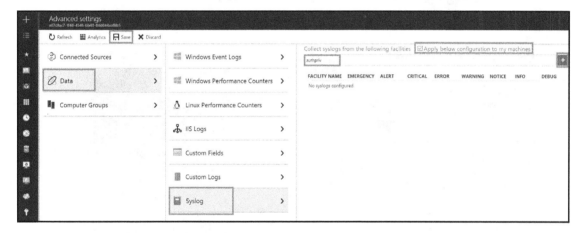

Figure 9.8

7. Click on **Save** at the top of the page to save the configuration.

Once a syslog facility is added to your workspace for collection, you can also remove the facility in your Log Analytics workspace.

How it works...

Syslog is a common event logging protocol on Linux systems. Linux system and applications will write messages to syslog, and you can configure syslog events and performance counters to collect. Once you install the OMS agent for Linux, the agent configures the local syslog daemon to forward messages to the agent, which then relays the messages to Log Analytics. Log Analytics supports collection for syslog messages sent by both the `rsyslog` and `syslog-ng` daemons. The OMS agent for Linux will only collect events with the facilities and severity specified in its configuration. Follow the steps in the preceding *How to do it* section to configure syslog in your Log Analytics workspace. To configure syslog on the machine, edit the configuration file and restart the syslog daemon. The files are located at the following:

- For rsyslog: */etc/rsyslog.d/95-omsagent.conf*
- For syslog-ng: */etc/syslog-ng/syslog-ng.conf*

The default settings for rsyslog are shown in the next figure:

```
codika@ODIKSUbuntu14:~$ cd /etc/rsyslog.d/
codika@ODIKSUbuntu14:/etc/rsyslog.d$ dir
20-ufw.conf  50-default.conf  95-omsagent.conf  postfix.conf
codika@ODIKSUbuntu14:/etc/rsyslog.d$ cat 95-omsagent.conf
# OMS Syslog collection for workspace a07c0ac7-1f48-4546-bb48-8dd844aaf8b5
kern.warning          @127.0.0.1:25224
user.warning          @127.0.0.1:25224
daemon.warning        @127.0.0.1:25224
auth.warning          @127.0.0.1:25224
syslog.warning        @127.0.0.1:25224
uucp.warning          @127.0.0.1:25224
authpriv.warning      @127.0.0.1:25224
ftp.warning           @127.0.0.1:25224
cron.warning          @127.0.0.1:25224
local0.warning        @127.0.0.1:25224
local1.warning        @127.0.0.1:25224
local2.warning        @127.0.0.1:25224
local3.warning        @127.0.0.1:25224
local4.warning        @127.0.0.1:25224
local5.warning        @127.0.0.1:25224
local6.warning        @127.0.0.1:25224
local7.warning        @127.0.0.1:25224
```

Figure 9.9

By default, the configurations will collect syslog messages sent for all facilities with a level of warning or higher. You can remove a facility by modifying the configuration file through changes in the Log Analytics workspace or directly on the agent.

As you can see in the preceding figure, the OMS agent listens for syslog messages on port 25224 on the local machine. To change this port, you will need to create a Fluentd configuration file, and an rsyslog or syslog-ng configuration file. Place the new Fluentd config file in /etc/opt/microsoft/omsagent/conf/omsagent.d and replace the value for the port entry with your desired custom port number:

```
<source>
    type syslog
    port %SYSLOG_PORT%
    bind 127.0.0.1
    protocol_type udp
    tag oms.syslog
</source>
<filter oms.syslog.**>
    type filter_syslog
</filter>
```

For the syslog configuration file, if using rsyslog, create a new file in /etc.rsyslog.d/ and change the value for %SYSLOG_PORT% to your custom port number:

```
# OMS Syslog collection for workspace %WORKSPACE_ID%
  kern.warning              @127.0.0.1:%SYSLOG_PORT%
  user.warning              @127.0.0.1:%SYSLOG_PORT%
  daemon.warning            @127.0.0.1:%SYSLOG_PORT%
  auth.warning              @127.0.0.1:%SYSLOG_PORT%
```

If using syslog-ng, modify the syslog-ng config file by adding the following entry to the end of the syslog-ng config file in /etc/syslog-ng:

```
filter f_custom_filter { level(warning) and facility(auth; };
destination d_custom_dest { udp("127.0.0.1" port(%SYSLOG_PORT%)); };
log { source(s_src); filter(f_custom_filter); destination(d_custom_dest);};
```

Restart the syslog daemon and OMS agent service to effect the configuration changes:

```
sudo /opt/microsoft/omsagent/bin/service_control restart
sudo service rsyslog restart
```

Once the OMS agent for Linux sends a syslog message to Log Analytics, the message is indexed in the service and a corresponding data record of type syslog is created for the message in the OMS repository. You can use the following log query to retrieve syslog records and see a count of the records created by various syslog facilities in your workspace:

```
Syslog
| summarize AggregatedValue = count() by Facility
```

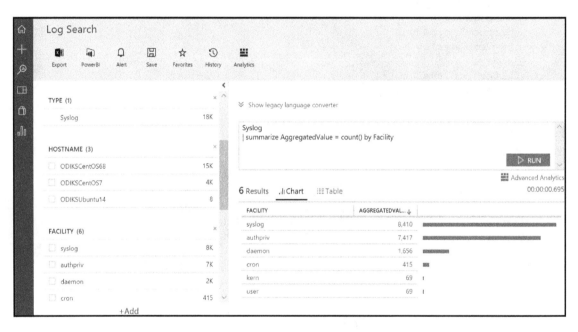

Figure 9.10

Monitor containers with OMS Log Analytics

Containers facilitate the modularization of systems into components that are easier to manage and maintain and that are resilient to failure. At its core, a container is an isolated user space environment that is used for a discrete set of functionalities. Many organizations are deploying Docker and other containerization technologies in their environments to optimize their DevOps initiatives and digitally transform their service delivery. Containers, therefore, have a widespread and growing application which makes it necessary to have a means to centrally monitor and manage container deployments. The container monitoring solution in OMS Log Analytics enables you to view and manage your Docker and other hosts from a single location. The solution supports various container orchestrators, including the following:

- Kubernetes
- DC/OS
- Docker Swarm
- Service Fabric
- Red Hat OpenShift

How to do it...

To install and configure the container solution, perform the following steps:

1. Navigate to the Azure portal (`https://portal.azure.com`) in your browser and sign in.

2. Select **+ Create a resource**; then, click on **Monitoring + Management** and then on **See all**:

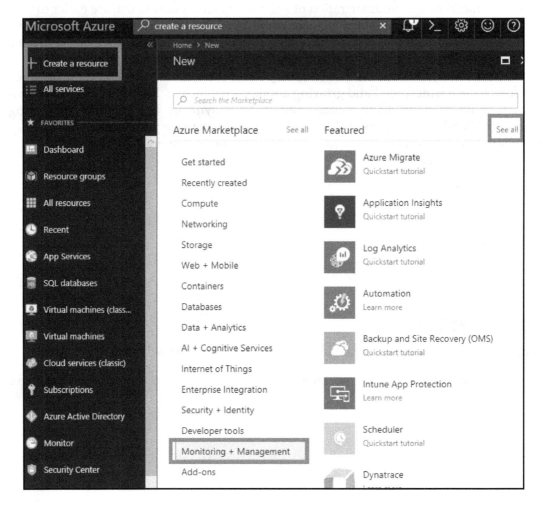

Figure 9.11

3. On the **Monitoring + Management** screen, to the right of **Monitoring + Management**, click on **More**.

4. In the **Management Solutions** blade, select the **Container Monitoring Solution** from the list:

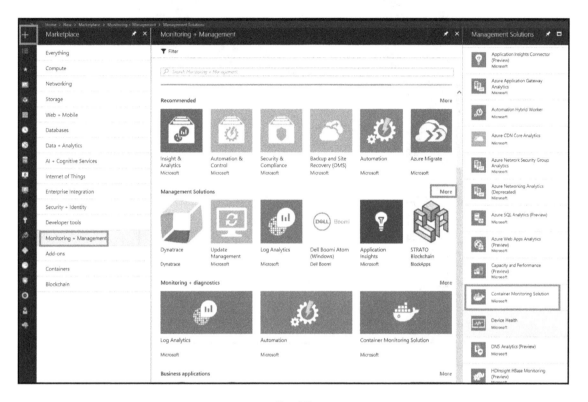

Figure 9.12

5. In the **Management Solutions** blade, read the information about the management solution, and click on **Create**.
6. In the **Container Monitoring Solution** blade, select your workspace to associate with the management solution.

7. Click on **Create** to finish installing the solution to your OMS workspace:

Figure 9.13

8. Once installed into your workspace, a new tile for the management solution will be visible in your workspace. Navigate to **Log Analytics**, select your workspace name, and click on **Overview** to see the tile for the installed management solution.
9. Install and use Docker with the OMS agent for Linux.

How it works...

The container solution is part of the insights and analytics solution offering in OMS. The solution provides you with a centralized way to view and manage your container hosts, track container usage and diagnose failures across your environments. The solution requires the OMS agent for monitoring and diagnostics of container hosts and clusters. The OMS agent for Linux is required on Linux computers that are container hosts, and the Microsoft monitoring agent (Windows agent) is required on Windows computers that are container hosts. Agents can be installed either manually or using some other method, such as the extensions for Azure VMs. The agent enables the collection of various logs, which generate data records in the OMS repository. You can run queries against the container data to glean insights into your Docker environment.

Ensure that Docker is running on your Linux container hosts before installing the OMS Agent for Linux. You will need to reinstall the agent if you install it before installing Docker. Once the container solution is added to your workspace, the solution adds the container tile to your OMS dashboard. The tile displays summary information about your container hosts and the containers running in the hosts:

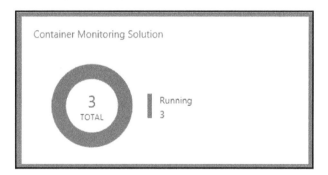

Figure 9.14

Click on the tile to open the solution dashboard. The dashboard groups solution data into the following blades:

- **Container Events**: This shows the status of containers and any computers with failed containers.
- **Container Logs**: This blade shows a chart of container log files generated over time and a list of computers with the highest number of log files, and it shows a count of log files.
- **Kubernetes Events**: This blade shows a chart of Kubernetes events generated over time, and it lists the reasons why pods generated the events.

- **Kubernetes Namespace Inventory**: This blade shows the number of namespaces and pods, and it lists them and shows counts for each.
- **Container Node Inventory**: This blade shows the number of orchestration types used on your container hosts and nodes.
- **Container Images Inventory**: This blade shows the total number of container images used. It lists and counts the image types.
- **Containers Status**: This blade shows the total number of container nodes and host computers that have running containers.
- **Container Process**: This blade shows a chart of container processes running over time. It lists containers by the running processes within the containers.
- **Container CPU Performance**: This blade shows a chart of the average CPU utilization over time for container hosts, and it lists the container hosts based on average CPU utilization.
- **Container Memory Performance**: This blade shows a line chart of memory usage over time.
- **Computer Performance**: This shows line charts of the percent of CPU performance over time, percent of memory usage over time, and megabytes of free disk space over time.

You can hover over any line in a chart to view more details:

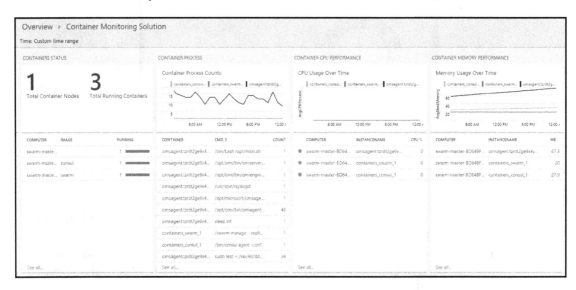

Figure 9.15

The container-specific data types generate records in the OMS repository. Some of the container-specific log types that are collected include:

- **Perf**: This consists of performance counters, such as container memory, network traffic, CPU, disk I/O, and other metrics from container host machines. Container perf counters generate Log Analytics records of type *Perf*.
- **ContainerInventory:** These logs contain information about the names, location, and images for containers. Once collected, a corresponding record of type *ContainerInventory* is created for this log type in the OMS repository.
- **ContainerImageInventory**: This log type contains information about deployed images, sizes, and running state. Records of type *ContainerImageInventory* are generated for this log type.
- **ContainerLog**: This log type contains information about various log entries and errors logs. Data collected for this log type generates records of type *ContainerLog* in the OMS repository.
- **ContainerServiceLog**: This log type contains information about Docker daemon commands that have been run. Records of type *ContainerServiceLog* are created for this log type.

Other container-specific data types that generate related records in the OMS repository include: container process, container node inventory, and Kubernetes inventory and events data types. For example, to determine the number of orchestration types used on your container hosts, you can run the following query:

```
ContainerNodeInventory_CL
| summarize AggregatedValue = count() by Computer, DockerVersion_s,
OrchestratorType_s
| sort by Computer asc
```

You can also see some of the performance counters collected and used by the solution by running the following query:

```
Perf
| where ObjectName == "Container" and CounterName == "Memory Usage MB"
| summarize AvgUsedMemory = avg(CounterValue) by bin(TimeGenerated, 30m),
InstanceName
```

The query looks at memory usage on containers, and shows a chart of memory usage over time, with a line chart that shows the data points in 30-minute intervals as shown in both the log search and the Advanced Analytics visuals here:

Figure 9.16

In the Advanced Analytics Portal, the query results are as shown in the following figure:

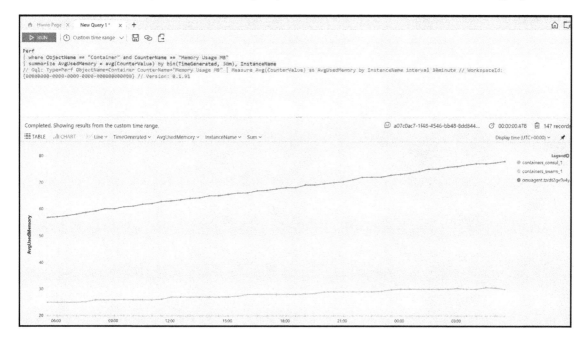

Figure 9.17

The container solution is available to all OMS pricing tiers, including the **Free**, **Standalone (Per GB)** and **OMS (per Node)** tiers. The solution is also available to legacy **Standard and Premium (OMS)** tiers.

Other Books You May Enjoy

If you enjoyed this book, you may be interested in these other books by Packt:

Learning AWS - Second Edition
Ritesh Modi

ISBN: 978-1-78839-739-1

- Familiarize yourself with the components of the Azure Cloud platform
- Understand the cloud design patterns
- Use enterprise security guidelines for your Azure deployment
- Design and implement Serverless solutions
- See Cloud architecture and the deployment pipeline
- Understand cost management for Azure solutions

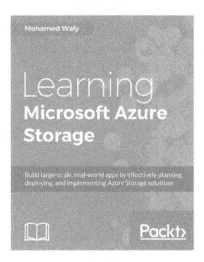

Learning Microsoft Azure Storage
Mohamed Waly

ISBN: 978-1-78588-491-7

- Understand Azure Storage types and determine the appropriate one for your needs
- Design Azure Storage for Azure VMs according to best practices
- Design and implement your SQL Database on Azure according to best practices
- Learn how to work with Azure Backup
- Learn how to work with Azure Site Recovery
- Extend Azure Storage to StorSimple
- Monitor storage metrics and logs and customize the Azure monitoring dashboard
- Monitor and troubleshoot Azure Storage

Leave a review - let other readers know what you think

Please share your thoughts on this book with others by leaving a review on the site that you bought it from. If you purchased the book from Amazon, please leave us an honest review on this book's Amazon page. This is vital so that other potential readers can see and use your unbiased opinion to make purchasing decisions, we can understand what our customers think about our products, and our authors can see your feedback on the title that they have worked with Packt to create. It will only take a few minutes of your time, but is valuable to other potential customers, our authors, and Packt. Thank you!

Index

www.ingramcontent.com/pod-product-compliance
Lightning Source LLC
Chambersburg PA
CBHW060646060326
40690CB00020B/4538